Reason and the Radical Crisis of Faith

American University Studies

Series VII
Theology and Religion

Vol. 30

PETER LANG
New York · Bern · Frankfurt am Main · Paris

Shabbir Akhtar

Reason and the Radical Crisis of Faith

PETER LANG
New York · Bern · Frankfurt am Main · Paris

Library of Congress Cataloging-in-Publication Data

Akhtar, Shabbir
  Reason and the radical crisis of faith.

  (American university studies. Series VII,
Theology and religion ; vol. 30)
    Includes index.
    !. Faith and reason. I. Title. II. Series:
American university studies. Series VII, Theology
and religion ; v. 30.
BT50.A26 1987   231′.042   86-27563
ISBN 0-8204-0451-9
ISSN 0740-0446

CIP-Kurztitelaufnahme der Deutschen Bibliothek

Akhtar, Shabbir:
Reason and the radical crisis of faith / Shabbir
Akhtar. – New York; Bern; Frankfurt am Main;
Paris: Lang, 1987.
  (American University Studies: Ser. 7,
  Theology and Religion; Vol. 30)
  ISBN 0-8204-0451-9

NE: American University Studies / 07

BT
50
,A26
1987

Printed by Weihert-Druck GmbH, Darmstadt, West Germany

To my mother and father

TABLE OF
CONTENTS

PREFACE

Theism is today everywhere under attack. Secular humanists deride the hopes which it advertises; theistic convictions are, we are told, nothing but dangerous myths inherited from a bygone age. As a result, in the advanced industrial communities of the world, indifferentism and atheism, along with a politically expedient religious pluralism, have won the day.

The purpose of this book is to investigate the problem of the rationality of traditional Christian conviction in the modern world.

I am indebted to many people but especially to Kai Nielsen, Terence Penelhum, C.B. Martin, Hugo Meynell, Jack MacIntosh, John Bishop, Anthony Parel and John Collier for valuable discussion of the issues raised in the text.

Jack MacIntosh alerted me to the sexism implicit in my choice of traditional language. I should say, in defence of my choice, that it is extremely difficult to use non-sexist locutions without an ensuing loss in elegance, style, and occasionally, clarity. I hope that this is an acceptable excuse.

I am grateful to Maggie Kohl for typing and other assistance in preparing the manuscript for publication.

Finally, despite the help of so many able people, many original errors no doubt remain. In a work on the limits of reason, however, that is perhaps not an altogether inappropriate failing.

Shabbir Akhtar
February 1986

Chapter I
A Perennial Problem

- I -

No metaphysic of human experience could avoid
superficiality if it failed to record the deeply felt
tension between the rational and the non-rational. It
might be an exaggeration - but it cannot be a very
great one - to say that the conflicts between the mind
and the heart, the intellect and the passions, and
faith and reason are woven backwards and forwards into
the entire pattern of our thought and experience.

The problem of the relationship between faith and
reason may not be an exclusively theological one. It
arises apparently as a general philosophical puzzle
about the status of the non-rational element in all
experience and knowledge. The antagonism between
religious faith and secular reason may be seen as a
special instance of the larger conflict between the
non-rational and the rational strands in all cognition
and thought. If the polarity between faith and reason
is pervasive, it is perhaps most acutely felt in the
religious experience of mankind. The Fall of the
human race is already a product of this very tension.
God exiled Adam from the Garden of Eden after Adam had
become reasonable: let no man put together what God
hath put asunder.

In some of the Eastern religious traditions, the
religious and the philosophical components were so
closely interwoven as to be well-nigh indistinguishable; but, as an accident of history, the Judaeo-
Christian-Islamic traditions encountered the philosophical tradition of the Hellenic world and had to
interlace their own independent religious insights

with this autonomous philosophical fabric. The discipline of theology is itself the by-product of this attempt to express religious insight and experience with the coherence, rigour, and clarity that rational thought demands. This is true of the early Church Fathers who established the theological traditions of Christendom; and it is especially true of an originally simple and literalist Islamic theology which became philosophically ramified under the impact of Greek scholarship.

Within the traditions of the Western faiths, one could distinguish, in very general terms, two different reactions to the problem of the relation between faith and reason: one which uses reason to amend the tradition of faith and another which tries to insulate faith from reason. The Hebrew-Christian tradition was in essence and origin independent of the Greek one. After the historic encounter, however, some religious thinkers insisted on the need for establishing some form of continuity between religious insight and rational philosophical thought in the larger attempt to adjust faith to rational demands. By contrast, others insisted on some form of essential discontinuity, even hiatus, between rationality and the content of faith. Again, in the Islamic tradition, the attempt to defuse the tension between philosophy and theology and to harmonize rational thought with traditional dogma begins as early as al-Kindi with his influential attempted reconciliation of Hellenism with Islamic orthodoxy, continues with al-Ash^{c}ari - the Muslim Aquinas - culminating in Ibn Rushd (Averroes). Paralleling these developments, Muslim orthodoxy recruited conservative thinkers (like the al-Ghazzali of the anti-philosophical Tahafut al-Falasifah[1]) to expose as baseless the pretensions of those who attempted a constructive synthesis of Koranic monotheism and pagan Greek philosophy.

The partial or complete rejection of reason _qua_ arbiter of truth in matters theological is as old as rational theology itself. Just as the metaphysical tradition in philosophy developed alongside the sceptical tradition and engaged in dialectical exchanges with it, similarly, rationalism and fideism in religious circles have grown together and interacted. As soon as the enterprise of philosophical theology had been conceived, fideistic foes of philosophy began to affirm passionately the utter uniqueness and even "absurdity" of faith when viewed from the perspective of an external rationality. The ultimate mystery represented by the religious revelation defies rational articulation and appraisal. The attempt to adjust faith to secular rational demands results at the very least in an unacceptable subordination of faith to human reason if not in positively heretical distortions. Tertullian - a famous early Church Father - is convinced that "it is philosophy that supplies the heresies with their equipment".[2] There were voices heard from the other camp too. In his inaptly named Decisive Treatise (Kitab Fasl al-Maql), the rationalistic Ibn Rushd argues against Sheikh al-Ghazzali's claim that belief in the divine law is a supernatural gift appropriated by means of a suprarational faculty. The divine law, Ibn Rushd contends, neither disregards nor supercedes the original natural constitution of the human reason.[3]

Historically, fideism has been one of the most influential attempts to meet the philosophical and scientific challenges to religious belief. Fideism is the theological doctrine according to which religious faith does not stand in need of rational justification and is, indeed, in religious domains, the arbiter of reason and its pretensions. Those who espouse this doctrine usually also hold - either as a corollary or as a ground of the above claim - that faith and reason are incommensurable and that the former is actually reinforced by the noticeable incompetence of the latter in religious matters. More specifically, fideism is the view that theological propositions are factual statements whose status is illumined not by the use of reason or by the accumulation of evidence but rather by the exercise of "faith", volition, or choice. This is a comment on our capacity for discovering or recognising theological truth - not a comment on the capacity of theological propositions to be true or false. Argumentation, rational investigation and other forms of ratiocination are, of necessity, futile in the attempt to discover whether or not a particular theological proposition is true: faith alone determines whether or not a man recognises the truth of an objectively true doctrine. This construal constitutes, I think, a partial characterisation of the theological outlook of some believing fideistic thinkers - especially Søren Kierkegaard and the neo-orthodox theologians he has influenced.

One cannot fully appreciate the appeal of fideism to so many very able religious thinkers both today and in the past unless one understands the predicament that evokes it. Imagine a man who has been deeply

convinced of the truth of a theological affirmation
before his encounter with philosophy. Suppose now
that he comes to see that any impartial assessment of
the relevant evidence shows or strongly indicates that
the religious doctrine under scrutiny is false or even
incoherent. Suppose further that two of his religious
concerns are, firstly, to avoid apostasy (i.e.,
abandonment of his professed faith) and, secondly, to
avoid heresy (i.e., abandonment of some doctrinally
crucial part of his professed faith). Additionally,
he may wish to avoid confusion and self-deception in
an attempt to preserve his intellectual integrity; he
may refuse to espouse any interpretation of the original doctrines so radical that, in effect if not in
intention, it amounts to a surrender of the original
claims under the guise of acceptance in a modified
manner. The best way, it seems, for such a man to
achieve both his religious and his intellectual ends
is by entering the fideistic camp. The reasoned
consideration of evidence, he may come to believe, is
utterly irrelevant to the issue of the truth or
falsity of the central pronouncements of the faith.

- III -

It is a commonplace of modern theological thought
that to be of service to the people in any period,
religion must minister to the needs and interests of
the age. The whole history of Christian theology, for
instance, may be viewed as a history of new restate-
ments of theological doctrine designed to bring the
Christian message into a significant relationship to
men and women facing new problems in new social contexts. The underlying motivation behind this
endeavour has been the correct observation that a

living religious tradition becomes ossified if it
isolates itself from the scientific and cultural
influences which give structure to the lives of
ordinary believers.

The crisis of religious faith in virtually every
era has been due, in large part, to the liberal
influence of scientific and rational philosophical
thought. Movements of secular thought vary in their
impact on religious belief. The spectacular increase
in the authority and scope of the sciences of nature
and society, during the last two centuries, has had an
unprecedented influence on the development of Christianity. The sceptical rationalism of the eighteenth
century[4] did not, arguably, radically damage the
traditional outlook of Christianity; that catastrophe
was reserved for the succeeding century. As the
historical mentality took deeper root in the nineteenth century and as thinkers began to supply the
historical sense with a metaphysical foundation, the
historical study of the Scriptures came to assume a
central importance in theology. Religious documents
and writings became subject to rational inquiry with
its strict canons of historico-literary criticism.
Many writers came to the conclusion that traditional
ideas concerning revelation, miracle, inspiration and,
in general, the whole thrust of literalist exegesis,
were difficult to maintain in their original form.[5]

As if the intellectual climate were lacking in
inclemency, Darwin's epoch-making theory of evolution
appeared on the scene at about this time. The revolutionary ideas of natural selection, mutation, and
the simian origins of the human race were a direct
affront to ancient scriptural views concerning the
fixity of species and the creation, fall and redemp-

tion of man. The implications of these new doctrines were cataclysmic. Darwin's doctrine gave to the concept of nature a depth and consistency and, most importantly, an autonomous application, which were the death-warrant for the purposive interpretation of nature so dear to the pre-Darwinian Christian teleologists. Furthermore, it came to be thought, if indeed man is a part of nature and his physical constitution is scientifically explicable, why shouldn't his mental and moral constitution be similarly subject to laws analogous to natural scientific laws?

Historical and scientific studies could indeed, it came to be believed in some liberal circles, discredit religious assumptions. It was time for revision. While Catholicism remained, for the most part, obstinately committed to the past, Protestantism acutely felt the need to accommodate itself to an age in which science, technology, art, and social revolution had led to seismic shifts in popular and intellectual thought concerning the status of inherited religious norms. Both Catholicism and Protestantism had to defend their dogmatic traditions against various secular critiques which threatened to effectively isolate them from the dominant modes of thought. Either faith would need to rely on an uncompromisingly absolute authority or else it must concede the importance of accommodation to and compromise with a hostile secular culture.

Christian thinkers can, of course, flatly oppose the empirical- rational trend of modern intellectual culture. But they can do so only at the cost of compartmentalizing their religion and thereby insulating it from the mainstream of current thought. On the other hand, the attempt to accommodate the

Christian message to the language and methods of the contemporaneous science and philosophy carries with it one signal danger. Christianity is at root relevant only to men's basic and unalterable condition - a condition of sin and estrangement. If it does not offer a remedy for our fundamental ailments, its own distinctive message will degenerate into a mere echo of some ephemeral orthodoxy destined for oblivion in the course of time.

- IV -

Ever since the Enlightenment, it has become a genuine question whether or not belief in the God of the ethical monotheistic tradition is either intellectually defensible or morally necessary. It is often said that recent advances in scientific and rational thought have exposed much of the monotheistic tradition to be making embarrassingly fantastic and barely credible if not wholly false and incoherent claims.

In this book, I examine several defences of the rationality of Christian conviction in the modern world. I begin with fideism which, in effect, holds that Christianity does not set out to be rational and hence cannot be convicted of irrationality. There are, in the writings of orthodox and neo-orthodox thinkers, both philosophical and theological objections to the use of reason in determining the true status and proper content of theology. I argue that the claims of the Christian religion cannot escape rational scrutiny and that Christian theology is not an autonomous discipline.

A significant concern of twentieth century Christian thought has been the attempt to identify the essence of the faith by separating the central or essential elements from the extraneous or peripheral ones. Several modern philosophical positions on the status of Christian religious belief incorporate the claim that what is essential to the Christian faith remains intact despite secular critique. I examine three such positions in this essay. Of these, two of them are examined briefly. Both have, for different reasons, been labelled "reductionist" on the ground that, in different ways, both fail to preserve the propositional character of religious belief. I have very little new to say about these two positions. I do argue, however, while examining them, that the tradition of Christian theism sets identifiable limits to the secularization of Christianity and that it has a normative significance for Christian theology.

The third is a position I label "theological revisionism" and this is examined at great length. It is a position much in vogue among secularized religious thinkers who reject theological reductionism. Theological revisionists endorse the autonomy of secular reason; religious claims must, if necessary, be attenuated, we are told, in the face of current scientific and rational philosophical challenge. I contend that theological revisionism is a deeply problematic position which fails to provide an adequate defence of the rationality of Christian conviction in our secularized age.

Finally, I offer some suggestions for a defence of religion in the modern world. Different religious traditions must, naturally, develop their own projects for protecting their respective belief-systems against the corrosive influences of modernity. All the monotheistic religions would, however, benefit from the

provision of a successful natural theology. And
in order to obtain that, we should, I suggest, set
ourselves the artistic task of reviving a religious
vision of the world - the task par excellence for a
theology of the future.

Notes

[1] Incoherence of the Philosophers. See Islamic Theology and Philosophy: Studies in Honour of George F. Hourani, Michael Marmura (ed.), (Albany: State University of New York Press, 1984).

[2] The quote is from Tertullian's The Prescriptions against the Heretics, as reprinted in Classical Statements on Faith and Reason, E.L. Miller (ed.), (New York: Random House, 1970), p.3.

[3] See Muhsin Mahdi's "Remarks on Averroes' Decisive Treatise", in Marmura, op. cit., pp. 188-202.

[4] See especially Thomas Paine's iconoclastic The Age of Reason (Secaucus: Citadel Press, 1948, 1974). First published in 1794.

[5] Bernard Reardon's anthology Religious Thought in the Nineteenth Century (Cambridge: Cambridge University Press, 1966) gives a good picture of the gradual collapse of traditional views.

Chapter II
The Exile of Reason

The view that reason is incompetent to serve as arbiter between truth and error in religious doctrine has a long and distinguished intellectual ancestry in the works of Tertullian, Luther, Pascal, Kierkegaard and Barth. These thinkers have together raised both theoretical (philosophical) and religious objections to the use of reason in determining the true status and proper content of theology. In dealing with the philosophical criticisms of rational theology, I confine myself to an examination of Kierkegaard's writings since most of the relevant objections to the use of reason are found in them. As for the theological objections, I examine both Kierkegaard's contribution as well as that of some of the neo-orthodox thinkers influenced by him.

- I -

Søren Kierkegaard is far and away the most influential religious thinker of the nineteenth century. In assessing the significance of his work (or that of any past thinker), there is always the danger that one might denature his thought by placing it in an alien intellectual nexus. The dominant mode of philosophizing in the English-speaking world today is, of course, analytical. But an analytical critique of Kierkegaard's position goes, in a significant sense, against the whole tenor of his own anti-academic approach to religious issues. And yet there seems to be no real alternative to a systematic rational critique or defence of any position - even, in the special case, a position which advocates enmity to method, system, or reason. Indeed, Kierkegaard himself gives not only an external theological critique of reason but also an internal theoretical one for only the latter will receive a sympathetic hearing in the rationalists' court.

Two preliminary remarks are in order. Firstly, it is natural to protest that if Kierkegaard distrusts reason, he cannot also assume the validity of reason for the purpose of undermining any claims - including claims made on behalf of reason. But Kierkegaard does not regard reason as incompetent for every task; it is only the task of investigating issues of "infinite" human concern that falls outside its scope.[1] The real issue here is: Can human reason be employed self-reflexively (i.e., in the determination of the limits of its own jurisdiction) even if it is indeed incapable of determining the content of theology (i.e., incapable of dealing with issues of infinite human involvement)? The answer to this question is, perhaps, in the negative: if reason can so doubt itself as to stand in need of a delimitation on its sphere of jurisdiction, it cannot also trust itself to define precisely its own relation to the realm of what is allegedly beyond its scope. And to this it might be objected that it can indeed do so. I do not intend to settle this question here. It is safe to assume, however, I believe, that no grand a priori dismissal of anti-rationalism is justified; the arguments proffered should be assessed on an individual basis.

Secondly, the conception of reason varies from thinker to thinker. For Kierkegaard, "reason" does not signify simply Descartes' rationalism according to which one discovers truth by doubting all which can be doubted and building a structure of deductive truths on a foundation of indubitable axioms. Nor is it limited to Kant's critical method or to the method of empirical science. Kierkegaard sees reason as the accumulated and critically organized common sense of our species with a normative kernel containing an awareness of human values and ultimate ideals. Such a reason expresses itself concretely as the self-sufficiency of human nature. It would be misleading, therefore, to characterize reason in terms of purely theoretical or academic categories such as the a priori or the self-consistency of human reflection, and so on.[2]

In the Concluding Unscientific Postscript, Kierkegaard draws a contrast between the "world-historical" (or objective) and the "subjective" per-spectives.[3] Consider a phenomenon such as death. On the world-historical level, Kierkegaard tells us, it can be discussed as a natural event which befalls all of us, has many causes, is inevitable, and so on. But there is also a subjective attitude towards death and its significance - an attitude that is not, Kierke-gaard continues, an inference from the objective data about death. The inevitability of death may, for example, strike us as making all our ambitions vain and pointless in the manner of the lugubrious jeremiad of the author of Ecclesiastes in the Old Testament. Suppose that a philosopher seeks to know whether or not he is immortal and whether or not there exists a being to whom human allegiance - his own included - is owed. The philosopher is asking an ultimate question here about his own eternal destiny. But how can any thinker conduct a dispassionate inquiry into a theme which must involve a large emotional investment for him? Kierkegaard answers that he can only do so at a high price since "an eternal happiness is rooted in the infinite personal passionate interest, which the individual renounces in order to become objective, defrauded of his interest by the predominating objectivity".[4]

Kierkegaard does not deny that objectivity is possible in some kinds of inquiry. Detachment has a place in mathematics, natural science, and history.[5] These sciences deal with the choice of means, not of ends or ultimate ends. The scientist merely needs detached and systematic observation and disinterested reflection in order to, say, classify a new species of butterfly. But there are, Kierkegaard contends, some things which can only be known through subjective experience. Love and friendship, for example, are not the subject of rational disinterested thought; without a participant's understanding and appropriate experiences, one cannot properly have knowledge of them. One could, of course, study the behavioural manifestations of love - fond glances, reddened cheeks, a quickened pulse, and so on - and yet remain ignorant of the nature of love. A woman in love, however, could, even without the dubious advantages of knowing psychology, recognise what love was. Things which are, by nature, impersonal can be known only impersonally; what is by nature personal can be known only personally. Anything truly and fully personal both within myself and in others can be known only by "subjectivity". I learn what love is in myself by actually loving someone and I also learn what love is in other persons only by loving someone.

With respect to God, there is only one standpoint from which we can truly know him, namely, the perspective of an infinitely concerned, dependent creature with an ultimate emotional interest in the issue of his own destiny.[6] Certainly, one can treat paganism objectively - but not Christianity with its personal stake for the thinker.[7] To investigate Christianity is, in effect, to investigate the human subject's own eternal destiny, the one comprehensive object of infinite personal concern. Where the object of inquiry really is biblical Christianity (and not some speculative modern substitute) objectivity is impossible. In this connection, Kierkegaard warns us, to assume an air of detachment or the unconcern of the spectator is to ruin all perspective right from the start.

Kierkegaard disputes the efficacy of reason to lead to objectivity in religious matters mainly on the ground that there are extraordinary emotional pressures behind one's apparently intellectual dealings with issues of human purpose and destiny and that these pressures conspire to completely jeopardise objectivity. This is one of his arguments. Another argument - which Kierkegaard himself does not clearly distinguish from this first argument - is that even if objectivity were attainable in religious discussion, it would be futile since, with things such as love and friendship, one must actually experience them (i.e., have a "subjective" perspective on them) in order to know what they really are. These are different claims and need separate assessment.

Now, to be sure, having a personal stake in the answer makes it undeniably difficult to inquire with objective detachment into the question of our destiny. But why does Kierkegaard infer (as he seems to) that having a personal interest makes it inappropriate, even incoherent, to seek objective detachment? Is it not arguable that one may be more concerned to achieve objectivity precisely because one has an interest in the answer?

Admittedly, in matters of profound concern, a perfect intellectual disinterestedness is impossible. But all that seems to be requisite is the occasional cool hour during which one could subject one's own experiences of commitment and passion to rational examination. This does presuppose the ability to alternate in the roles of participant and critical spectator. But there is no good reason to think that we are incapable of this. I suspect that part of the reason for Kierkegaard's refusal to concede the possibility of this kind of objectivity in religion is that he is unclear in his own mind about the differences between objectivity and other related but distinct concerns such as neutrality, disinterestedness, indifference, unconcern, detachment, impartiality, dispassionateness, and non-partisanship.[8] For example, the mood of detachment which rational inquiry demands does not necessarily imply indifference to or unconcern for its deliverances. Thus even detached investigators in scientific disciplines often experience psychological dislocations of a kind that give the lie to the claim that they are unconcerned about the results of their investigation. Again, to be objective is not always tantamount to being non-committal; not every partisan position is partial. And, finally, neutrality need not entail objectivity: one can be objective without being neutral (although not without being unbiased) and neutral without being objective. Kierkegaard fears that objectivity in religious matters would amount to being indifferent and non-committal. But, as we have seen, neither of these is necessarily implied by the espousal of an objective stance: disinterestedness as a virtue of inquiry does not require uninterestedness.

Kierkegaard maintains that actually having the experience of some things (such as love and friendship) is essential to knowing what they are. This is not an implausible view; we do tend to think that it is one thing to know something and another to really know it i.e., know it as an _experienced_ reality. For instance, there is an emotional residue to the experience of starvation which does not require new words for its description and yet it is an experience which is indeed unavailable to someone who has never gone without food for a long time. But surely one can learn what it _means_ to starve without actually having starved. Wittgenstein has persuasively argued that a man's understanding of a concept such as pain or hunger is shown by his ability to use the word "pain" or "hunger" correctly i.e., by his ability to make the appropriate connections between certain kinds of behaviour and the word "pain" or "hunger". Wittgenstein counsels us to subdue the powerful inclination to view the mental as somehow irreducibly inner and subjective, as an inner realm susceptible only to introspective attention. Thus, a man who has mastered mental language - knows how to use correctly words such as "pain", "pleasure", "love", "anger", and so on - has acquired an understanding of mental concepts even if he has not had the relevant experiences. The suggestion is that we should explicate mental concepts in terms of abilities (including linguistic abilities) and behavioural capacities alone so that a man's full repertoire of abilities to use the appropriate words correctly would indicate an understanding of the relevant concepts.[9]

Kierkegaard is right to insist that God is known only from a personal perspective of involvement and concern on the part of his creatures. But it does not follow from this alone that there can be no purely theoretical understanding of the reality of God. If we apply to Kierkegaard's thought the anachronistic Russellian distinction between "knowledge by description" and "knowledge by acquaintance",[10] we can see that someone could know about God without knowing God. These two kinds of epistemological relations are supplementary but distinct. In order to know God, one has to encounter him; in order to know who God is, one merely needs to have some true ideas about him. A man may know who God is without knowing God - the situation of most ordinary believers and of some (practical) atheists. But a man cannot know God without also knowing who he is: one cannot know God without having some true ideas about him.

There is an important truth in Kierkegaard's claim that God is fully known to the believer only under some personal ("subjective") description such as "My Lord and Saviour", and not under some abstract or impersonal one. The concept of God - like the concepts of person, teacher, friend, and enemy - is a titular one. With all titular concepts, the object of one's experience is the subject of moral appraisal; the attitude of the perceiving subject makes an ineliminable contribution to the experience. The term "God" does not refer, so to speak, just to the identity of an object; rather it describes the nature of an object by identifying its status as an object of a certain kind. It is true that God is to the infinitely concerned believer - as the mother to the young child - a wholly personal reality. But it does not follow from this feature of his experience that there cannot be any objective knowledge of God in the sense of demonstrable truths isolated from any personal commitment. The distinctive advantages of Christian faith - for example, a trustful relationship with God - can be <u>defined</u> apart from the mode of acquisition of those advantages.

- II -

Kierkegaard offers several arguments to show that objective reasoning in support of religious faith is rendered futile or undesirable by the very nature of such faith. He defines faith as "an objective uncertainty held fast in the appropriation process of the most passionate inwardness".[11] An "objective uncertainty" is a proposition which cannot be shown by objective reasoning to be certainly true; and a given piece of reasoning is objective if it attempts to demonstrate impersonally and generally that the conclusion in question is true or probably true. Now a central problem for Kierkegaard is the following: Is it possible to base an eternal felicity upon historical knowledge given that the latter is always tentative? Kierkegaard answers that it is not possible to base an eternal happiness on objective reasoning about historical facts. It is possible, however, to base an eternal happiness on a belief in historical facts that is independent of objective evidence for them.[12]

The greatest possible certainty with respect to any historical belief or proposition (including any Christian historical belief) is an approximation since historical evidence, objectively considered, never completely excludes the possibility of error.[13] There

is some finitely small probability of error in the
objective grounds for all historical beliefs; the
probability of error in our belief that, for example,
Karl Marx flourished in the nineteenth century may be
infinitesimal but it is not necessarily negligible.
Genuine faith, Kierkegaard tells us, is only present
where the believer is infinitely interested in the
object of his faith; but if we have an "infinite
passionate interest" in something, there is no possibility of error too small to be worthy of attention.[14]
It follows, Kierkegaard thinks, that objective ratiocination cannot justify the believer in disregarding
any possibility of error about the object of faith.

Doubts can always disturb decisions about historical problems, Kierkegaard avers. Faith is the
radical act of will whereby a man decides to eliminate
his doubts and resolves to disregard any possibility
of error. Religious belief cannot coexist with doubt;
genuine faith must be decisive and wholly exclude
doubt. Indeed religious belief is not so much a
conclusion one reaches but rather a resolution one
adopts.[15] The believer - acutely aware of the risk of
error[16] - decides to act on his beliefs without hed-
ging his bets to accommodate the possibility of error.
And thus it comes about that the transition involved
in basing eternal truths upon tentative historical
testimony requires the famous objectively unjustified
"leap" beyond the evidence. The "leap of faith" is in
the form of a commitment - an unconditional trust in
the correctness and meaningfulness of one's existential decision.

For Kierkegaard, decisions about faith should be
more or less indifferent to historical details. An
adequate knowledge of the events in the life of Jesus

is to be reached not by the methods of empirical history (which can at best yield probability rather than certainty) but rather only by a decision which brings one's will into conformity with the significance of what Jesus was and did. Kierkegaard insists, however, that an affirmation of the historicity of Christ is central to Christianity. Faith is directed towards something which has happened in history, which happened contingently and which happened in circumstances that render it impossible to show that it did happen.

Now suppose that the probabilities of historical research went contrary to faith. Let us suppose that it became highly probable, on the basis of new evidence, that, say, Jesus never existed or that he was really an imposter with purely political aspirations. Surely, this would and should cause concern among orthodox Christians. One may not be able to claim complete certainty for historical knowledge but equally one cannot simply ignore the problem of the relationship between faith and historical fact. One cannot view an event like the Crucifixion as merely a theological maxim whose truth and significance are wholly independent of the deliverances of historical research.[17] The acceptance of Christian doctrines cannot and should not precede historical investigation of their factual basis.

Kierkegaard's implicit response to this can be extracted from his discussion of the problem of "contemporaneity with Christ".[18] Two contemporaries of Jesus who witnessed the same incidents in his ministry could agree on empirical details while disputing their religious significance: one could accept and the other reject the claim that Jesus was the Christ.

Historical evidence may well show that Jesus was a religious man of extraordinary integrity of character but it cannot entail the special theological valuation that faith alone can put on him. After all, St. Paul saw in Jesus not merely a wise teacher but also a divine redeemer. Kierkegaard's contention is that the question of the deity of the historical character Jesus of Nazareth must be dealt with by faith (or rejection) and cannot be settled by an appeal to rational proof or sense-experience or purely historical evidence alone. The contemporaneity with Jesus can, at most, be crucial in forming the certain belief that Jesus existed and was a moral and religious personality of great stature; it cannot help us to reach certainty concerning the deity of Jesus. The distinction between "the disciple at first hand" and "the disciple at second hand" is, then, Kierkegaard concludes, religiously insignificant.

This reply is inadequate. It is true, of course, that both the contemporaneous generation as well as later ones have to contend with the uncertainty concerning the revelatory significance of events while only the later generations have to contend with the uncertainty concerning the relationship of the Gospel records to the actual events themselves. But the verdict on the authenticity of the biblical record - the deliverances of secular history, if you wish - has a bearing on a Christian's faith since faith cannot reasonably be directed towards the revelatory significance of events which did not actually occur. One simply cannot escape modern scepticism about the historical foundations of Christianity by an act of will or by an appeal to the "infinitely interested" subjectivity of the believer. There is work to be done.

But objective historical inquiry is, Kierkegaard retorts, an endless task. If someone wishes to base his faith on its deliverances, he will have to suspend his religious commitment indefinitely.[19] Total commitment to a belief entails, Kierkegaard seems to reason, that one be determined not to relinquish the belief under any circumstances. Now the thinker (to be objective) has to submit to the requirement of complete indecisiveness while the reasoning is in progress. Hence total commitment to a belief based on empirical data is indefinitely postponed and awaits upon further favourable evidence to be amassed in the future. It follows, then, for Kierkegaard, that one cannot objectively justify a total commitment to a belief $\underline{P}$ which one believes may stand in need of possible future revision. How could a tenacious religious commitment be sustained in an atmosphere of unpredictable changes in historical scholarship - some of which promise to consolidate the commitment while others threaten to erode it? In believing in God's existence, a man may of course decide to ignore once and for all any objections which have not yet been made.[20] Authentic religious faith, Kierkegaard triumphantly concludes, must shun any objective empirical justification as its basis and should indeed seek complete independence from it.

Kierkegaard is right to insist that rational empirical method fails to attain absolute and final certainty on issues of moment.[21] In important matters, all the crucially relevant evidence is never available. But the pursuit of objectivity does not imply that one is objectively justified in indefinitely deferring any commitment to a course of practical religious devotion. There is no suggestion

that one should refuse to make any decisions or suspend all practical commitments. Worse than believing
in what is inadequately supported by evidence is not
believing in anything at all: if one devotes oneself
to the most reasonable principles, one may still miss
the truth, but if one fails to devote oneself to any
principles at all, one is sure to miss the truth. The
reasonable course of action is to commit oneself to
principles which seem - all things considered - the
most reasonable. And critical rational inquiry could
help us in deciding which are the more and which the
less probable beliefs. The proper object of rational
search is not metaphysical or apodictic certainty but
rather the kind of certainty achieved when, within the
context of current human knowledge, a claim receives
favourable evidence from many quarters while little or
no hostile evidence conspires to dislodge it. If
rational evidence, at a given time, sustains belief in
God as more probably true than any known alternative,
we are being perfectly reasonable in decisively committing ourselves to this belief. But this does not
entail an unconditional determination to entertain
this particular religious belief even in the face of
overwhelming unfavourable evidence.

Objective historical reasoning cannot yield
complete certainty. But this failure, Kierkegaard
contends, is really a blessing in disguise. The
certainty that rational inquiry would per impossibile
deliver is inimical to genuine faith for such faith
can be induced only under conditions of uncertainty:
"Anything that is almost probable, or probable, or
extremely and emphatically probable, is something
[one] can almost know, or as good as know, or
extremely and emphatically almost know - but it is

impossible to _believe_".[22] The rational certainty which proof provides is fatal to faith;[23] for faith to exist, the central beliefs whose truth is necessary to the attainment of one's religious goal must be objectively improbable. Faith is not some complacent intellectually supported confidence but rather necessarily a great and painful risk.[24] Only an "uncertainty of knowledge with respect to an eternal happiness"[25] could make possible that "most vehement gesture of the passion that embraces the infinite".[26] The attempt to establish religious beliefs on a foundation of objective probability, then, is _religiously_ undesirable. The believer should resist the temptation to seek guarantees of success; rather he should recognise the paradoxical nature (even absurdity) of his beliefs - objectively considered - and achieve faith through a strenuous exertion of the will.[27] Kierkegaard fears that the availability of guarantees will jeopardise faith: one cannot strive in an absolute fashion for something when success in the endeavour is guaranteed in advance. The man who risks everything for his faith in the truth of Christianity, knowing that it is objectively highly probable or certain that Christianity is true, has less passion, according to Kierkegaard, than the man who risks everything for his faith in the truth of Christianity knowing that the truth of Christianity is perhaps objectively possible but objectively highly improbable.

Three remarks are in order here. Firstly, even if there is greater (i.e., more intense) passion involved in striving for what is _not_ guaranteed in advance, the fact that a man strives for what _is_ guaranteed in advance does not necessarily entail that he _has_ less passion than the man who strives for what is _not_ guaranteed in advance; it may merely imply that the man who makes his effort in the presence of guarantees _exhibits_ less passion. Secondly, the integration of reason and passion is not, in the final analysis, inimical to faith. It is true, of course, that if a man's intellect and will are in harmony, a kind of passion due to inner emotional conflict is indeed absent. But if one pits one's will against one's reason, the danger is that all the battles one fights are within oneself. Surely there is enough of a discordance between what one takes to be the will of God and the state of the world to create sufficient tension to engender enough passion to sustain faith. And finally, it is not at all obvious that Kierkegaardian infinite passion should be or even could be a part of the religious ideal of life. Is Kierkegaard's ideal of religiousness humanly attainable? Even if religious faith is indeed the highest of human passions[28], it is certainly not an absolute and continuous passion. A continuous mood of agapeistic love, for example, may be possible but - few men (if any) can live in the heat of any single active passion. Nor does one need such a passion in order to obey the religious injunction to love. Moreover, a model of religious passion on which even the seminal religious figures of the Judaeo-Christian-Islamic tradition - Moses, St. Paul, Umar - turn out to be merely mediocre instances naturally gives rise to the suspicion that some unrealistic yardstick is at work. These men made great sacrifices - perhaps not the greatest possible sacrifices: Muhammad's staunch companion, Umar, gave only half of his wealth for the cause of Islam - but they did so apparently completely

convinced that their religious beliefs were certainly
true and the chances of ultimate success very high.

Kierkegaard was a profound thinker. It would be
surprising if there were no significant truths about
religious faith in a corpus which reverberates with
spiritual seriousness. In bringing this section to a
close, I comment on two of Kierkegaard's sound
insights. Firstly, Kierkegaard's antipathy towards
detachment is inspired by the correct observation that
to recognise the availability of religious knowledge
is also partly to recognise the importance of pursuing
it and implementing it through a course of practical
religious devotion. One cannot fully grasp the truth
about the nature of religious belief without also
realising that it characteristically inspires specifically religious responses to reality. This is why
faith cannot be based, Kierkegaard reasons, on the
"indifferent objective knowledge"[29] which academic
philosophy provides. But Kierkegaard mistakenly
concludes that the possession of religious faith and
the pursuit of objective truth are incompatible as if
our interest in having properly grounded beliefs
necessarily frustrated our interest in exercising our
religious passion. Secondly, Kierkegaard is surely
right to insist that, for most of us, religious
commitment involves whole-hearted affirmation under
conditions of uncertainty. Christian faith involves
the usual uncertainty attaching to all decisions about
interpretations of historical events and the peculiar
uncertainty involved in giving assent to claims for
which one can adduce as evidence only comparatively
complex data requiring controversial interpretation.
Kierkegaard wrongly concludes, however, that one could
escape from such ineliminable uncertainty by a gratuitous act of will.

- III -

Kierkegaard has profoundly influenced the development of Protestant theology in the twentieth century. Many religious writers, notably Karl Barth, Emil Brunner, and Reinhold Niebuhr, have taken to heart Kierkegaard's passionate distrust of rational approaches to religion. There have been calls for a return to the theology of the Reformation and for a revival of the religious tradition of such influential thinkers as Tertullian, Luther, and Pascal. The knowledge of God is, we are told, not subject to rational criticism or rational support; we should put a religious veto on any intellectual approach to faith. Traditionally, many ordinary religious believers have condemned as impious the entire programme of philosophy and especially a philosophy whose practitioners have the audacity to question (allegedly) divine truths. The impiety of such an enterprise derives from the fact that man is a fallen, sinful and depraved creature whose reasoning faculty has been irreparably damaged. Only the pride and foolishness of this created being could account for his claim to fathom God's intentions or appraise divine matters. It is as irreligious to defend faith as it is to attack it; faith is the judge of a sin-riven reason and its claims and could scarcely stand in need of the defence it provides. The important things, we are told, are revelation, divine grace, preaching, and submission to God. There is no place for any experimental natural theology; the revealed Word of God suffices to give us knowledge and salvation.

Karl Barth has expounded and defended this neo-orthodox position.[30] He champions the orthodox view that Jesus was the earthly embodiment of a perfect and

peerless Creator who made man for his own glorification and enjoined him to submit to him. While
created perfect, man had through disobedience fallen
from grace into sin and error thereby spoiling the
perfect handiwork of God. This radical sin corrupted
not only Adam's own nature but also that of the entire
race of his descendants who therefore stand condemned
before their Maker. But fortunately, a way of atonement and salvation had been provided through the
propitiatory sacrifice of God's only begotten son.
While helpless in themselves to avert the just wrath
of God, men were to be permitted (through his mercy
and grace and by their own humility and obedience to
his will) to obtain forgiveness for their sins and to
live in a manner which pleases their Creator.

Some modern Christian theologians may have felt
somewhat uneasy throughout their perusal of the preceding paragraph. Barth admits that these claims are
embarrassingly old-fashioned - but they are true. And
that makes all the difference. The work of the
Christian thinker is cut out for him. This work is
emphatically not that of constructing a theology using
his own reason nor that of making an idol out of human
logic and conscience. Theology and philosophy are
idleness at best and blasphemy at worst. If God has
spoken, the only correct response is to listen - in
silence.

Religious knowledge is <u>sui generis</u> since its
object is God - a reality totally other (<u>totaliter
aliter</u>) than any mundane reality. God is a being
known only to faith and is completely unknowable
(indeed unimaginable) by any natural human faculties.
This wholly alien reality stands in stark contrast to
anything in this world and irrupts inexplicably into

the contingent spatio-temporal continuum. But nature
does not reveal God. The revelation of God is solely
in his word. But it is not in the Bible if by that
one means that one can find it through biblical herme-
neutics. Critical biblical scholarship could throw
light on the historical Jesus but not on the theological Christ. The Bible is, Barth tells us, indeed
the Word of God but we do not come to know this
through our own natural gifts or by asking questions
about its authenticity and reasonableness. It is
blasphemous to appraise divinity by human tests.
Indeed, it is sinful to commend the truth of the
Christian revelation to non-Christians on the grounds
that the character of Jesus is exemplary his life
being a revelation of the moral excellence of deity.
Some men do have knowledge of God but this knowledge
differs from all other kinds of knowledge in its
content, origin, and mode of communication. Philosophy, religion, and academic theology are human
inventions; Christian faith is a gift of divine grace.

Neither reason nor experience can be trusted as a
basis for religious faith. Human reason as corrupted
by sin is not only inadequate to provide a saving
knowledge of God, it is actually a positively perver-
ting influence. "Religion" is the product of human
experience and human belief; faith is based on divine
revelation and divine action. God can become known to
us only through some totally nonrational process of
revelation. The only legitimate task of reason in
matters of faith is to make revelation clearer.
Reason must submit to the authority of revelation as
it submits to the authority of the experientially
given and the factual.

The self-disclosure of God in Christ may seem gratuitous and even foolish in the eyes of the most refined human sagacity. But faced with genuine revelation, the right response is not understanding but worship. How does one recognise an authentic revelation and distinguish it from a false rival? Barth replies that one cannot claim one has recognised a bona fide revelation for this would imply that the fallen finite creature can comprehend the perfect infinite Creator. Men can neither recognise revelation nor respond to it. But revelation is greeted with an appropriate response from those elected for the privilege and yet this response is not even partly due to men's own prior efforts. Revelation is recognised through revelation via the impetus that faith receives through revelation: revelation creates its own response. Similarly, while faith enables one to know God, faith itself is not a human faculty. The faith that recognises God is itself the work of the mysterious and gracious God. We have nothing to contribute - except sin, error, confusion, and pride.

Barth's theology is a threnody about our spiritual hopelessness: there is no path from humanity to deity, no way of gaining knowledge of the divine reality through ordinary human experience or through interpretation of that experience. There is, properly speaking, no such discipline as natural theology; its actual existence, Barth informs us, is due to a radical mistake. There is, however, a path from deity to humanity - the somewhat circuitous path that Christ travelled in his Incarnation. This is, then, the truth about that singularly colossal reality which demands human loyalty and veneration; and it is a truth which divine grace alone could enable a man to recognise for it transcends human ability altogether.

In the writings of Kierkegaard and the neo-
orthodox writers influenced by him (of whom Barth is
characteristic), we find an impressive collection of
theological objections to dependence on reason in
matters of faith. Now it needs to be said that there
is, of course, some supporting evidence for anti-
rationalism in the biblical canon: there is some
religious sanction for questioning the authority of
our reasoning faculty. In Scripture, the authority of
human reason may, for example, be questioned in order
to emphasise the importance of some religious values
(such as trust and obedience) which require a suprarational belief in the ultimate goodness of the divine
purpose for men.[31] There is, however, no theological
warrant for the exaggerated disparagement of reason so
characteristic of fideistic and revelationist positions; such a denigration of reason is rooted in an
unreasonable biblical exegesis which emphasises too
exclusively one legitimate scriptural concern while
ignoring other opposed but equally important ones.

There is no explicit rejection of reason, as a
means of learning or testing truths about God and
salvation, by Jesus or by St. Paul; and there is some
implied recognition of the role of reason in the
religious life.[32] Indeed, what is scriptural is that
reason is limited and subject to perversion - not that
it is totally incapable of bringing us to truth. Thus
even Paul's much-quoted remark about the "wisdom" of
the Gentiles and the "foolishness" of the Cross is not
so much a lament against reason per se as against a
particularly high estimate of the efficacy of reason
in the ethico-religious life. Paul, in effect if not
in intention, questions the Hellenistic philosophical
reliance on an impartial reason which is alleged to

supply the supreme motivation in human conduct i.e.,
the Socratic thesis of the adequacy of rational knowledge for doing the good.[33]   Against this worldly
wisdom, Paul holds up a remarkably insightful estimate
of the sheer depth of human depravity and perversity
seeing that men may rationally choose evil and indeed
choose evil while knowing the good.   The apparent
irrationality of the Cross - a stumbling-block to the
Jews and an affront to the Greek intellect - is, then,
to be interpreted more in terms of men's tragically
limited self-understanding than in terms of what may
appear as the unreasonableness of God.

Let us suppose, for the sake of a case, that
men's rational powers are indeed limited by the sin-
fulness of their nature.   But even if we grant this,
there is still something theologically suspect about
that extreme denigration of reason which some Protestants relish.   Is it credible that the reason which
God has given us has been so irremediably estranged
from its proper object as to render all human attempts
to know God utterly futile?   For one thing, it certainly seems unworthy of reverence to conceive of God
as being so indifferent to men's earnest search for
him that he reveals himself to whomsoever he wills and
at whatever arbitrary juncture he pleases; the search
for him does not at all affect his speaking the
decisive word when it suits his own good pleasure.
More generally, the total distrust of the natural man
- his conscience, his mental constitution, and so on -
seems religiously offensive.   In theological terms,
the Fall may have damaged human nature but it seems
harder to believe that it corrupted it completely.
St. Thomas Aquinas is a good guide here.   According to
St. Thomas, men can prepare themselves for God's

revelation by the use of their own natural reason
since "grace does not supplant nature, but perfects
it".[34] God's grace is not a substitute for but rather
a supplement to human effort: we need to tie the
camel _and_ trust in God. And theologically, given the
implied optimism about human nature in Jesus' willing-
ness to bless the children and in his peculiarly
moving claim that the coming Kingdom belongs to such
as these,[35] it is hard to believe that the later
ecclesiastical theories of _total_ depravity (and perhaps even the doctrine of _peccatum originale_) conform
to the original teachings of Jesus himself. Moreover,
if indeed "Wisdom leads us back to childhood",[36]
childhood could scarcely be a corrupted state.

The objections raised in the preceding paragraph
are, a defender of neo-orthodoxy is likely to retort,
just the ones which a human reason (defiled by sin as
it is) would raise against the divine truth. The
absoluteness of God's truth, our protagonist continues, must not be subordinated to human rationality
for it is precisely as a corrective to the limitations
and errors of a contaminated human reason that God
revealed his message in the first place. Furthermore,
to allow reason to determine the status of a particular religious doctrine is theologically objection-
able: it is intellectual idolatry. Reason may of
course decide between truth and error in mundane
matters but it is presumptuous to attempt to decide by
reason whether God exists or whether one ought to fear
him. Whether reason leads to acceptance or rejection
of God, isn't reason the highest god before whom even
God must be sacrificed? Faith in the efficacy of
reason is idolatrous. As Reinhold Niebuhr has
famously said: "...[T]he reason which asks the

question whether the God of religious faith is plausible has already implied a negative answer to the
question because it has made itself God and naturally
cannot tolerate another".[37]

These are important objections but they are
easily answered. Two comments will suffice. Firstly,
if a man refuses to worship a god who, he believes,
does not actually exist, and does so refuse under the
guidance of reason, his action is not only not idolatrous, it is positively virtuous. It is wrong -
sinful, in religious parlance - to worship what one
believes does not exist. Since it is as possible to
believe in false deities as in genuine ones, the
tutelage of reason is necessary for detecting idols
and making the right choice. Secondly, to question
the truth or reasonableness of the Christian faith is
not, contra Niebuhr, tantamount to sitting in judgement upon the Christian deity. One can sit in judgement upon God only if one says of what is known and
acknowledged to be a bona fide divine revelation that
it merely expresses God's opinions and that it remains
an open question whether or not these opinions are
worthy of credence until human reason has issued its
verdict. But a man cannot be taken to be judging God
merely in virtue of the fact that he uses his own
reason to decide the outcome of the theoretically
prior puzzle, namely, whether or not any particular
alleged revelation is actually genuine. In general, a
man may justifiably use his own reason as long as he
does not think that his judgement could, per absurdum,
override God's judgement once the latter has been
decisively determined. While it is obviously hubri-
stic to reject God's judgement after it has been
decisively determined, a believer is not culpable if

he uses his own reason merely to determine what God's judgement is. God has the <u>decisive</u> word in the affair - not the <u>sole</u> one.

But isn't this the voice of that presumptuous human - all too human - reason all over again? A man may appear as if he were preserving his intellectual integrity in raising such questions before giving his allegiance, the objection will run, and yet, in fact, he is just a doubter whose pride and sinful condition are making him resist surrender to the divine will. Surely, the objection continues, the true explanation for men's desire to validate divine truth by the use of their own reason lies in their dishonest refusal to countenance their defects as human and fallible creatures. Kierkegaard thought that the principal obstacle to the acceptance of Christian belief was men's unwillingness to obey God caused by an arrogant self-will rather than sincere doubt or disbelief. Doubts concerning the truth of Christianity are not rational or intellectual in character; they are due to moral causes produced as they are by sin and expressing as they do sinful pride.[38] And such doubts are not to be answered by intellectual proofs. Amassing evidences for or against Christianity is pointless; indeed, rational apologetics is a disservice to the faith. The cause of doubt is not reason but sin; the cure for doubt is not reason but faith. Without faith, reason is useless for the sinful heart will corrupt reason too; with faith, reason is unnecessary. If it is only sin and selfishness rather than reason which cause rejection, it is only grace rather than reason which confirms the truth of Christianity in the human heart.

Now it needs to be said that some doubt is indeed the result of rebellion and "sinful pride". If a man wishes to evade his religious duty - a duty he acknowledges to be entailed by his religious convictions - he may fabricate specious objections or induce insincere doubts in order to seek release from his duty. Once a given objection or doubt is answered, such a man generates a new one because his religious convictions imply sacrifices and require submission to unwelcome demands. But one cannot thus impugn the motives of all those who reject the Christian faith. Many seekers after truth seem to be beset by doubts which are, to all appearances, utterly sincere. Some of these doubts have intellectual grounds. Take, for example, the rejection of some doctrinal and moral Christian claims by Jews and Muslims. The deity of Jesus is rejected by Jews and Muslims on what seem prima facie reasonable grounds. The Christian moral injunction "Turn the other cheek" is rejected (with some apparent justification) by Islamic ethics in favour of the perhaps less noble but more practical maxim "Act honourably but there is no need to turn the other cheek". Again, Nietzsche's disturbingly powerful assault on the Christian forms of the virtues of humility and compassion could scarcely be seen as groundless.[39] It is one thing for a Christian (i.e., an avowed follower of Christ) to invent, say, a biblical exegesis which employs evasive casuistical tactics to arrive at relatively pleasant interpretations of ostensibly harsh commands or to ask "Why?" once too often with respect to religious claims he does accept; but it is another thing, for those who reject Christianity, to develop, with intellectual integrity, rival schemes of thought. The avowed

Christian may be evading his duty but the non-Christian may well experience serious misgivings about the authenticity or truth of the Christian faith. And if it is said that a Jew's or Muslim's refusal to see his life in terms of specifically Christian theological categories can only be understood as the last refuge of the sinful self in an ultimately pointless Promethean rebellion against the Creator, then the correct response is that this is a straightforwardly question-begging assumption.

A _tu quoque_ is also in place here. There is no lack of pride among those who insist that reliance on reason leads to sinful presumption. Presumably, presumption has other sources too. Barth and Kierkegaard at times betray insufferable hubris and vanity in their pronouncements. If the arbitrament of reason is rejected, a man may be tempted to think that his own opinions coincide exactly with those of God while those of his sinfully deluded opponents are inspired by the Devil. It is a notorious truth, however, that God's views on any subject are difficult to ascertain. How is it, then, that Barth is so well acquainted with God and his purposes? The audacious tone and method of some of Barth's writings provide for some of the finest instances of pride. If one speaks in the very accents of the voice of God, confuses oneself with deity as a matter of principle, one loses the right to pretend to humility. And if hubris be unacceptable in ordinary men, how much more so in a man of God. In fine, then, the fideistic anti-rationalist has a tendency to hubris since his decisions concerning what is revelatory or theologically genuine are not open to normal rational scrutiny and hence the unquestionable authority of the divine may occasionally be claimed on behalf of what is only human thought - in a context in which no appeal to evidence, coherence or rationality is allowed.

The defender of neo-orthodoxy will, at this stage, probably attempt to put an end to this entire dialectical exchange. God has spoken in history through Christ, he will re-iterate, and it is with this reality alone that we should be concerned. The rest is mere "philosophy and empty deceit".[40] When asked for a validation of faith, we should either decline to accommodate the request or else appeal to the authority of Christ, the Bible, and the Church. We must recognise the urgency of our situation and the momentousness of our religious decisions. Life is short; we must prepare ourselves for death and divine judgment. We are incurably sinful folk; we must recognise our desperately alienated state and simply accept the Christian offer of salvation. The cure for sin is faith - not philosophy. A decisive passionate commitment to Christianity could alone save us. And if we cannot understand or come to believe the para-doxical claims of Christianity, then let us heroically "endure the crucifixion of our understanding".[41]

It is true, of course, that once God has spoken, it is irreverent to ask for further evidence or even to raise questions or doubts. But the problem is that the intuition expressed by the proposition "I am now hearing the voice of God" accompanies contradictory beliefs - as is evidenced by the (apparently) con-flicting claims of different prophetic traditions. This is unfortunate but true. And scepticism about claims to revealed knowledge is both natural and justified. One simply has to decide whether or not God really has spoken and to wonder if the experience in question is not due just to such less sublime causes as an upset stomach or a surfeit of theological learning. If there is some revelation by which a man may know God, the validity of that revelation must be established by rational reflection. Reason must decide between truly revealed doctrine and teaching that is falsely claimed to be revealed; if there is a true revelation and it has false rivals, we need to judge which is which. It is not an argument to inform an unbelieving opponent that he is contradicted by no less an authority than God himself. This has to be shown to be the case. And that this is difficult to do is palpably obvious. Only an unusual dispensation of hubris could lead anyone to speak with any pretence to infallible authority concerning such matters.

Furthermore, why should one accept the Christian offer of salvation in a world in which such offers abound? Given that our knowledge of rival religious traditions today makes it quite feasible - a live option, if you wish - for, say, a man in Alberta to choose the Hindu offer of salvation, it does seem unforgivably occidocentric and insular if a man insists on choosing the Christian offer and declines to justify his preference. Now even if it is true that life is short and our state desperate, we still have some time - a few years, perhaps - to make critical judgements. It would be wrong to make a capricious choice. And if our eternal destiny does indeed depend upon some urgent "leap of faith" unsupported by any metaphysic, upon the rightness of some arbitrary choice, that would hardly be a compliment to the fair-mindedness of God.

These responses are not likely to impress the neo-orthodox thinker who is secure in the conviction

that men are contentious and wicked creatures more
obedient to the voice of reason than to the voice of
God. But even granted that we are sinful and captious
creatures, the worries persist. Why has God concen-
trated his blessings on a group of affluent Christian
nations? Why does God choose to favour certain men
and certain communities in a manner that is, to all
appearances, arbitrary and unfair? Why are religious
experiences that seem qualitatively very similar
revelatory in Sweden but illusory in Saudi Arabia?
Again, on what grounds is any doctrine or event or
person to be regarded as ultimately authoritative for
religious believers? Is the Bible God's revelation?
Does the Koran supersede the Bible as the final revelation of the divine purpose for men on earth? And,
more fundamentally, why should anything at all be
regarded as God's revelation in contrast with what is
humanly known and humanly discoverable? The list of
troubling issues does not end here. Nor is this the
stuff of which artificial puzzles are made of but
rather that which genuinely agitates thoughtful human
beings. Is Christianity the culmination of the prophetic tradition? If so, why? If not, why not? Is
Christianity uniquely true such that all other religions are, at best, partially true or, at worst,
entirely false? If so, what are we to make of God's
apparent lack of justice in placing some peoples in,
from the point of view of salvation, a specially
favoured position? These questions and others like
them are not the invention of atheistic critics;
reasonable believers do and should address them.
Unless one's choice of faith can be justified in the
language of a universal reason, one cannot reasonably
affirm one faith rather than another. But, surely,

both the defenders of neo-orthodoxy and its opponents have heard this song before. The dispute has reached a deadlock.

- IV -

In order to see why there is a deadlock and whether or not it can be broken, I shall need to shift the focus of the discussion now onto a few problems of theory and method. Consider then the following question: How does philosophy of religion differ from theology? I take it that philosophy of religion treats all types of religion and religious faith as its domain, not presupposing the privileged position of any type, but aiming at discovering what religious truths, if any, are implied by the psychology, sociology, and history of religion. And, although this is a controversial claim, I assume that a philosophy of religion may legitimately aim at discovering, through rational interpretation of human experience, both the truth of religious beliefs, if indeed they are or even could be true, and the value of religious practices and attitudes. Now, theology, as I understand it, simply starts with the faith of some particular religion - the Jewish or the Sikh, for example - and expounds that faith while accepting the central tenets of the religion in question as revealed or otherwise authoritatively grounded truths. More precisely, theology typically consists of (a) putatively true statements of historical fact concerning religiously significant events; (b) statements about the meaning and interpretation of scriptural writings; (c) metaphysical inquiry concerning such central theological concepts as sin, grace, miracle, eschatology and, in the case of some of the Eastern religions, concepts

such as karma, nirvana, dukkha, atman, and so on; and
(d) systematic discussion of the relationship between
rational (or humanly accessible) knowledge and
revealed (or ordinarily inaccessible) knowledge and of
the exact epistemological status of each.

Let me say a little more about this distinction -
a distinction which is, incidentally, not a sharp one
since items (c) and (d) above may well be, in effect,
a part of the philosophy of religion. Any theology is
a distinctive metaphysical theory which supplies
answers to a certain range of religious questions. A
revealed theology stands within a certain tradition by
taking some particular events or documents to reveal
the nature and purposes of a certain type of God. To
be a specifically Christian theology, a theory must
take it that, in the person and life of the historical
Jesus, the nature and purposes of the divine Creator
are, to some degree, perhaps even definitively,
revealed. Now, each revealed theology has a corresponding philosophical theology which examines the
rationality of various religiously central assumptions. The philosophy of religion is the business of
constructing various philosophical theologies, perhaps
comparing them, and seeing if any of them are true or
warranted. Philosophy of religion is, in fine, essentially the search for religious truth.

We are now in a position to examine the neo-
orthodox claim that Christian theology must not take
the norms or criteria by which it conducts its case
and evaluates its conclusions from some other intellectual discipline such as the philosophy of religion
or even the philosophy of the Christian religion; it
should rather develop its own distinctive criteria. A
Christian theology, unique among our intellectual

activities, is founded upon a recognition of God's
truth as he himself has made it known to mankind.
Consequently, the methods of theology must be responsive to God's self-revelation. The divine revelation
is the ultimate standard in terms of which all human
conceptions must be judged; one must not judge
revelation by inadequate human criteria. Theology
cannot be, we are told, the true interpretation and
explication of Christian faith if it deviates from
norms and criteria secreted by divine revelation
itself - criteria which are faithfully responsive to
God's self-disclosure without regard to the criteria
or conclusions of secular science and philosophy. The
method of theology must, then, be _sui generis_ and
independent of all other intellectual activities;
theologians should reject the methods and criteria
indigenous to non-theological disciplines. In fine,
theology is an internal enterprise, isolated from
secular intellectual norms, whose task is to lay bare
the meaning and implications of God's revelation.

How is one to interpret the claim that religious
faith is totally autonomous? Presumably, what is
meant is that religion is somehow independent of
secular science and philosophy - that our judgements
about the truth of religion are actually independent
of our judgements about the nature of experienced
reality as a whole. Understood thus, one can see that
such a claim stands in need of elaborate justification. The _onus probandi_ seems to be on the advocate
of autonomy for religion. Complete autonomy would
presuppose a distinctively Christian basis to theoretical thought; God would be taken to be sustaining the
world epistemologically by, for example, letting the
Holy Spirit underwrite the truth of every (true)

proposition. The notion of such a culturally independent theological norm may well be unformulable if not
unintelligible in the last analysis. One would need
to argue carefully to show that this is so. I do not
intend to do that here. I suspect that the kind and
extent of independence for theology claimed by writers
like Kierkegaard and Barth is impossible to attain.
Disciplines are inter-dependent; autonomy is limited.
For example, even if religion could be freed from the
shackles of philosophical and metaphysical scrutiny,
it could not escape scientific investigation. The
admittedly veridical experiences of religious men had
arisen not _in vacuo_ but rather in a specifiable historical and socio-psychological context. The sciences
of history, sociology, and psychology are entitled to
investigate the rise and development, institutional
embodiment, and psychological structure and function
of religion _qua_ socio-historical phenomenon. If one
wishes to derive connections between the results
offered by these disciplines and our experience in
general and to appraise the various connections or
distinctions effected while doing so, some recourse to
general theoretical, perhaps rational philosophical,
thought is inevitable.

The neo-orthodox view is, I shall now argue,
mistaken. Whatever may be said about the autonomy of
theology, it cannot be interpreted to mean a radical
independence from other ordinary intellectual activities. Christian theology cannot rightly claim to be
the sole area of human understanding which is immune
from rational assessment: the ideal of complete
theological epistemic autonomy must be rejected.

If theological method is to be formulated on the
basis of God's revelation, we need, as a first step,

to locate God's truth. If such a truth could be located, then it would indeed serve as the ultimate court of appeal in theology. Now the Bible, for example, cannot be taken, uncritically, to be the place where divine truth resides. On one level, the Bible is simply a collection of many documents recording the cultural history of Israel, Egypt and other nations. It is written in the vernacular of a people and reflects the general political and cultural situation of the Hebrews living in the Near East. Again, if revelation is said to find its locus in Jesus of Nazareth, one needs to remember that Jesus was, in an important way, simply a man shaped by his culture and social context. The messianic status accorded him can be made intelligible only against the background supplied by the political aspirations of the Jewish people.

The underlying error in neo-orthodoxy is its view of religious faith as a _fait accompli_ sustained by an arrogant finality and sitting in glorious isolation from man and and his predicament. But Christian theology does not derive its appeal from the fact that it expounds _divine_ truths (even supposing, for the sake of argument, that it does) but rather from its logically prior concern with providing an enlightening perspective on the _human_ condition. If there are compelling experiences with which it cannot adequately deal, it will become irrelevant to us even if it is, in fact, an explication of eternal religious truths. The neo-orthodox thinkers celebrate the notion that Christian faith requires a radical rupture with ordinary human experience and imagination and with normal worldly pursuits and ambitions. Thus, Kierke-gaard boasts that Christianity does not accommodate

itself to the frailties of our nature while Barth is
happy in the conviction that the Church has a higher
calling than the service of mankind. But, surely,
while God is indeed a "wholly other" reality in the
sense that his existence is independent of men's
knowledge of it, it does not follow that our experience of God occurs in complete irrelation to or in
utter independence of ordinary mundane events. Again,
while Christianity aims at transcending human nature
by emancipating men from a purely natural existence,
it continues to serve human interests in the deepest
sense. By putting God at the centre, one is not
mutilating or disparaging human welfare but rather
enhancing it: men's true interests are secured, it is
thought, not by excessive materialism, sensuality, or
arrogant self-absorption but rather by whole-hearted
submission to the divine will.

The preceding paragraph may have seemed like a
digression. But the insistence on autonomy and on the
need for some separate criterion of religious truth
is, I believe, essentially tied up with the conviction
that genuine religious faith (unlike science, philosophy, and bogus religion) is a response to an exclusively other-worldly reality. Religious belief, it is
argued, is not the kind of belief that rests on empirical or scientific evidence. Indeed, the acquisition
of such belief is not an intellectual act subject to
ordinary volition or inhibition since it is not a
human act at all but rather a gratuitous descent of
grace. (Small wonder then that religious writers are
not content with the criteria that are applied in
science and daily life to detect the presence of truth
or falsehood.) The very attempt to grasp ultimate
religious truth by reason is, we are told, misguided

since it will be flouted by the object which it attempts to comprehend. To explicate or to defend Christianity by the use of unaided human reason is to denature it: one changes the whole character of the Christian message from the revealed Word of God to a human metaphysic facing various philosophical rivals and seeking the coveted approval of human reason.

But isn't Christianity just that i.e., a human metaphysic in competition with other belief-systems and aiming at winning the hearts of reasonable men? Kierkegaard and his neo-orthodox disciples merely assume that Christianity is the gift of an eternal God. Religion, science, and philosophy are all responses to the same reality, namely, the empirical reality of this world. If the Christian religion is indeed the repository of revealed truths about some transcendent realm and its relation to us, this has to be shown to be the case. And dramatic dogmatism is not an adequate substitute for argument.

It could not have escaped anyone's notice that the neo-orthodox claims on behalf of the Christian dispensation rest on an entirely arbitrary and indefensible basis which could stand unquestioned only as long as it was assumed that God had in fact revealed himself in Jesus Christ. This assumption is present both in the writings of Kierkegaard and in the writings of the neo-orthodox theologians influenced by him. Kierkegaard, for example, assumes that faith cannot be conceived in non-Christian terms or directed towards objects other than the Christian deity even though this assumption introduces a dominant inconsistency into his system. Now at times, Kierkegaard seems to think that through existential commitment "the individual is in the truth even if he should

happen to be thus related to what is not true".[42]
Kierkegaard explains:

> If one who lives in the midst of Christendom
> goes up to the house of God, the house of
> the true God, with the true conception of
> God in his knowledge, and prays, but prays
> in a false spirit; and one who lives in an
> idolatrous community prays with the entire
> passion of the infinite, although his eyes
> rest upon the image of an idol: where is
> there most truth? The one prays in truth to
> God though he worships an idol; the other
> prays falsely to the true God, and hence
> worships in fact an idol.[43]

The whole burden here, it seems, is on the integrity
of the inward attitude we take towards whatever is the
object of our worship. But Kierkegaard is actually
showing us Potemkin villages here for he still speaks
of a "true conception of God". And yet, surely, it is
obvious that if truth and faith are defined as subjectivity, one cannot consistently speak of a "true
conception of God" that could be made available independently of the subjectivity of the passionate believer.
Far from regarding faith as a wholly subjective
expression of a man's wishes or of what a man merely
imagines to be true, Kierkegaard here seems to be
implying that faith is actually a form of knowledge.
Faith does not remain wholly within the confines of
the individual's will or intellect: it comes into
contact with reality. Kierkegaard realised, of
course, that while integrity and sincerity may have
intrinsic value, the inward attitude cannot be sound
if the worship is directed towards an illusion or an

idol. In effect, then, Kierkegaard is encouraging Christians to become authentic: the faithful should not believe the truth in a false spirit. But he has no doubts about what the truth is.

The truth of subjectivity, then, has to do with the quality of the believer's relationship to the object of worship. No such quality can determine the reality of that object and Kierkegaard knows that. And yet if discipleship to Christ is the criterion of faith, then the truth of Christianity is assumed ab initio. And so, for all his talk of passion and pure subjectivity, Kierkegaard insists, without argument, that the correct solution to the problem of faith is personal faith directed towards the one living Christian God. It is difficult to see how, in that case, his proposal is anything more than a counsel of perfection aimed at getting hypocritical Christians to develop greater sincerity. The problem of truth has, for Kierkegaard, already been resolved.

But faith entitles us to claim confidently, the neo-orthodox thinker will respond, that Christianity is indeed true. Philosophical speculation is theologically pointless for it cannot help us construct true religious doctrines; God can be truly known only by revelation. The central core of Christianity - the self-disclosure of God in Christ - is an unanticipated creative divine act. There is no point, our protagonist tells us, in attempting to demonstrate the existence and unity of the Godhead since such knowledge, by itself, would be futile unless God were a moral personality; and our knowledge of the moral excellence of God is derived from his self-disclosure in Christ and not from any purely human rational proof. The arguments of natural theology are philosophically inconclusive; the methods of natural theology (i.e., inference from and analogy with the world as data) are inherently unsuited to gaining genuine religious insight. Moreover, intellectual criticisms of religious doctrine are irrelevant. One must extricate the biblical conception of faith from the alien matrix of a pagan Greek philosophical enterprise which had imparted a foreign ideal of secular reason to the nascent Christian religion. Rational or philosophical method has no place in theology.

There is an important confusion in this response. Even if the kernel of Christianity is an unanticipated divine act, it does not follow that the appraisal or assessment of its significance _ex post facto_ is carried out in utter independence of or in irrelation to our ordinary human canons of validity and ordinary criteria of truth, falsity, coherence, rationality, and profundity. Philosophical reason may not be the instrument of religious knowledge in the sense of producing religious insight in the first place; but it does not follow from this alone that it cannot undertake the more modest task of judging the truth and validity of revelatory claims once they have appeared. And that revelation must be judged by human standards is no more to belittle revelation than the fact that salvation depends on God's decision to offer it belittles salvation.

The neo-orthodox rejoinder to this argument is predictable: revelation goes to set the standard for judging truth and falsehood in matters of religious faith and could hardly be itself subject to the strictures of a sin-stained reason. Indeed, revelation is a total offence to our understanding. The very character of the Christian Gospel, it will be proudly

54

granted, betrays its irrationality. There are metaphysical antinomies: God and man are wholly distinct
and yet God became man in history. And there are
moral antinomies: How can the sinless God be cruci-
fied by sinful men? The emphasis on the paradoxical
character of Christianity runs from cover to cover in
Kierkegaard's Postscript: faith is irremediable
uncertainty but demands unconditional trust, revelation reveals God and yet indicates his mysterious
nature, the facility of God's grace is available yet
difficult to appropriate for oneself, and the promise
of ultimate felicity is tied up with inexplicable
present suffering. Christianity is an absolutely
irresolvable paradox. The writers of the epistles of
the New Testament knew that; the glorification of
paradox was no mere accident. And Tertullian's much-
maligned self-congratulatory irrationalism was no mere
hyperbole. From the standpoint of human reason, then,
Christianity is morally absurd and logically incoherent - but it is true nonetheless.

What are we to make of this? It is, of course,
true that apparent absurdity can conceal important
truths. And, moreover, what is contrary to reason
(i.e., irrational) may still be actually true (although
what is incoherent cannot be true). Irrational
beliefs can be true just as rational ones can be
false. Even so, however, Tertullian's prodigal doctrine ("I believe it because it is absurd"[44]) is
unacceptable. The truth in it can be put less extra-
vagantly (and perhaps less memorably); "I believe P
even though the evidence tells against it" is acceptable but "I believe P because the evidence tells
against it" is not - just as a man may believe P,
contra mundum, despite universal opposition but not

<u>because</u> of such opposition. Now, relatedly, reve-
lation need not (and indeed cannot) be a total affront
to our understanding. It may challenge our preconcep-
tions, set new standards, and cause us to revise our
previous judgements and intuitions. We may do all of
these things under its impact but revealed criteria
must necessarily be recognisably linked to ordinary
human criteria of judgement and rationality. Again,
paradox can certainly help us to direct our attention
towards neglected aspects of our experience, aid us in
coming to a profounder understanding of the way in
which, for example, material existence is essentially
foreign to creatures destined for eternal life, and so
on; but the truth resides not in the paradox but in
the rational synthesis which transcends it. A theological method based on a belief in the superiority of
paradox cannot be sound since paradox in religious
thought is always a means to an end - never an end in
itself.

To be sure, the worry is that a straightforward
trust in reason implies a denial of the paradoxical
claims of the Christian faith. At the risk of
sounding polemical, Christianity is indeed, in a
perfectly ordinary sense of the word, an unreasonable
religion.[45] Now if one allows, even commends, absurdity, contradiction, and irrationality in allegedly
profound matters, why not elsewhere? What is the
criterion for deciding where absurdity is evidence of
profundity and truth and where evidence of superficiality and falsehood? Moreover, why tolerate only
<u>Christian</u> absurdities in a world in which absurdities
are never in short supply? Why not countenance para-
doxes and absurdities beyond neo-orthodox Christianity? Why is the Incarnation - that paradox <u>par</u>

excellence - a profound truth? Or is it? In a passage of peculiar pathos, a Nietzsche on the verge of insanity writes: "A god come to earth ought to do nothing whatever but wrong: to take upon oneself, not the punishment, but the guilt - only that would be godlike."[46] Hasn't Nietzsche here seized an even greater profundity than the Christian religion? Doesn't Nietzsche have an even profounder paradoxical insight into the Incarnation than Kierkegaard? Are there any limits to unreason? Among paradoxical religious truths, reason has a very hard time indeed.

- V -

To rest one's case here would be premature. Certainly, the life of faith is not primarily an attempt to gratify the intellect but rather to make possible a trustful and loving response towards God. Revelation is not given to us for its own sake: we do not have the revealed truth merely in order that we may know the truth. The hope is that by knowing the truth we may be freed from selfishness and hypocrisy. Thus, a believer's motives in seeking to learn God's purposes from the teaching of Scripture should primarily be practical and personal rather than academic and controversial. Even so, however, we must recognise and understand the truth before we can appropriate it. To be sure, the way to know God is not just through theistic argument; there must also be a personal struggle between the divine will and a man's own will. But there has to be a prior conviction that there is a God who demands such a struggle. Religious belief and commitment are parasitic on an understanding of the world - not independent of it.

Kierkegaard and Barth correctly insist on the human need for God's all-sufficient grace. But they choose the wrong way to effect this emphasis. The temptation to pity man - a creature who, in his finitude, depravity and intellectual bankruptcy, stands in stark contrast to a perfect and powerful God - is usually part of the impetus behind anti-rationalism in religion. But even if there is room for pity in genuine religion, one hardly needs to banish reason to accommodate pity.

Fideists like Kierkegaard rightly emphasise the fallibility and limitations of human reasoning in general and in religious matters in particular but they wrongly recommend us to abandon it. Owing to our intellectual limitations, the ultimate truth about God and the world is of course only partially attainable. Surely, however, some truth is preferable to none at all.

Kierkegaard is deeply convinced that life's supreme values are at stake in religion and that rational investigation threatens to dislodge or imperil them. My own position on this matter is that it is an egregious error to attempt to safeguard a truth by insulating it from rational inquiry. The protection of religious beliefs from critical investigation naturally arouses the suspicion that religious beliefs cannot withstand rational scrutiny. (After all, why should religious beliefs be exempt from the rational scrutiny to which our other beliefs about matter, mind, culture, history, and art are regularly subjected?) There is, I think, absolutely no ground whatsoever for the supposition that a truth is more profound or more graphically graspable if its own delineation and relation to other truths are deliberately kept obscure. Where supreme values are involved, it is our moral duty to investigate and appraise. One loses nothing in the process. If they are genuine, their worth has now become evident; if they are false, one avoids running the risk of mistaking falsehood for supreme value.

Fideism is, in its impulse, if not in its ultimate character, an apologetic movement in religious thought. (How strange that one often opposes apologetics to fideism!) Men of faith wish to resist the encroachments of rational and scientific thought in the field of religion by circumscribing some area of doctrine belonging to faith and declaring its truth and value guaranteed by revelation and thus independent of the vicissitudes of mundane criticism and historical changes of intellectual climate. The right and capacity of reason to judge between truth and error in affirmations of religious belief is questioned in the larger attempt to safeguard such belief and thereby satisfy the religious impulse to locate some eternal landmark of faith amid all the promiscuous relativism of the age.

- VI -

The remarks in the preceding section may appear somewhat desultory. In bringing this chapter to a close, let me see if I can impart some order into them by giving a brief and provisional characterization of reason and some account of its proper role in religious debate.[47] In its broadest sense, "reason" is any human activity directed by the purpose to discover truth. Reason should not be identified with the procedures of the natural sciences (or with these added to the analogous methods of the social sciences). The inadequacy of scientific method as a universal test of truth is obvious when one examines men's experience of value: ethics is the first casualty of scientism. Now the relevant data to be considered in the special sciences is limited; the range of materials relevant to the evaluation of human conduct is, however, much broader and less clearly defined. Presumably, problems about the ultimate significance of human experience bring the whole range of our experience into the arena of relevance. Kierke-gaard is right to insist that a self-imposed temporary impoverishment of our experience is an appropriate technique for attaining truth only in the empirical disciplines.[48] In seeking the truth about the purpose and destiny of mankind, one needs to be immersed in maximum wealth of experience. A broad conception of reason - a more comprehensive construal than mere analytical abstraction - is needed for dealing with issues of destiny and purpose. We need, that is, a reason more broadly grounded in the total experience of our species.

These are very abstract considerations. More concretely, a conception of reason which is incapable of effecting a fair assessment of religious convic-tions is that of a reason which is by definition or assumption opposed to the possibility of genuine revelation, even though it is philosophically mature and otherwise comprehensive. If "reason" signifies simply the inquirer in quest of truth, there is a priori no reason why revelation, as a significant human experience, should be debarred from making its own independent contribution to the task of finding the truth. (That the initiative of God plays an indispensable role in the revelatory process is not in dispute.) Experiences which may be regarded, and perhaps rightly, as divine revelations are also data to be assessed in a rational inquiry. Of course, we need to decide first whether or not it is reasonable to believe that there are any revealed data and moreover to judge which data, if any, have this unusual status.

Many religious writers who demand a separate criterion of religious truth are, in fact, in need only of the assurance that the reason which judges religion be rooted in the totality of our experience. In other words, religion must be judged neither on the basis of a priori considerations alone nor on that of purely secular non-religious ones. There must also be an attempt to evaluate and interpret the actual evidences supplied by the religious experience of mankind; religious claims must make an independent contribution to the evidence on which the final verdict is based. Hence, for example, a naturalistic thinker who operates with a provincial conception of reason, according to which belief in revelation is assumed a priori to be a superstition, is likely to arrive at judgements prejudiced by this initial stipulation.

Notes

[1] Søren Kierkegaard, Concluding Unscientific Post-script (Princeton: Princeton University Press, 1941), translated by David F. Swenson and intro-duction, notes, and completion of translation by Walter Lowrie. See p. 28, pp. 135-136. Kierkegaard used pseudonyms for some of his early works. I assume that this technique was intended to represent the various phases of Kierkegaard's own complex thought.

[2] Søren Kierkegaard, Philosophical Fragments (Princeton: Princeton University Press, 1962), translated by David F. Swenson and translation revised by Howard V. Hong in second edition, with introduction and commentary by Niels Thulstrup. See Chapter III, pp. 46 ff.

[3] Postscript, pp. 147 ff.

[4] ibid., p. 28.

[5] ibid., pp. 135-136.

[6] ibid. pp. 50-52.

[7] ibid., p. 54.

[8] I assume that the translations from the Danish can be trusted.

[9] I cannot pursue this issue here. For details, see Ludwig Wittgenstein, Philosophical Investigations (Oxford: Basil Blackwell, 1963), passim.

[10] Bertrand Russell, The Problems of Philosophy (London: Oxford University Press, 1957), pp. 46 ff.

[11] Postscript, p. 182. Emphasis removed.

[12] ibid., pp. 25 ff.

[13] ibid., p. 41.

[14] ibid., p. 26, p. 28.

[15] Postscript, p. 69; Fragments, p. 104.

[16] Postscript, p. 182.

[17]Cecil J. Cadoux argues persuasively for this view in his The Life of Jesus (West Drayton: Pelican Books, 1948).

[18]Fragments, pp. 68 ff.

[19]Postscript, p. 28.

[20]Fragments, p. 52.

[21]Postscript, pp. 16-27, 34-35, 75.

[22]ibid., p. 189. Emphasis in original.

[23]ibid. p. 31.

[24]ibid. p. 182.

[25]ibid., pp. 381-382.

[26]ibid., p. 381.

[27]ibid., pp. 189-190. For Kierkegaard, incidentally, faith is not an act of will in the sense of being initiated by human volition or of being within human power to acquire. God supplies the condition of faith i.e., the Paradox of the Atonement.

[28]Søren Kierkegaard, Fear and Trembling (Garden City: Doubleday and Co., 1954), published along with The Sickness Unto Death in one volume, translated with introduction and notes by Walter Lowrie, p. 131.

[29]Postscript, p. 53.

[30]I choose to expound Barth's position here because it is characteristic of this school and is, moreover, the most influential of any writer of this persuasion. My concern here is not with locating differences between Barth and other thinkers of a similar doctrinal outlook; nor am I concerned to trace with scholarly precision the development of Barth's complex theological scheme. For Barth's views, see the following works by him: Knowledge of God (London: Hodder, 1938), translated by J.L.M. Haire and Ian Henderson; The Doctrine of the Word of God (New York: Charles Scribner's Sons, 1936); and Dogmatics in Outline (New York: Harper, 1959), translated by G.T. Thompson. For some standard criticisms of Barth's theological outlook, see Brand Blanshard's piece, "Critical Reflections on Karl

Barth", in Faith and the Philosophers, John Hick (ed.), (New York: St. Martin's Press, 1964), pp. 159-200.

[31]See, for example, the anti-philosophical passage in Colossians 2:8 ff and note its context.

[32]See, for example, Matthew 5:46-47, I Thessalonians 5:21, Isaiah 1:18.

[33]St. Paul's famous lament is in I Corinthians 1:20-25. For the Platonic-Socratic view that a fully rational comprehension of the ultimate good is necessarily determinative of conduct, see, for example, Meno, 97 b-c, 100a.

[34]This is the essence of Thomas' thought. See Nature and Grace: Selections from the Summa Theologica of Thomas Aquinas, Alan Fairweather (ed.), (Philadelphia: Westminster Press, 1954).

[35]Matthew 19:14

[36]The remark is found in Pascal's Pensees (Remark No. 82) and derives from Matthew 18:3.

[37]Reinhold Niebuhr, The Nature and Destiny of Man (New York: Charles Scribner's Sons, 1949), Vol. 1, pp. 165-166.

[38]The locus classicus for this view is Romans 1:18-23.

[39]See especially Nietzsche's The Anti-Christ (Harmondsworth: Penguin Books, 1968), translated by R.J. Hollingdale in one volume along with Twilight of the Idols, although Nietzsche's other books also offer powerful criticisms of Christianity.

[40]Colossians 2:8.

[41]Postscript, p. 500.

[42]ibid., p. 178.

[43]ibid., pp. 179-180.

[44]"Credo quia absurdum".

[45]For a particularly powerful indictment of Christianity as an unreasonable, even absurd, religion, see Thomas Paine's audacious The Age of Reason

(Secaucus: Citadel Press, 1948, 1974), p. 83, p. 186.

[46]Friedrich   Nietzsche,   _Ecce   Homo_   (Harmondsworth: Penguin Books, 1979), translated by R.J. Holling- dale, p. 45.   Emphasis in original.

[47]For   further   discussion   of   this   theme,   see Chapter VI.

[48]But compare John Rawls' technique of "the veil of ignorance" in his influential _A theory of Justice_ (Cambridge: Harvard University Press, 1971).

Chapter III
The Christian Tradition

- I -

The terms "tradition" and "modernity" are often used antynomously in religious debate as if modernity itself had no tradition. What characterises religious modernism is not, of course, any lack of tradition but rather the conviction that traditional teachings can no longer be affirmed in traditional ways. Even a conservative theology must, the modernists urge, concede the necessity of accommodation to and compromise with a hostile secular culture and its dominant intellectual norms.

Ever since the sceptical currents of eighteenth century rationalism struck the knell to the stark literalism of the older theology, those who have resisted the encroachments of the critical temperament have, it is thought, merely helped to render their religious systems obsolete. Once historical biblical criticism had shown that the Scriptures could not be seen as a repository of materials for the construction of a self-consistent doctrinal matrix, liberal-minded theologians began to question the received opinion about the centrality of religious dogma. To be sure, the experience behind religious doctrine may, they claim, remain constant; but its expression must change if obsolescence is to be avoided. Doctrine simply is, it came to be thought, experience interpreted in accordance with the contemporaneous intellectual framework. The attempt to endow meaning and structure to religious belief-systems had to be a perennial one - it could not have permanence. Doctrine in theology was subject to revision from time to time.

The doctrinal cleavage of the sixteenth century was only the first step in rupturing the unity of Christendom. The liberalizing tendencies which threatened religious conservatism in the nineteenth century were resisted mainly by Catholic writers unwilling to qualify their staunchly traditionalist views; most Protestant thinkers began to endorse the doctrinal revisions forced upon them by the advance of rational and scientific reflection. For Protestant theologians, the climacteric issue was not whether or not revision was necessary - that question had already been settled in the affirmative - but rather the extent to which revisions of doctrine could be effected without sacrificing the essence of Christianity in the process.

A dominant concern of modern Christian philosophical thought has been the issue of the essence of Christianity. This worry has taken the form of attempting to separate the essential or central from the peripheral or extraneous and to indicate the possibility, the need, and the legitimacy of such a separation. Kant's seminal Religion Within the Limits of Reason Alone[1] is an early attempt to separate the primary from the secondary elements in Christianity. The touchstone Kant applies is the moral consciousness: whatever fails to satisfy this cannot be truly essential to the faith. Kant famously insisted on the autonomy of morality and on the consequent subordination of religion to morality. The substance of the true faith is ethical: the good life is what pleases God. The religious consciousness, according to Kant, seeks to view its duties as divinely sanctioned imperatives. Christian doctrine is more or less an external supplement to Christian morality.

A signal achievement of the Kantian system was the removal of the metaphysical element from religious belief. Faith is not a by-product of metaphysics or a defective philosophical understanding of the world; it is not a form of theoretical knowledge for which we have only inconclusive evidence. It is rather a practical mode of apprehending reality. Even the existence of God is not theoretically provable; it is guaranteed only in and through our apprehension of the moral law.

Neo-Kantianism in theology gained in influence as the need for some bulwark against secularism became more pronounced. Under the impact of Kant's critical philosophy, Protestant writers began to affirm that "proof" in matters theological should be addressed to the seat of faith - the feeling and willing self - and not to the intellect. Piety cannot be founded on intellectual propositions. Scientific and rational philosophical thought cannot, it was thought, help us in locating the ground of religious belief.

Not every religious thinker endorsed Kant's own somewhat pedestrian moralism. But many championed his anti-metaphysical outlook. Friedrich Schleiermacher, for example, steered between the rigid moralism of Kant, on the one hand, and the extravagant intellectualism of Hegel, on the other, only to locate an emotional impulse (Gefuhl) at the core of Christianity which sustains its distinctive character.[2] Faith, for Schleiermacher, is a feeling of absolute dependence upon God in Christ. Faith is neither the culmination of metaphysical reflection (in the sense of involving the acceptance of theological propositions) nor the rational interpretation of inner religious experience but rather the experience itself.

Once religion was freed from the constraints of science and philosophy, a writer took himself to be at liberty to pursue intellectual inquiry into the history of religion qua social phenomenon, develop disciplines like comparative religion and even philosophy of religion. The believer need not even fear that a historico-scientific investigation of the origin and primitive state of the Christian religion would endanger his faith. Historical biblical criticism is not theology. Orthodoxy should look to the undefiled religious consciousness itself for the defence and justification of religious ideas i.e., ideas which have no place in history and speculative philosophy and are, in consequence, not subject to historical or philosophical judgement. Hence, the true essence of Christianity, its immutable spirit, so to speak, was to be identified with whatever was independent of secular rational thought. The rest was ephemeral, incidental, and probably false.

A significant concern of twentieth century Christian theology and philosophy of the Christian religion has been the attempt to distinguish between the alleged quintessence of Christian belief and its supposedly more or less incidental (i.e., historically and culturally specific) features. Several modern philosophical positions on the status of Christian religious belief incorporate the claim that what is essential to the Christian faith remains intact despite secular critique motivated by perceived advances in rational and scientific thought. Many writers have, however, urged that most of these positions in the philosophy of religion are, in fact, reductionist since they fail to give a philosophical account of the nature of actual Christian belief and

are instead content with offering analyses of various
emaciated versions of the faith. Before giving a
critical assessment of these positions, we must offer
some coherent characterization of these positions
which does not beg crucial questions. It is not at
all obvious, however, that this can be done. There
are several reasons for this scepticism. A major
substantive worry is the one caused by the alleged
success of historical studies in showing that there is
no unitary Christian tradition and that, in consequence, any charge of reductionism must flounder for
want of a generally acceptable account of what is
apocryphal and what canonical to Christianity. After
all, just what, if anything, is common to all the many
forms of what passes for Christianity in this age?
Another major perplexity, methodological in character,
stems from the use of the label "reductionism" in the
philosophy of religion. J.C. Thornton has contended
that accusations of reductionism can legitimately be
levelled only if one has an adequate account of the
real (as opposed to _prima facie_) logical status of
Christian religious belief and of the implied inadequacy of currently available analyses of such belief -
and that it is an open secret no-one has supplied such
an account.[3]

- II -

I shall now argue that, firstly, it is possible
to give a non-questionbegging account of the nature of
Christian belief and, secondly, that, _pace_ Thornton,
we do not need a fully adequate analysis of the nature
of religious belief in order to identify reductionism
in the philosophy of religion.

The Christian religion centres in the personality of its founder. This is theologically unsurprising once one realises that Christians (unlike Jews and Muslims) deify and worship the founder of their faith. It is now widely recognized that this is a characteristic and peculiar feature of Christianity setting it apart from its sister religions of Judaism and Islam. Thus "Muhammadanism", for example, is not, certain engage non-Muslim critics to the contrary notwithstanding,[4] an alternative label for "Islam": it is an utterly erroneous appellation. In an attempt to identify the essence of Christianity, one cannot ignore this most characteristic feature - that much-noted Christocentricity which thinkers of many different Christian denominations regard as central. Hence, Anders Nygren's claim that Christianity is distinguished from all other religions by virtue of its insistence on the revelation of the eternal in the person of Jesus Christ is typical of Christian writers and believers in general.[5]

The religious description of Jesus may vary but all Christians have been united in a sense of loyalty to Jesus of Nazareth - the historical personage - and, in principle at least, in acceptance of his moral and spiritual leadership. By contrast, Christians do not accept, in any straightforward sense at any rate, the ethico-religious hegemony of any of the Jewish patriarchs; and they completely reject the religious authority of the Arabian Prophet. The acceptance of the ethico-spiritual leadership of Jesus (and, perhaps arguably, of those whom he may have appointed as his successors) is unique and central to the Christian faith.

What is the essence of Christianity? There are
three necessary (minimum) conditions for entry into
the Christian fold:[6]
(1) Belief in the existence of one God - a uniquely
     perfect transcendent individual.
(2) Acceptance of the ethico-religious authority and
     leadership of Jesus of Nazareth - the historical
     personage.
(3) A commitment to viewing the life of Jesus as a
     disclosure and human exemplification of the moral
     excellence of deity such that the imitation of
     Jesus' behaviour is already a moral action in the
     believer's life.
Condition (3) deserves comment. Firstly, it
makes a claim that is not equivalent to claiming
divinity for Jesus: it is not a doctrinal comment on
his nature. Secondly, it deliberately leaves room for
controversy over whether Jesus' ministry is an exclusive expression of God's manifold wisdom and righteousness or merely a pivotal and distinctive one.
Relatedly, condition (3) leaves it an open question
whether or not the historical Jesus is the acme of
human development in moral consciousness. Perhaps,
all we need is that he was without sin and stood in
right relationship with God without necessarily
denying the possibility of the occasional moral
failing. And thirdly, the imitation of Christ
(imitatio Christi) is tantamount to a participation in
the moral life of God in a way in which, say, the
imitation of Muhammad (imitatio Muhammadi) is not: to
imitate Muhammad is to imitate an arguably excellent
but undeniably human moral exemplar.
A man who rejects (1) is not a monotheist and is
consequently not a Christian (or a Jew or a Muslim for

that matter). If he rejects either any or all of the above conditions, he is not a Christian. If he accepts (1) in conjunction with other appropriate beliefs but rejects (2) and (3), he may be a Jew or a Muslim (or even a Sikh). What is characteristic of and unique to Christian theism is contained in conditions (2) and (3) while what is common among the different but related traditions of ethical monotheism is contained in condition (1).

The delicate task of supplying a set of sufficient conditions for being a Christian is, fortunately for us, primarily a theological one. Certainly, the religious views which an exemplary Christian orthodoxy would want men to espouse are more robust and controversial than the meagre requirements given above as necessary conditions. Even so, this discussion is not without religious significance especially in an age in which men's capacity for self-deception has reached such proportions that they imagine that a man can be a Christian while rejecting belief in the existence of a supreme author of nature. The three necessary conditions given above are, one might say, the conditions for successful heresy. A man who rejects any or all of these conditions is not even a heretic; he is either not a Christian at all - he may, that is, be an atheist or a member of some non-Christian religious group - or he is an apostate consciously repudiating the faith of former days. Rejection of, say, the ethico-spiritual leadership of Jesus, to take one of the defining features of the Christian faith, constitutes an alternative to the Christian outlook, not a variation on it. (It is instructive to note how Christian heretics wanting to win approval for their own views typically claim that their interpretations of Scripture alone conform to the <u>real</u> teachings of Jesus.)

Christianity is rich in doctrine. The over-whelming majority of Christians have not only enter-tained the necessary minimum beliefs but have also discerned a unique religious significance, for the whole of fallen mankind, in the salvific life, death, and resurrection of Jesus, deified him as the mundane incarnation of the triune Godhead, and seen him as the divine deliverer whose messianic status is recorded in the Old Testament and whose advent consequently ful-fills Jewish prophecy. Woven around this central doctrinal framework are further doctrines about Jesus' Virgin Birth, the paradoxical union of the fully human and the fully divine in his unique personality, his Crucifixion and Ascension. Virtually all Christians have, in addition, seen the attempt to create commu-nity based on these convictions as a corollary of their commitment to the faith. Now, among these and other related doctrines and beliefs, there is scarcely any which has not, at one time or another, been the subject of intense sectarian controversy. But, it may fairly be said, that a group whose members rejected any of the necessary conditions listed earlier would not even be a sect within Christianity for they have, in denying the existence of God or the authority and moral excellence of Jesus, placed themselves outside the bounds of the Christian religion.

All this is perhaps fairly misleading. I am not suggesting that I have, within the space of about two pages, successfully resolved a long-standing and religiously sensitive dispute about the essence of a faith whose complexity hardly needs advertisement. The truth is, of course, too obviously the other way.

After all, if one could give an account of what it
means to be a Christian, one would simultaneously
supply, many Christians believe, a body of theory
about the means necessary for the acquisition of
salvation - the ultimate goal of the religious life.
And the fact that there is such a religiously relevant
dimension to the debate about the essence of Christianity renders it highly unlikely that any religiously
uncontroversial solutions will be available.

The criteria I have suggested, someone might
reasonably object, are easy to formulate but difficult
to apply. What precisely, for example, does "acceptance of the moral and spiritual leadership of Jesus"
come to? The sad fact is, the objection might run,
that we know directly neither the content of Jesus'
own teaching nor that of his first disciples; the
nascent Church's doctrinal commitments need not be a
faithful reflection of either Jesus' own preaching or
that of his early followers. Modern critical biblical
scholarship has convincingly argued, the objection
continues, that it is impossible to cut through the
Gospel records (themselves based on an unreliable oral
tradition and subjected to extensive later revision)
to the original documents and the events they allegedly record.[7] Furthermore, our independently available knowledge of the conditions of life and thought
in the age in which the Christian Church initially
spread abroad is very limited. The deep philosophical
problems involved in the attempt to characterize the
Christian tradition are rendered all the more intractable, it is urged, by our limited knowledge of the
historical foundations of Christianity.

One possible response to the scepticism engen-
dered by critical biblical scholarship is simply that

there must be a tradition since, after all, the Church exists in the present. The <u>regula fidei</u> - a statement of apostolic faith used by the early Church as a canon of orthodoxy - has been transmitted, it might be contended, in its pristine form from Jesus himself to all subsequent generations by a Church committed to condemning doctrinal innovations and distortions. There is thus a unified and definite corpus of essential doctrine; the deposit of faith has been carefully preserved from heretical distortion or adulteration.

This is a weak and unconvincing response unless it can be supplemented by some kind of reasoned assurance that the Church is indeed apostolic and stands in continuity (if not conformity) with the Church of the preceding centuries. As it happens, it may be impossible to prove (or even show with some degree of plausibility) that the Church's present beliefs are the same (or essentially the same) as those of Jesus and the first disciples; and it is equally difficult to show that the Church has maintained a single identity throughout the past two millennia safeguarding itself against the corrosive influences of secular culture. One would need to develop a criterion of continuity for identifying the link between current doctrinal pronouncements and any previous doctrinal pronouncements. The continuity criterion would take the form of a concern with apostolicity and would be used to detect any serious discontinuity with previous doctrinal promulgations. Clearly, both the development and formulation of this criterion and the demonstration of the integrity of the Christian message presuppose a knowledge of the origin, primitive state, and development of the faith; and it is precisely this which may not be available.

This is a powerful objection which may, in the end, be unanswerable. It is indeed difficult to know, for example, whether or not all the early Christians regarded Jesus as God incarnate and, more importantly, whether or not he declared himself as such. But there can be little doubt concerning the early community's belief in the ethico-religious authority and moral excellence of Jesus for it was precisely this which distinguished it from the rest of Jewry. To be sure, this fact (if it be a fact) does not help us resolve the really crucial issues: Does the content of Christian faith constitute a coherent totality from its inception? Is the content determinate ab origine or did the early Church impart a definiteness to it at a much later date? Did the founder of the faith intend that this content should remain forever unchanged? Should it? These questions cannot be resolved by any purely a priori method requiring as they do a thorough knowledge of the historical foundations of Christianity for their successful resolution to be possible. With respect to them, all one can say is that, rather unhelpfully, if we could locate Jesus' own views amid the labyrinthine profusion of apostolic interpretations and elaborations, they would rightly be seen as being canonical to Christianity. But my concern is not with providing satisfactory answers to these questions but rather with resolving the problem of providing a criterion for distinguishing Christian convictions from non-Christian ones given the actual tradition of Christian theism as we know it.

Consider the question: "What is Christianity?" One answer to this question is the formally correct but unhelpful one to the effect that Christianity is what Jesus and his sincere early followers took it to be. To give substance to this, one needs to make use of the deliverances of historical research. Another answer to this question is that Christianity is, at root, what subsequent Christians in each age have taken it to be. These are both sociological ways of settling the issue concerning the nature of Christianity just as one could settle the question "What is philosophy?" by seeing what people who call themselves philosophers do. The natural objection to this procedure is, of course, that Christians have taken Christianity to be so many very different and incompatible things. Do Christians of denominations as varied as Catholic and extreme Protestant hold different positions within the same tradition even though these positions represent the limits of the Christian spectrum? Or do they have different traditions and, by implication, worship what they take to be different entities? My answer to this is implied in my earlier discussion of the essence of Christianity: all Christians are characteristically committed to a belief in the ethico-spiritual leadership and supreme moral rectitude of Jesus, whatever other doctrinal differences may exist among them. There have undeniably been many developments, in the history of Christianity, concerning the concepts of redemption, atonement, incarnation, and other central theological concepts. The interpretations of these religious categories vary, sometimes widely, among Christian thinkers of different doctrinal leanings. Even with respect to the existence of the Godhead, there are internal disputes: Catholics maintain that it is possible and necessary to demonstrate the existence of God from non-theistic premises while many Protestants hold that it is not in principle

possible to prove the existence of God from non-
theistic premises and hence necessarily not
necessary. But these are all domestic disputes
recognisably internal to the household of faith.

- III -

In a pungent discussion of reductionism in the
philosophy of religion, J.C. Thornton has contended
that we need to ascertain whether or not our criteria
for appraising the extent to which a given analysis
succeeds in characterizing Christianity adequately are
themselves arbitrary.[8] Thornton argues that the
attacks on reductionism by both orthodox traditionalist and secular humanist thinkers are often vitiated
by a tendency to employ question-begging criteria for
identifying reductionism.[9] Such allegations of reductionism are, Thornton tells us, generally controversial since the issue concerning the essence of
Christianity is itself a controversial one.

One of the orthodox traditionalist writers
singled out by Thornton for special censure is Hugo
Meynell.[10] Let us now examine Thornton's criticisms
of Meynell's attack on reductionist analyses of
Christian doctrine.

Meynell's criterion for distinguishing reductionist from non-reductionist theologies is simple:
the latter include assent to statements of historical
and eschatological fact as belonging to the essence of
Christian belief whereas the former regard such statements as more or less inessential. The traditionalist, unlike the reductionist, does not see the
factual statements as merely the vehicle of religious
experience but rather as their ground; unless the
factual statements are true, the experiences and

attitudes associated with belief in such statements
are arbitrary and groundless. Meynell argues that
some of the claims in the Apostles' Creed either are
or imply historical statements. The belief in the
Virgin Birth, for example, rules out, by implication,
the belief that the activities of a man were causally
responsible for Jesus' conception. Again, the Ascension implies the belief that Jesus vanished in a
physically inexplicable manner and was never seen
again in vicinities in which previously he had been
seen. Now, while none of the clauses of the Apostles'
Creed is an historical statement in any unproblematic
sense, Thornton concurs, each of them does seem to
imply or presuppose an historical statement.

Thornton is not unsympathetic to Meynell's claim
that an analysis of Christian belief (such as R.B.
Braithwaite's[11]) which claims that the truth of
Christianity is logically independent of the truth of
all historical beliefs is indeed reductionist. The
logical dependence of specifically Christian religious
beliefs on certain historical beliefs serves to distinguish the Christian tradition from the other extant
religious traditions of the world. An analysis which
obscures or denies the essential historicity of
Christian belief, Thornton concedes, may be seen, at
least prima facie, as being reductionist. But, continues Thornton, while it may be justifiable to
believe that the truth of the Christian religion is
logically dependent on the truth of certain historical
statements, it is difficult to know what is the mini-
mal set of historical claims to which the Christian
believer is logically committed. Hence, while Meynell
is entitled to maintain that any interpretation of a
particular religious belief (say, the belief in the

Resurrection) which is logically independent of any historical claim whatever is properly to be viewed as reductionist, the claim that a particular religious belief implies a specific historical entailment is tantamount to begging crucial questions concerning the exact logical status of this belief. If historical beliefs are entailed, they must be specifiable ones but, Thornton tells us, it is question-begging to specify which historical statements are entailed and then use the acceptance or rejection of these specific statements as the criterion for distinguishing between reductionist and non-reductionist theologies.

The question "What is the logical status of religious beliefs?" - a question which any philosophical analysis of religious belief is centrally concerned to investigate and answer - cannot be settled, Thornton insists, prior to an analytical investigation of the status of these beliefs. The philosophical analysis will include an investigation of which historical statements are indeed entailed by particular religious beliefs. Even the assumption that religious beliefs entail or presuppose any historical statements at all is an assumption about the logical status of religious beliefs and does indeed stand in need of justification. Thornton invites us, however, to accept this very general assumption for "... there is some excuse for regarding as 'reductionist' any analysis of Christian beliefs which denies that any of them entails historical statements, because if this denial were justified, the logical status of these beliefs would be almost <u>totally</u> different from what appearances would suggest".[12] The central question to ask in any philosophical analysis of religious belief is: "What is the real (and not

merely the apparent) logical status of theological
propositions?" Meynell's criterion for distinguishing
reductionist from non-reductionist analyses, Thornton
concludes, begs the central question at stake by
effectively identifying the prima facie logical status
of religious beliefs with their actual logical status.

Now, to be sure, one cannot ab initio identify
the actual logical status of religious propositions
with their apparent logical status. But, presumably,
Meynell is arguing for such an identification in the
case of some religious beliefs basing his argument on
some background theoretical assumptions about the
nature of (Christian) religious conviction. And there
is, of course, no alternative to such a reliance on
general theoretical assumptions. Meynell's general
assumption, namely, that there is, in Thornton's
words, "an historical core"[13] to the Christian faith,
is accepted by Thornton at some structural level but
not in detail. And yet the concession that there may
be such an historical kernel amounts merely to paying
lip-service to an abstract characterization of the
historicity of the Christian religion unless one is
prepared to allow and seriously consider, as Meynell
does, specific historical statements as the entail-
ments of such religious beliefs and, moreover, to do
so in the absence of a fully adequate analysis of the
nature of such belief. In determining what is the
essential feature of a metaphysical position which
makes it a Christian theology, one can say that it has
some historical implications - implications about the
life and activity of Jesus of Nazareth. But any
particular Christian theology will have to be
reasonably precise as to just what its historical
implications are.

Furthermore, Meynell is entitled to an <u>ad hominem</u> argument against Thornton: even Thornton's own view that the actual logical status of religious beliefs does not differ <u>in toto</u> from their <u>prima facie</u> logical status is, in a significant sense, a presumption at the very least if not a <u>petitio principii</u>. Suppose, for the sake of a case, that the logical status of religious beliefs turns out to be completely different from what one would expect from their linguistic garb. How are philosophers to discover this if the whole burden of their analysis rests on a presumption in favour of the opinion that there is indeed necessarily some essential similarity between the logical structure and the grammatical structure of a religious belief? Such an initial presumption would effectively beg the question against at least one possible analysis of religious belief. Moreover, if Thornton can allow himself the liberty of making some initial assumptions about the logical status of religious beliefs prior to the availability of a fully adequate analysis, he can hardly refuse such an amenity to other writers (like Meynell) who wish to make different provisional assumptions.

Now, certainly, the onus is on the side which seeks to rule out certain interpretations as possible Christian views. And, admittedly, Thornton is more justified in wondering why the position of those who say that Christian theology has no historical implications at all should count as genuinely Christian than Meynell would be in wondering why people who want to give less traditional (and hence less obvious) historical implications of various Christian doctrines (such as the Virgin Birth and the Resurrection) might want to call themselves Christians. But Meynell is

entitled to make general assumptions about the status
of religious belief in the absence of a complete
account of the nature of such belief although, of
course, he is not entitled to assume without argument
that Christianity has just those historical implications that have usually been taken to be the ones
following from the Apostles' Creed. In fine, then,
Meynell may legitimately argue that a religious belief
such as the Resurrection has a specific historical
implication: the belief in an empty tomb may well
have the status of an implied historical statement.
It is no argument against an opponent to insist that
such a claim is question-begging on the sole ground
that it is controversial. I conclude, therefore, that
Thornton's argument against Meynell is nugatory.

Thornton's next assault is on two secular
humanist critics of reductionism - R.W. Hepburn and
A.C. MacIntyre - each of whom is taken to task for
using allegedly question-begging criteria for identifying reductionism. Hepburn has argued that "belief
in the cosmological relation", as he calls it, is
essential to Christian belief.[14] The "cosmological
relation" is that relation between the universe and
the Godhead which is implicit in the cosmological
argument for God's existence. The belief in this
relation is logically embedded in, and hence required
by, that strand in Christian thought in which God has
the status of an individual - an individual who acts
in human history, reveals himself to men, and who
therefore cannot be identifiable simply with human
attitudes towards the world or with some purely
symbolic construction out of experienced realities.
For Hepburn, an analysis is reductionist if it avoids
or omits "the cosmological relation" or if it

interprets its logical status to be other than what it prima facie is; analyses which interpret it in terms which make religious belief just a useful emotional stimulant to moral concern (a la Braithwaite, for example) or simply a way of seeing the world (in the manner of writers like D.Z. Phillips and Kenneth Sayre[15]) are, in fact, reductionist. But, Hepburn argues, there is another strand in Christian discourse which logically insists that God must not be concep- tualised as an individual to whom the world stands in a relation of dependence. And the presence of these conflicting demands is, Hepburn concludes, evidence for suspecting a deep incoherence in Christian thought.

But why couldn't one interpret the evidence which Hepburn takes to be indicative of incoherence as being indicative rather of a defective analysis of the logical status of the "belief in the cosmological relation"? Thornton explains:

> ...[Hepburn] classifies as "reductionist" any analysis which suggests that this belief in the cosmological relation has anything other than its prima facie logical status, and then observes that when interpreted along non-reductionist lines this belief is both demanded by, and incompatible with, Christian discourse taken as a whole. Surely an equally reasonable and less question-begging conclusion to draw would be that the evidence from Christian discourse taken as a whole suggests that the logical status of the belief in question is other than what on the face of it, it appears to be.[16]

Thornton applies here, in effect, a principle of charity: perhaps we have misunderstood the true import of the cosmological relation. We should explore the route of re-interpretation - even if, in the process, the "belief in the cosmological relation" loses its _prima_ _facie_ meaning - before we are in a position to conclude that Christianity is essentially incoherent.

Two comments are in order here. Firstly, note Thornton's claim that his suggested interpretation of the evidence leads us to the (allegedly) "equally reasonable and less question-begging conclusion" that the actual logical status of the belief in the cosmological relation is different from its apparent status. But while this interpretation may be equally reasonable, it is certainly not any the less question-begging than Hepburn's: it merely begs the question against different opponents. If Hepburn's analysis supposedly begs the question against those who divorce the actual status from the apparent one, Thornton's analysis would, by parity of reasoning, beg the question against those who take the actual linguistic formulations of Christian belief to be adequate to the true import of Christian convictions (i.e., identify the actual status with the apparent one) in the larger attempt to convict Christianity of incoherence. Thornton's interpretation is also question-begging: it begs the question against those who believe in the cosmological relation in a relatively literal sense. Nor will it do, incidentally, to retort that Thornton will merely beg the question against those who want to persist in incoherence for that would be to presuppose the soundness of Thornton's contention - which is precisely what is at issue here.

Secondly, neither Hepburn nor anyone else need or should deny that the status of the belief in the cosmological relation may be other than what it appears to be. Indeed, it would be a mistake to deny this for the status of any proposition or belief may be different from what its typical linguistic formulation would lead one to expect. Thornton is right to insist that the grammatical form is not always appropriate to the logical form. There are many classes of linguistic formulations - for example, "systematically misleading expressions"[17] - whose grammatical form is not faithful to their real (logical) form. And the dangers of being misled by language are real enough in the philosophy of religion. The ontological argument, for example, has been permanently punctured by analysts who showed that because "men exist" and "men eat", or "men are existent" and "men are mortal", are sentences of the same grammatical form, we are liable to suppose that they also express the same form of proposition. And yet "God exists" and "God is powerful" do not express the same form of proposition. Not every theological sentence expresses propositions of a subject-predicate type. But, and this is the other side to the story, one cannot deduce from these correct observations that the actual status of a belief is never identical with its prima facie status: there may be fortunate accidents where the linguistic garb does not disguise the logical structure of a belief but rather perspicuously displays it rendering the actual status identical with the prima facie status. While we may not know the precise logical form of the propositions putatively expressed by theological sentences, it would be fruitlessly dogmatic and unempirical to assume that the linguistic formulation of every Christian theistic belief is necessarily misleading as to its actual logical status.

Finally, Thornton considers MacIntyre's accusation that, in the hands of modernist interpreters of Christianty - writers like Paul Tillich and Rudolf Bultmann - Christian belief has been extensively evacuated of its traditional theistic content while a potentially misleading theistic vocabulary has been retained.[18] MacIntyre produces a dilemma for those who attempt translations of the language of traditional Christian theism into a secular idiom in the larger attempt to make Christianity a live option for modern man in twentieth century industrial society. Either the theologians succeed in their translation - in which case what they are saying has become transformed into the atheistic parlance of their audience; or else they fail in their translation - in which case their audience is drastically reduced for no-one understands them except themselves. In either case, the theologians fail to achieve their original goal.

Thornton takes MacIntyre to task for the latter's "tacit assumption that we all know what the substance of theistic belief is, and that furthermore we know it to be of the essence of Christianity".[19] This tacit assumption must be at work, Thornton reasons, for how otherwise could MacIntyre know that the analyses offered by thinkers like Tillich and Bultmann are indistinguishable from atheism. But what is wrong with MacIntyre's tacit assumption? Presumably, MacIntyre thinks not that he knows exactly what theism is (for, I suppose, no-one does) but rather that whatever theism may reasonably be said to be, an account like Tillich's must be a clear instance of one that isn't true to it at all. If one emasculates traditional Christian doctrines to _that_ extent, one loses the right to say that what one is proffering is a _theistic_ account. The gruel is simply not thick enough. Now there are accounts of Christian theism which seek to interpret traditional Christian doctrine in the context supplied by an aggressively secular culture and which, unlike the accounts given by Tillich and Bultmann, seem to recognisably preserve the link with the traditional conception of the nature, status, and content of theistic belief.[20] The status of these accounts is harder to ascertain. And this is why MacIntyre's superficially clever dilemma won't do - a dilemma which Thornton rightly rejects as being based on question-begging assumptions.

Thornton insists that the decision to use the appellation "reductionist" (with respect to a suspect analysis of Christian belief) ought to succeed rather than precede actual investigation of the status of such belief.[21] And yet this seems to presuppose that an analysis could proceed to attain complete adequacy first and then we could retrospectively judge its legitimacy. Surely, however, the task of judging the legitimacy of an analysis neither fully precedes nor fully succeeds it: it accompanies it.

The main error underlying Thornton's critique of MacIntyre is the "Socratic fallacy" of confusing a question such as "What is a physical object?" with a question such as "What is the definition or analysis of the concept of a physical object?" A failure to produce an adequate definition or analysis of X is not and does not necessarily entail a failure either to understand the concept of X or to use the appropriate words. Hence, knowing what Christian belief is is a necessary precondition of giving an analysis of it, but being able to give an analysis of it is not a necessary precondition of knowing what Christian belief is.

Thornton seems to suggest that an account of the nature of religious belief could start from entirely neutral or at least unquestion-begging presuppositions. Now, giving analyses of religious belief (as of any other phenomenon) requires that we make certain assumptions which guide research. These assumptions are, naturally, made prior to obtaining a fully adequate analysis and they may come to be modified or rejected under the pressure of subsequent critical analysis and disciplined research. But, in a perfectly valid sense, virtually every analysis begs questions against some position or other just in virtue of the fact that it relies on some unargued assumptions - any unargued assumptions. Every analysis necessarily operates on some initial premiss whose legitimacy or truth cannot be checked against the deliverances of a fully adequate analysis for the simple but sufficient reason that, ex hypothesi, no such analysis is actually available. Even Thornton's own apparently innocuous assumption about the presumed partial congruity between the apparent grammatical status and the actual logical status of religious beliefs is, as I remarked earlier, actually question-begging. Thornton is aware of this; and promises that he would justify even this assumption in a lengthier work. But the kind of justification that Thornton is seeking would need to be given in vacuo i.e., in utter disregard of and in irrelation to any logically prior view about the contents of a fully adequate analysis of religious belief. And this is an incoherent demand.

Having established that we do not need a fully
adequate analysis of the nature of religious belief in
order to identify reductionism in the philosophy of
religion, we are in a position to examine various
allegedly reductionist analyses of Christian belief.
It will be our task to show that the Christian
tradition sets identifiable limits both to the emascu-
lation of Christian doctrines and to the secularization of Christianity.

Notes

[1] Immanuel Kant, _Religion Within the Limits of Reason Alone_ (New York: Harper, 1960), translated with an introduction and notes by Theodore Greene and Hoyt Hudson.

[2] Friedrich Schleiermacher, _On Religion: Addresses in Response to its Cultured Critics_ (Richmond: John Knox Press, 1969), translated with introduction and notes by Terence Tice. First published in 1821. See especially the Second Address.

[3] J.C. Thornton, "Religious Belief and 'Reductionism'", in _Sophia_, Vol. V, No. 3, October 1966, pp. 3-16.

[4] Professor Sir Hamilton Gibb, in his regrettably influential _Mohammedanism: An Historical Survey_ (London: Oxford University Press, 1969), writes: "[I]n a less self-conscious age Muslims were proud to call their community al-umma al-Muhammadiya". (p.2). Muslims are still proud of that title because they are indeed the people of Muhammad (al-umma al-Muhammadiya). But the label "Mohammedanism" does carry the unwelcome implication that Muslims, like Christians, worship the founder of their faith. I suppose, in this matter, Professor Gibb prefers falsehood to truth.

[5] See Anders Nygren's _Essence of Christianity_ (London: The Epworth Press, 1960), pp. 49 ff. Translated from the Swedish by Philip Watson.

[6] I suppose someone could argue, reasonably enough, that these three conditions are _central_ rather than _necessary_. My own intuitions concerning this matter tend to vary.

[7] For powerful statements of this view, see Cecil Cadoux's _The Life of Jesus_ (West Drayton: Pelican Books, 1948) and Maurice Bucaille's _The Bible, The Qur'an, and Science_ (Paris: Seghers, 1983), 10th edition, translated from the French by A.D. Pannell and Maurice Bucaille.

[8] Thornton, _op. cit._

[9] Thornton (Thornton, _op. cit._ pp. 4-8), criticises the work of E.L. Mascall. These criticisms are well-taken. See Mascall's reply in _Sophia_, Vol. VI,

No. 2, July 1967, pp. 3-5 and also see Thornton's reply to Mascall in the same issue of Sophia, pp. 6-8.

[10]Hugo Meynell, Sense, Nonsense and Christianity (Sheed and Ward, 1966).

[11]See Chapter 4 for details of Braithwaite's analysis.

[12]J.C. Thornton, "Religious Belief and 'Reductionism'", in Sophia, Vol. V, No. 3, October 1966, p. 10. Emphasis in original.

[13]ibid., p. 10.

[14]Ronald W. Hepburn, "From World to God", in The Philosophy of Religion, Basil Mitchell (ed.), (Oxford: Oxford University Press, 1971), pp. 168-178.

[15]See Chapter 4 for details.

[16]Thornton, op. cit., p. 12.

[17]Gilbert Ryle, "Systematically Misleading Expressions", in The Linguistic Turn, Richard Rorty (ed.), (Chicago: The University of Chicago Press, 1967), pp. 85-100.

[18]Thornton, op. cit., pp. 12-13.

[19]ibid., p. 12.

[20]The revisionist accounts of Christian theism, discussed in Chapter 5, fit into this category.

[21]ibid., p. 12

Chapter IV
Faith and Modernity

No theorist of culture could ignore the con-
spicuous decline in religious observance in twentieth
century Western societies. Generations craving to be
reared in the lap of divine providence were succeeded
by ones who spent most of their creative energy consciously repudiating the whole religious Weltanschauung
of their predecessors. In the process, the Christian
religion has increasingly retreated into the realm of
private idiosyncrasy deserving, it has been thought, an
amused tolerance if not outright condescension.

Unsurprisingly, the task of a modern Christian
theology has been a delicate one. Christian thinkers
want, on the one hand, to make Christianity a live
option for contemporary man in industrial society but,
on the other, they have felt the need to ensure that,
in the process, the content of traditional Christian
doctrines - which many modern educated Westerners find
repugnant - is not so extensively eroded that it
renders the resulting ostensibly Christian theism
virtually indistinguishable from atheism.

A doctrine usually only needs to be defined
explicitly after the appearance of some unorthodoxy;
similarly, a word does not usually receive or need
sustained attention until it has come to be misused.
It would be difficult to examine the career of the
words "Christian" and "Christianity" in recent years
without feeling that some writers are taking undue
liberties in their usage of these words.

At times, in the hands of some writers, the
traditional theistic content of Christian belief has
been excessively eviscerated. Doctrinal statements

about God are to be understood, it has been claimed, not as referring to a metaphysical deity (as the Christian tradition apparently maintained) but rather in terms of an attitude towards the world or in terms of a particular moral outlook encapsulated in an appropriate way of life. In this chapter, I argue that there are identifiable limits to the secularization of Christianity. I begin with a brief examination of two allegedly reductionist analyses of Christian belief.

- I -

A characteristic feature of philosophical practice in this century has been a marked scepticism concerning the pretensions of traditional metaphysics. This scepticism has been buttressed by a somewhat cacophonous theory of meaning developed by the logical positivists.[1] Positivist thinkers developed a criterion of cognitive significance designed to lend substance to certain epistemological intuitions generated by their work in the mathematical and scientific disciplines. With all the zeal of a political party, and in a rather programmatic if not insouciant manner, they applied this criterion to areas (like theology and metaphysics) remote from the criterion's original context of inspiration.

According to this criterion, a proposition P would qualify as cognitively or factually meaningful if and only if its truth or falsity could be verified at least in principle if not in practice. In general, metaphysical utterances, such as "The impersonal forces of history influence individual human destinies" or "The absolute oneness with nature is the goal of life", seemed utterly impervious to any empirical verification which could help in ascertaining their truth or falsity. In particular, religious utterances had a metaphysical dimension which seemed resistant to empirical verification; religious utterances like "God is the ruler of the celestial kingdom" or "Men are iniquitous sinners trapped in the Cimmerian darkness of mortal life" were, therefore, declared devoid of cognitive significance. The very notion of an utterly transcendent deity active in the spatio-temporal continuum, it was thought in some quarters, was sense-less i.e., cognitively meaningless. Nothing could count for or against the truth of the non-anthropo-morphic religious beliefs of the mature Judaeo-Christian-Islamic tradition; such beliefs were there-fore devoid of factual significance. Religion may stir pious sentiment in the hearer but it (if properly understood) neither claims nor conveys any intelligible factual meaning.

The metaphysical dimension of Christian belief was, the empiricists thought, the real thorn in the flesh. It had to be expunged if Christianity was ever to gain intellectual kudos. There followed, predict-ably enough, a whole programme of constant trimming of theological doctrine by religious writers to accommo-date verificationist demands and criticisms. If one could remove the reference to the supernatural elements in Christian belief and practice, the residual non-metaphysical content of such belief would be expres-sible as verifiable (and hence cognitively meaningful) propositions.

A famous attempt to re-interpret Christian beliefs in such a way that they met the requirements of the contemporaneously popular verificationist criterion of meaning was that of R.B. Braithwaite.[2] The question of the truth of religious claims could only arise,

Braithwaite reasoned, after that of coherence and intelligibility had been positively settled. The fundamental question is: How are we to verify as true or false the claims of orthodox Christian theism given that the meaning of any statement is supplied by its method of verification?[3]

For Braithwaite, belief in God amounts to a commitment to a specific way of life: it is, in effect, a commitment of the will to a morally excellent life coupled with a recognition of the psychological aid provided by certain "stories" which exemplify and represent vividly the moral ideals whose realisation is regarded as worthy by the believer. A religious assertion is "the assertion of an intention to carry out a certain behaviour policy, subsumable under a sufficiently general principle to be a moral one, together with the implicit or explicit statement, but not the assertion, of certain stories".[4] Like moral belief, religious belief is not belief in a proposition; a religious belief, Braithwaite argues, is a moral belief (i.e., an intention to behave in a certain way) in alliance with "the entertainment of certain stories associated with the intention in the mind of the believer".[5] In the case of Christianity, these "stories" are the putatively factual biblical claims about the origins of the world, the Last Judgement, and the divine nature of Jesus of Nazareth. A man is not a professing Christian, Braithwaite tells us, "unless he both proposes to live according to Christian moral principles and associates his intention with thinking of Christian stories; but he need not believe that the empirical propositions presented by the stories correspond to empirical fact".[6] The relation between one's intention to follow an agapeistic way of life, on the

one hand, and one's thinking of Christian stories, on
the other, is causal: entertaining these stories is
efficacious psychologically since it helps subdue
inclinations which are contrary to one's moral intentions.[7]

The moral commitments of Christianity are, in an
important sense, detachable, Braithwaite reasons, from
the metaphysical matrix in which tradition had placed
them. What makes impact upon us when reading the
Gospels is Jesus' remarkable moral character. This
facet of the Gospel narratives is as relevant now to us
as it was to the earlier generations. The rest - the
mythological paraphernalia from a bygone era - can, we
are told, be confidently ignored.

Braithwaite's reductionist analysis of theistic
belief has excited much critical comment.[8] I am
inclined to think that the case against Braithwaite has
already been made by contemporary philosophers of
religion. In any case, since reductionism is not my
central concern in this essay, I will examine Braithwaite's analysis only very briefly.

It is widely believed that Braithwaite's account
immunizes Christian theism against verificationist
assault but only at the cost of emptying it of all its
traditional metaphysical content. The Christian
religion cannot be seen as providing just an outgrown
(and largely discredited) historical matrix for
Christian morality. The link between Christian doctrine and Christian ethics is much more intimate. The
distinctive moral commitments and aspirations of the
Christian believer require something like the traditional supernatural trappings; these alone can supply
an appropriate rationale for the characteristic commitments embodied in Christianity. The metaphysical

shackles which confine Jesus as the imperishable
exemplar of moral perfection cannot be removed without
rendering the characteristic moral demands of Christianity unfounded and indefensible. Hence, a defence of
the continuing relevance of agape as a cultural and
moral ideal cannot be convincing if the corresponding
religious view of reality is thought to be untenable.
The viability of the normative (or attitudinal) component in religious conviction presupposes the truth of
some factual assertions about the nature of God and of
his relationship to creation.

Moreover, claims such as "Love thy neighbour" and
"God loved you; therefore love one another" derive
their Christian character from the total context of
doctrine in which they are embedded. These claims may
retain their emotional and moral character even outside
of any doctrinal context but their religious character
is destroyed when they are torn from their doctrinal
moorings. One cannot perpetuate the moral values of
the Christian religion if one totally disengages them
from their traditional doctrinal setting. Christian
moral ideals must be grounded in a Christian conception
of reality.

Suppose someone says: Why couldn't the ideal of
agape be defended on purely secular metaphysical
premisses? After all, the objection may run, the fact
that the religious character of Christian moral claims
is destroyed once the Christian metaphysic is rejected
does not entail that the moral claims cannot be perpe-
tuated. Indeed, the objection concludes, their status
as moral claims is enhanced once they are disengaged
from their traditional religious context.

But this is unconvincing. Agape as a moral ideal
cannot be justified on purely secular grounds. Agape

is a moral ideal with a specific religious foundation; it is, if you like, a <u>Christian</u> moral ideal. To be sure, one could tear it away from its normal Christian foundation and let it stand independently of doctrine. But to do so would be similar to the case of a Muslim who scrupulously observed his five daily prayers but rejected the Muslim doctrinal foundation which gives that ritual its customary sense and religious significance. Something would be amiss indeed. The religious character of Christian moral ideals is not simply an outer layer that can be peeled off to reveal an inner kernel. This religious character is internally related to the very basis and nature of Christian moral conviction.

Braithwaite himself revealingly insists on the use of <u>Christian</u> "stories" to reinforce <u>Christian</u> moral behaviour. But if one uses religious beliefs simply as possible stimuli to moral actions (with their truth or falsehood regarded as being of merely incidental interest), one has no good reason for restricting the range of possible stories to Christian ones. Any stories (including stories with no or no obvious basis in reality) should be allowed to supplement the ethical claims. Indeed, if some Arabian fairy-tale or Hindu myth has the required effect, it should be entertained as seriously as any of the Christian stories. Admittedly, there is an impropriety involved, in one's practical life, if one associates, say, Buddhist stories in one's mind with Christian moral intentions but, on Braithwaite's account, there is no theoretical reason for prohibiting the entertainment of non-Christian stories.

Braithwaite is a subjectivist about the morality that he takes to be of the essence of Christianity.

His "behaviour policies" are more or less freely chosen; there is no objective validity going for them. Intention and resolve call the tune here. But if moral principles are mere conventions or preferences, unrelated to the fundamental structure of that reality which is independent of human thought and feeling, then they cannot be espoused under that description by any traditional Christian. Braithwaite's answer to this objection (and to the related objection that his proposed analysis of Christian belief distorts its structure as that structure is commonly understood) is predictable: so much the worse for common and traditional interpretations. The fact is, he might well reply, that Christianity can only be salvaged if its central claims can be re-interpreted so as to have some sense. If such a task requires, among other things, the imposition of a tortured or strikingly artificial interpretation on Christian doctrinal and moral claims, then so be it.

As an inquiry into the emotional and behavioural accompaniments of hypothetical credal formulations i.e., the psychological antecedents and consequences of theological quasi-assertions made, so to speak, as if there were a God, Braithwaite's account is worth serious study. It is not an unworthy contribution to the psychology of pretence. It is, however, one thing to provide an informative description of the subjective experiences which accompany religious belief and another to pronounce on the validity of such belief itself by giving some account of the factual (cognitive) element embodied in the creed. Braithwaite pretends that the cognitive issue need not trouble us since the supernatural element in Christianity is, in any case, dispensable.

Nothing is, in fact, further from the truth. Once we jettison the supernatural accoutrements of Christianity, we have, as Nietzsche prophetically declared, no longer any right to the Christian moral scheme. It is an English sense of consistency, Nietzsche acidly comments, that allows us Christian values without Christian doctrines.[9] For Nietzsche, "the death of God" - a picturesque way of enunciating the demise of the supra-sensible realm - precedes and heralds the demise of the religious virtues.[10] Nietzsche is, significantly, hostile not just to Christian doctrine but also to the whole associated Christian ethic. The ascetic ideal with its hatred of the purely natural instincts and its demand for an extirpation of the sensual element in our nature - "Life is at an end where the 'kingdom of God' begins ..."[11] - is itself anchored in a view of God as the sovereign ruler who makes these particular moral demands on his creatures. One cannot promote the moral ideals of Christianity without appealing to a distinctively Christian propositional framework.

- II -

If in previous ages there was a need to disabuse believers of the concept of an anthropomorphic deity, there is a need today to lessen the appeal of that characteristically modern notion that the concept of God is a theoretical construct i.e., a convenient way of referring to a distinctive viewpoint on the world. In this century, several philosophers of religion have emphasised the role of theological statements in providing those who assert them with a characteristic viewpoint on reality. Believing in God, it has been urged, is in effect a specific manner of experiencing

the _world_. Theological propositions, while not literally true, are factual claims about mundane phenomena:
they are compressed versions of the familiar facts of
human experience. The referential model of religious
belief (according to which "God" refers to a unique
incorporeal being who can be identified in some
specifiable way) should be jettisoned. The correct
replacement, it has been said, is some construal of
theological belief according to which such belief
essentially amounts to a distinctive perspective on
human experience.[12]

No writer has been a more indefatigable advocate
of this position than D.Z. Phillips. It is an error,
Phillips contends _ad nauseam_, to construe the divine
reality as if it were the reality of an object.[13]
Indeed, "['God'] is not the name of an individual; it
does not refer to anything."[14] One misconstrues
religious belief if one regards religious utterances as
descriptive literal propositions about a transcendent
being. Religion does not provide supernatural information: we need to be cured of the old metaphysical
impulse. The whole model of correspondence to the
facts is inappropriate here, Phillips continues, since
on a literal factual interpretation, religious beliefs
are superstitions.[15]

Religious language is, for Phillips, it seems,
non-cognitive. It is expressive of certain attitudes
and intentions: "That a man says that God cares for
him in all things is the expression of the terms in
which he meets and makes sense of the contingencies of
life".[16] And again:

> ...[R]eligious expressions of praise, glory,
> etc. are not referring expressions. These
> activities are expressive in character, and

what they express is called the worship of
God. Is it reductionism to say that what is
meant by the reality of God is to be found in
certain pictures which say themselves? If we
mean by reductionism an attempt to reduce the
significance of religious belief to something
other than it is, then reductionism consists
in the attempt, however sophisticated, to say
that religious pictures must refer to some
object; that they must describe matters of
fact. That is the real reductionism which
distorts the character of religious belief.[17]

Phillips insists that his position faithfully
records the original import of Christian doctrines.
Genuine Christianity, he tells us, was never meant to
be metaphysical: theological claims do not and were
not originally intended to refer to or describe any
transcendent reality. The Bible has been misread. The
language of the Apostles is a literary one; it is not
meant to express technical, scientific or factual
truths. Indeed, Hume has demonstrated the conceptual
impropriety involved in inferring either the existence
or nature of God from features of the world of experience. But bona fide religious belief is, Phillips
continues, generally free from the metaphysical
assumptions which the Humean critique rejects as
unwarranted.[18] Hence, for example, a sentence such as
"God is infinitely wise" yields grammatical remarks
about God; far from having the role of putting forward
true propositions concerning God, it has the role of
determining what can possibly be true or false propositions concerning such a reality. "God is infinitely
wise" is a grammatical comment which indicates how the
divine reality, as regards wisdom, finds no parallel
with human reality.[19]

Phillips dismisses with withering contempt the familiar view that recent advances in scientific and rational thought have exposed part of the monotheistic tradition to be making straightforwardly false or incoherent claims. The criteria of meaning and justification for theological propositions are, he argues, intrinsic to religion itself. Religion is not answerable to any external scientific or philosophical tests: it is an autonomous "form of life". Religious beliefs are, Phillips assures us, actually immune to the kind of philosophical and scientific criticism that is regularly directed against them. The modern critique of religion is inspired by a particular (and mistaken) understanding of the nature of knowledge and its ultimate grounds. He counsels us to reject this monolithic "foundationalist" construal of the epistemological enterprise in favour of the later Wittgenstein's methodology - a methodology which might, perhaps tendentiously, be described as a form of linguistic relativism according to which one should proceed by seeking and providing detailed descriptions of actual instances of knowledge and its professed grounds (i.e., what are taken as grounds by the participants in the relevant language-games). The method of philosophy is descriptive: it cannot be the task of the philosopher to justify or refute religious claims since, as Phillips' mentor - Wittgenstein - would have us believe, "Philosophy leaves everything as it is".[20]

Phillips' neo-Wittgensteinian analysis of religious belief has been much criticised.[21] A powerful if hackneyed criticism has been that Phillips' account trades on a false antithesis between expressive language and descriptive language: expressive language can also be descriptive. Indeed, it seems natural to suppose that typically it is both. The man of faith who says that God loves him can confidently face the tribulations of life while entertaining the (putatively) factual belief that there is a God whose love and mercy encompass the failings of our common humanity. Religious language is, _inter alia_, a vehicle for the expression of intentions and attitudes. But it has other uses too; and, in particular, it has factual uses. Hence, it is implausible to argue that an utterance such as "There will be a Judgement Day", while ostensibly a putatively factual or literal assertion about divine retribution, can, in fact, only be understood as a poignant guide to moral choice in daily life or as an emotional stimulant to feelings of accountability and moral responsibility.

Religious attitudes cannot subsist entirely _in vacuo_ i.e., in utter independence of some background convictions. Supporting religious observance (if such observance is to be rationally justifiable) must be, in the case of ethical monotheism, a set of metaphysical beliefs about the existence of an eternal and peerless Creator. Hence, for example, underlying the Muslim prayer "Guide us in the straight path; the path of those whom Thou hast blessed..."[22] are such (putatively) factual beliefs as, most fundamentally, that there is a God, and relatedly, that he hears praise and petition addressed to him, that moral rectitude is attainable through divine guidance, and so on. Psychologically, of course, men can and do take up religious attitudes (like trust) towards the world without sensing the need for the appropriate metaphysical underpinnings. But such attitudes are irrational; it is irrational to maintain, say, an emotional state of trust in the universe if one recognises that this trust has no objective foundation. If the relevant objective beliefs are unjustified or known to be false, the advocacy of religious attitudes is tantamount to recommending wish fulfillment. And, perhaps, once all is said and done, theism - like contracting second marriage - is indeed, to borrow a comparison from Dr. Samuel Johnson, the triumph of hope over experience.

Unless there is a rationale for a particular set of attitudes towards the world, any attitude is as acceptable as any other; and this implies that the attitudes actually adopted are arbitrary and ungrounded. Why should a believer regard his own way of interpreting human experience as being any more authentic than some alternative (say, atheistic) one? Why should he think that this heartless and indifferent world somehow disguises an underlying order in which righteousness is rewarded or human vicissitudes are ultimately meaningful? Moreover, on Phillips' construal, the attitudes adopted by the believer are as compatible with an atheistic metaphysic as they are with a theistic one. Resignation and trust are hardly the monopoly of religious men. Surely, however, what distinguishes the Stoic fatalism of a Nietzsche in personal distress[23] from the dignified resignation of a Muhammad in moments of eclipse is the fact that the former finds its roots in the tragic humanistic metaphysic of the godless man while the latter is grounded in a fierce belief in the ultimate supremacy of the divine purpose for men on earth.

Phillips claims that his account of Christian belief concurs with an accepted tradition. Now, prima facie at least, this seems palpably untrue. For the overwhelming majority of religious believers, theological utterances are used, it appears, to assert the

actuality of some state of affairs in a transcendent
realm and not merely to express their own attitudes.
More generally, any analysis of the meaning of religious utterances in entirely non-metaphysical terms
makes a mockery, it seems, of the convictions of the
faithful since the concept of truth is ultimately
vacuous on such an account. And, accordingly, most
Christians would, I suspect, reject the truncated or
"demythologized" versions of their religion - versions
concocted by a small group of intellectuals.

Phillips subscribes to Wittgenstein's potentially
dangerous slogan "Don't think, but look!"[24] As an
avowed follower of Wittgenstein, he claims to reject all
a priori blueprints of the religious life. We should
look at religious practices in situ rather than stipu-
late any unempirical definition of religious belief or
practice; we should rely on the empirical data provided
by the sociology of religion. But Phillips' philosophical account of theological belief is singularly
unfaithful to the reality it is designed to capture:
most reflective, sincere, and self-conscious believers
would reject an analysis according to which religious
belief had no metaphysical component. And who, after
all, if not the users of a certain type of language,
are, for a Wittgensteinian, the best judges of the
adequacy of a philosophical analysis of what the
function of that language is - if only its first-order
usage? Most Christians would reject Phillips' analysis
as an inadequate account of what belief in Christian
doctrines comes to. And if Phillips complains that his
concern is with real or genuine religious belief as
opposed to actual instances of it, one should reply
that the whole affair smacks of a surreptitious
epistemological elitism and an unwarranted essentialism

108

both of which are anathema to a true votary of Wittgenstein.

This is a perfectly legitimate ad hominem argument against Phillips. Phillips' involved attempt to extricate himself from this difficulty has resulted in ingenious manoeuvres and a voluminous output. And all this in deference to the maxim that the impossible takes a little longer. The assumption that genuine Christianity was never intended to be metaphysical is both self-indulgent and unempirical. It is adopted under the pressure of two irreconcilable a priori theoretical demands, namely, both to endorse the devastating Humean critique of religious belief and yet to preserve the truth and autonomy of religious conviction along Wittgensteinian lines.

Phillips is fond of quoting Wittgenstein's conservative dictum: "Philosophy leaves everything as it is". The only thing that Phillips' account leaves where it was is our understanding of religious belief. Phillips' anti-metaphysical and quasi-anthropological conception of Christianity is impossible to reconcile with the traditional presentation of that religion. If it is indeed the case that the truth of Christianity consists simply in its being a system of "pictures" acceptable to some men, then the traditional view of Christianity (as embodying cosmic claims whose truth is independent of what men happen to believe) is untenable. Phillips claims to accept the truth of the doctrines of Christianity. But can we take him seriously on this? Is eternal life indeed to be identified with the life of faith here and now? And how are we to construe notions such as revelation and grace when there is no-one to reveal his intentions or bestow his grace? Phillips' response to this - that the religious language-game is different from the scientific one, that there is a special grammar for religious language and that, in view of these facts, it is simply a misunderstanding to ask these kinds of questions since religion is insulated from this kind of external probing - is both evasive and entirely unconvincing.

It is hard to resist the suspicion that Phillips' account distorts Christian belief under the pretext of merely explicating it; the proffered analysis is not even compatible with the salient features of the reality it investigates, let alone commensurate with them. For Phillips, religious belief isn't, couldn't and shouldn't be what ordinary believers usually take it to be. And thus, for all its professed neutrality and apparent conservatism, Phillips' analysis of religious belief is actually thoroughly tendentious calculated as it is to promote a particular normative viewpoint on the nature of Christian religious conviction.

- III -

Some theists have, in the face of sustained philosophical critique and growing religious perplexity concerning the extent to which the literal traditional interpretations of the divine attributes are coherent, abandoned the orthodox view of God as a person or distinct being. Hence, for example, we have Paul Tillich's famous prohibition against affirming or denying the existence of God qua distinct being: "it is as atheistic to affirm the existence of God as it is to deny it. God is being-itself, not a being."[25]

At one level, Tillich's move is understandable and legitimate. He is rightly concerned to emphasise that

God is different in kind from other entities in the created realm. But at another level, compromising the ontological integrity of claims about God's existence in this way has some unpalatable implications. Sacred Scripture is replete with remarks about divine wrath, love, mercy, compassion, and so on. Unless God is a person, none of these psychological predicates can meaningfully be applicable. Relatedly, what are we to make of such traditional concerns as men's fear of God, worship of God, disobedience to God, and so on, if there is no distinct and identifiable being there who can be feared, worshipped, and disobeyed?

This is not the place to criticise Tillich's position directly.[26] I mentioned his view merely to emphasise, by contrast, the Christian view of God as a distinct personal being. What renders most reductionist positions unacceptable is precisely their denial of the personhood of God. The attempt to equate God with certain human values and experiences, as we saw earlier, effectively abrogates belief in God qua person. Thus, for example, while God may assist us in realising our moral aspirations, God cannot simply be some impersonal cosmic force which reinforces our moral efforts at living decent lives. Again, the victory of reason or of kindness in the world is not, in itself, equivalent to traditional theism. Christianity is not Taoism.

A Christian's belief in God must involve belief in an identifiable being before whom he has taken up the attitude of faith. Belief in God will affect the believer's attitudinal postures and moral convictions but it cannot be reduced to either or both of these alone. Divorced from the traditional believer's intended reference to an objectively real transcendent

being who makes moral demands on men, such distinctively religious postures as worship and supplication
become vacuous and irrational. Prayer, for example,
becomes an original and ingenious way of expressing
one's fantasies for it is no longer intended to relate
the believer to an independent being who commands human
loyalty and veneration.

One of the factual presuppositions of the normative religious practice of most ordinary as well as
sophisticated Jews, Christians, and Muslims is the
belief that there is a supreme personal being. Unless
there is a real being to do the judging, for example,
the typical believer may innocently reason, it is
irrational of men to live their lives in fear of divine
judgement. It is, of course, possible to fear an empty
threat: a man may fear God when, in fact, no such
being exists much as a dog may feel threatened by his
own shadow. But it is certainly irrational (and
perhaps psychologically impossible) both to recognise
the emptiness of a threat and yet to feel genuinely
threatened.

- IV -

Religious thinkers immersed in the ethos of
modernity frequently lament the fact that the demise of
Christianity today is in large part due to the sheer
incredibleness of its supernatural heritage. The
Gospels portray the central figure of Christ in a way
that no longer admits of unqualified credence: that he
was miraculously born of a virgin, cured demoniacs,
subdued Satan, rose from the dead, and so on, strike
the modernists as a hotchpotch of superstitions concocted by a generation incapable of discerning the true
substance from the false cultural trappings of the

faith. The incipient Church, it is alleged, embel-
lished a purely non-metaphysical religious reality with
the puerile myth of supernatural occurrences. The
whole notion of the transcendent order found its
natural home in some later suspect metaphysic. Indeed,
even the customary modern categories of theism and
atheism were alien to the Zeitgeist of the biblical
writers. In this age, it is urged, Christianity should
be divested of the metaphysical dogmas with which
primitive Catholicism had enshrouded it; stripped of
its mythological supernatural garment, Christianity
could yet become a live option for modern man.

The prevalent opinion has been that the "desuper-
naturalized" versions of Christianity proffered by
radical theologians like Rudolf Bultmann[27] and Paul van
Buren[28] are instances of a merely nominal Christianity
which rests on an essentially atheistic metaphysic; an
underlying atheistic substance is veneered with a
misleading religious vocabulary. It is one thing, the
argument has run, to eliminate the traditional literal
accounts of cosmogony and eschatology, it is another to
abolish the supernatural order altogether or to make
God a part of the furniture of this world. Surely, it
has been said, it would be less misleading, given how
fundamentally different the radical theologians' talk
of God is from what most ordinary believers take it to
be, if the former were to find new words for expressing
what are, in effect, new and different beliefs
altogether.

This is a standard, even stock, yet forceful
criticism. The distinction - indeed contrast - between
a mundane or natural reality (which ordinary human
experience discloses) and a supra-mundane or transcendent reality (which is inaccessible to ordinary

sense-perception) is fundamental and central both to
religious thought and to much of traditional metaphysics.[29] It is this "schizocosmic"[30] division of
reality - what one writer has referred to as a
"fundamental metaphysical-cosmological dualism"[31] -
that must find a place in any bona fide theistic
metaphysic. Nor is the problem simply one of concep-
tualising an other-worldly reality as against this
world by the use of imagery and language which find
their natural place in this world. The problem is not
linguistic but ontological: Is there an absolute
metaphysical reality to be set in meaningful contrast
to natural reality? It is worth noting in this context
that Bultmann's famous demythologization programme
leaves the ontological issues untouched. Having
reduced the lavish ontology of the biblical world -
angels, archangels, demons, and witches - Bultmann does
not proceed to pronounce on the crucial issue concerning whether or not there is a divine realm. Does
the Christian revelation originate in heaven or is it
all a product of men's febrile solitude in the desert?
Perhaps, the Word of God is merely eloquent poetry of
disturbingly intense beauty. The Bultmann programme
simply by-passes the worries that genuinely plague us:
the ontological puzzle (Does a supreme supernatural
being really exist?), the epistemological perplexity
(How do we know that there is another order of
reality?), and the sceptical worry (Do we really know
that God exists in some transcendent realm?)

A truly theistic metaphysic must make the transcendent and the supra-natural among its central categories. If it doesn't, then the use of a theistic
vocabulary is both unjustifiable and misleading.
Hence, if "God" is equivalent to whatever men cherish

as their highest moral ideals, "transcendent" signifies simply the unrealized potentialities of the human person, and "salvation" comes to symbolize merely a concern for the future of mankind on this planet or for individual self-realisation and social harmony, then the use of a specifically religious vocabulary can have no basis other than convenience or an inability to find better words.

Consider the following dissident construals of some central religious notions:

(1) The idea of <u>the Kingdom of God</u> has a symbolical function in pointing to the final purpose which history is internally directed to attain.

(2) <u>Eternal Life</u> is a figurative allusion to the ecstasy which accompanies the pious will.

(3) <u>Revelation</u> is not the record of an eternal voice speaking at a specific historical juncture but is rather man's progressive discovery of his own immanent divinity.

The import of (1), (2), and (3) is purely secular. If theistic language has a purely human referent, then even an atheist - who believes that the significance of life is to be understood in purely human terms - can happily believe in such (alleged) realities as the Kingdom of God, eternal life, and divine revelation.

- V -

I want to shift the focus of the discussion now. I shall explore briefly the motivations behind reductionism in philosophical theology and identify one feature of religious conviction which facilitates reductionism.

It is easy to lampoon reductionism because it seems so <u>obviously</u> unfaithful to the reality of men's religious experience. It hardly needs to be proved that the men who argue passionately or even take up arms in defence of their religious convictions think that the rejection of faith is tantamount to a dangerous deviation from objective truth and reality rather than, as Phillips and Braithwaite would have us believe, to merely an attitudinal idiosyncrasy. The typical religious dispute (whether sectarian or interreligious) is over the nature of the Deity and the character of the world; believers rarely question the propriety of various attitudes as such towards the world. Religious judgements are supported by arguments which typically do not rely on establishing new bio-graphical facts i.e., facts about, say, the believer's psychology. Again, at another level, the striking reality which addressed Job out of the whirlwind or disturbed Muhammad's solitude in his retreat at Mount Hira was apparently no mere symbolic principle of organization or theoretical construct or some other reductionist fantasy.

But this way of looking at the matter obscures the fact that a literal interpretation of most religious claims contained in the Bible or the Koran seems deeply problematic. Primary religious discourse (as opposed to the secondary discussions in systematic theology) occasionally perplexes even ordinary reflective believers of many denominations let alone philosophers and theologians. Who is God? How does an incorporeal agent mete out rewards and punishments? Where are Hell and Heaven? There is, no doubt, a certain prosaic literalism which characterises a mentality unsettled by these kinds of problems. Even so, however, the peculiarity of first-order God-talk scarcely needs demonstration.[32]

The stress on the primacy of practice so characteristic of moralistic and fideistic accounts of
religion is in large part motivated by the desire to
deflect the vexing cognitive issues of the truth and
validity of theological belief. This is clear in the
case of the Wittgensteinian fideists and, arguably,
Wittgenstein himself.[33] Wittgenstein seems to argue
that a distinctively religious utterance such as "There
will be a Judgement Day" is to be understood in terms
of a certain picture which plays the ethical role of
admonishing the person who entertains it. The picture
of the Last Judgement plays a regulative role in the
believer's life: he appeals to this picture in the
daily decisions concerning the forgoing or indulging of
pleasures, the adoption of a specific regimen, and so
on. Now it is fairly obvious that there must be some
difference between the content of the belief itself and
its practical normative function. The meaning-content
or import of a belief such as "There will be a Judgement Day" is captured by the claim "One day a supreme
Judge will judge men with de jure authority". How can
the belief perform its action-guiding function in the
believer's life unless he believes in the reality of
the Judge? The regulative function cannot be equivalent in meaning to the belief even though a particular
regulative function may be a natural corollary of one's
entertainment of the belief. A believer does not, in
the first instance, believe in the regulative function
or causal efficacy of the picture: he believes in the
reality of the Judge. If this were not so, the reci-
tation of an ostensibly factual credal proposition such
as "Credo in unum deum" would be, in one writer's
words, "...simply one form of religious behaviour, so
that what is 'said' can no more be thought of as true

or false or meaningless than can kneeling before an altar".[34]

The history of religion is replete with examples of the peculiar power of religious conviction to transform men's lives. Within the Christian tradition, considerable emphasis has always been placed on the "saving truth" of Christianity. Christianity, we are told, is not so much metaphysically or propositionally true as practically convincing: it enables us to live authentically.[35] "The Gospel", as one commentator puts it, "is not an intellectual system, but a salvation".[36] In fine, the end of Christianity is to save, not to inform.

Now Christianity is certainly not just an abstract metaphysical corpus of theological propositions. But the fact that Christian truth-claims offer more than static theoretical insights, the fact that Christian claims are indeed influential and powerful, does not alter their epistemological status any more than the fact that a man might have missed his wedding alters his actual status as a married man. A doctrinal claim such as "Christ is the Saviour of sinful Adam's progeny" is a claim about how the world really or truly is. It is intended (by those who assert it) to refer to an actual or possible state of affairs in the universe. The content of theological propositions is unaffected by the transformative power of religious conviction.

Unlike theoretical science, Christianity is not primarily descriptive although it does share with science an interest in the nature of reality. Much of the significance of Christianity lies in its power to change the world rather than to mirror it. But there is an ineliminable cognitive dimension to Christianity

which renders false the regrettably influential contrast between the moral-practical interpretations of
the faith, on the one hand, and the doctrinal-
speculative on the other. The normative component of
faith supplements the informational: it cannot replace
it.

Perhaps religion is all just superstition - the
unfortunate remnant of a discredited mythology. To be
sure, the fear is that attention to its cognitive
dimension would reveal this to everyone. Religious
beliefs may indeed be superstitions; but it remains a
cardinal blunder to think that a religion could consist
just of a beliefless practicality uninformed by any
vision or any distinctive metaphysic of man and nature.
Some belief (no matter how inchoate) about the final
ground and purpose of existence and the destiny of our
species - an eschatology, if you wish - is an indispensable ingredient in the formation of an ultimate
commitment to any lifestyle whether religious or
secular. A rational religious interpretation of human
experience must be sustained by certain metaphysical
beliefs about the ultimate nature of the universal
order.

The attempt to eliminate the cognitive dimension
of religion is, of course, aided by certain features of
religious belief. It is peculiarly human to seek an
arena where our innermost passions can have free play.
Now the attitude men actually display towards their
moral ideals (or any ideals which govern their deepest
impulses) is similar to the attitude recommended by
religion for us to display towards God: one is to
ascribe in both cases an absolute and unconditional
authority to the object of one's devotion and to feel
morally obliged to interpret lapses from complete

loyalty and commitment as instances for regret and possibly severe self-incrimination. Given this similarity between religious and moral conviction - reflected in the use of a quasi-religious vocabulary for describing the quality of moral commitment and lapse - it is no longer surprising that religious conviction should so often be reduced to some amorphous human passion to affirm, with a morally impressive pathos, the ultimacy of our most tragically human impulses. The tendency then is to reject the intellectualist strand in religious belief so that truth (in the sense of correspondence to the facts) or even the apportioning of belief to evidence (to achieve rationality for one's believings) is seen as being of merely incidental interest.

- VI -

Presumably, people don't go to church just to feel uncomfortable. They want to feel uncomfortable in some special way and for some special reasons. Otherwise a visit to the Philosophy Department of some major university would do just as well. To put the point more generally and less cryptically, the functions which reductionists attribute to religion can equally be fulfilled by non-religious modes of thought and practice. If the value of religion resides solely in the psychological states it engenders or in its moral effects, then religion is merely a vehicle for achieving an end which some purely secular technique may also, in principle, achieve. Hence, if prayer were just a therapeutic technique for reducing tension or alleviating distress, then it would, in principle, be no different from purely secular techniques for stress reduction.

In his seminal work, <u>Dialogues Concerning Natural Religion</u>, Hume makes the sceptic Philo argue that the concept of God is acceptable to the rational mind only if it is qualified to such an extent that theism and atheism eventually become merely alternative ways of describing the same facts.[37] Hume saw, of course, that any version of theism that was compatible with atheism would necessarily be a very attenuated one in which the doctrinal claims would have been so thoroughly eroded that no adequate basis for any <u>distinctive</u> inferences that could affect or guide human conduct would be available. It is no coincidence that the theological scheme of many reductionist thinkers points to a lifestyle that is, in most circumstances, indistinguishable from that of conscientious secular humanists.

One of the dangers of reductionism is the threat of trivializing the dispute between faith and rejection. If the dispute is to be genuine and not merely verbal, theism must minimally involve the affirmation of the existence of a transcendent reality and atheism must involve a denial of the existence of such a reality. The concern with a supernatural dimension of benefits and burdens for men is partly constitutive of the theistic outlook. The secularization of Christianity is unsuccessful precisely because it effectively assimilates the Christian ideal to an atheistic secular one thereby puncturing the distinctive aspirations that the former advertises.

- VII -

If one wants to show atheists that there are more things in heaven and earth than are dreamt of in their philosophies, it is generally an unsound policy to attempt to do so by altering the meaning of words like

"God" and "exist". By this colourable method, one could show many wonderful things. If belief in God merely amounts to, say, having a certain ungrounded optimistic assurance that the values we happen to prize most highly will be progressively realized, then we have won the optimists over to the cause of faith merely by linguistic legerdemain.

Some attempts at re-interpreting the concept of God are in effect, if not in intention, tantamount to abandoning the concept altogether. Take, for example, the "religious atheism" of Ludwig Feuerbach.[38] For Feuerbach, the traditional concept of deity should be humanized so that man himself is the true object of religious belief and thus the focus of worship. Man, not God, is the ens perfectissimum, the Scholastics to the contrary notwithstanding. One should reduce theology to anthropology: the proper study of God is man.

Now, if God simply is human nature objectified, then clearly Feuerbach's thoroughly human god is not the God of Abraham, Jesus, and Muhammad. But why should that matter? We are, after all, a defender of Feuerbach's views may remind us, re-interpreting the concept of God for the needs of a self-consciously secular age. The concept of God (like all concepts) evolves naturally in response to changes in intellec-tual and popular culture. It has now reached a stage where the concept is thoroughly de-transcendentalized and secularised. This is, I think, an important criti-cism which needs to be addressed. My response will be somewhat indirect appealing as it does to a rather complex point about the status of tradition in histo-rical religions. It is fairly obvious, I suspect, that throughout this chapter, I have assumed that the tradition of Christian theism is normative for Christian theology. It is time now to make this assumption explicit and to attempt to justify it.

Let me begin by emphasising the complexity of the issue under discussion. There are, it appears, three distinct but related issues here. Firstly, there is the empirical question about whether or not the early followers of Jesus took his sayings to be intended literally or metaphorically. It has been charged, no doubt unfairly, that the over-literal misconceptions of the Romanist Church are to blame for the supernatural superfluities whose presence still plagues us today. Now, if Jesus and his disciples really meant what the modernists claim they meant, why didn't the former say so? To this it may be replied that it would have been premature to have done so, just as feeding solid food or teaching calculus is thought premature for very young infants. (Presumably, the sophistication requisite for understanding Jesus fully had to await upon the appearance of D.Z. Phillips and Rudolf Bultmann in this world.) Another response would be to invoke a sort of argumentum e silentio: Jesus never explicitly forbade metaphorical interpretations of his remarks. This is, of course, true. But, equally, Jesus never expressly endorsed such interpretations either. The argument from silence is, in effect, tantamount to recording our ignorance concerning the whole matter.

This whole issue is, of course, at once related both to the psychological question concerning the workings of the Hebraic mind (i.e., the quality of the religious imagination of the Jewish people) and, more broadly, to the historical milieu of the reception of Christianity. My own position on this - and I cannot argue for it here but I need to assume its truth to proceed further - is that while the figure of Jesus may well have become enshrouded in later legendary adornments, themselves effected out of motives of piety and reverence, some supernatural references were indeed implied in Jesus' reported discourses. I believe that this assumption survives the objection that the historical authenticity of the Gospel records is itself in question.

Secondly, there is the <u>logical</u> issue concerning whether or not the distinctive commitments of the Christian believer logically require something like the supernatural baggage which tradition has always supplied. And thirdly, there is the <u>apologetic</u> concern with making Christianity intellectually respectable and culturally viable in an aggressively atheistic culture. Such a concern has, arguably, taken the form of reinterpreting Christian concepts precisely so as not to offend secular sensibilities.

Bearing in mind these different concerns, I shall now argue that the tradition of Christian theism sets limits to the secularization of Christianity. The traditional metaphysical elements in Christian belief cannot be eliminated, I believe, without doing violence to the very concept of Christian theism. The concern with pedigree of doctrine is fundamental to religious traditions with an historical foundation. Contemporary Christian doctrine should be judged for genuineness by comparison with the doctrinal prototype, and not vice versa as the radical theologians aver. Hence, a view obviously predominant in Scripture and in the Christian intellectual tradition (such as God's personhood or his moral perfection or omnipotence or, in the extreme case, his very existence in some ontologically serious

- i.e., literal - sense) cannot be lightly dismissed by the innovator in favour of some newfangled ephemera. If the whole tenor of a narrative (as opposed to merely isolated or incidental emphases) makes plain or implies that, say, the disciples took Jesus to be divine, the innovator who rejects this feature of Jesus' personality must justify his departure from tradition.

The natural and justified response to this is, of course, that such a position attributes _ab initio_ an extraordinary importance to tradition - an importance that is subsequently invoked to justify resistance to doctrinal changes. Such a conservative interpretation, the objection may run, effectively begs the question against the modernists and the radical thinkers by pontificating that "traditional" and "orthodox", on the one hand, and "modernist" (or "radical") and "heterodox", on the other, are always equisignificant characterizations in religious dispute. Anyone who is advocating change is, therefore, the objection concludes, _ipso facto_ advocating heresy and hence something religiously unacceptable.

This is a confused if natural response. Reliance on tradition does not necessarily imply that doctrinal novelties can never be more accurate interpretations of the original than what established orthodoxy would lead one to suppose. The point to note is that it is no coincidence that unorthodox thinkers often seek to win approval for their own views by claiming that their apparently novel or heretical interpretations conform to the real (i.e., original and unadulterated) teachings of the founder. Christian faith and theology are developing historical phenomena - living realities, if you like - whose present character and formulation are not _wholly_ determined by their past; but they are essentially determined thus. The Christian thinker must appropriate the contemporary religious experience in the light of a perspective which essentially derives from the past - the specifically Christian past.

Now, to assign a normative role to tradition is not to deny the possibility of change, even revolutionary change, in Christian doctrine. But while ruptures with the mainstream historical development of Christianity may occasionally be radical, they cannot be utterly discontinuous with the traditional understanding of the faith. All changes, whether gradual or revolutionary, must recognisably be continuous with the past - a past which has a normative-critical significance for all later generations seeking to reinterpret afresh the religious genius of the original for the needs of generations reared in other epochs. Any interpretation which works by rupturing all links with the whole tradition of thought on the nature of Christian religious belief is unacceptable for it has, ex hypothesi, no tradition to appeal to. It is therefore an arbitrary interpretation. Relatedly, no adequate interpretation of any established reality can be wholly indifferent to the tradition of the reality involved. Religion is not an exception; a nonarbitrary interpretation of any religion has to appeal to it as it has always been recognised to be.

Christianity is not an inert fact of nature: it has a history, a living and distinguished intellectual tradition, and an impressive record of development and schism. The theologian's task is to construe changes, modulations and refinements in doctrine and, relatedly, the concepts of religious originality, continuity and individuality, against the background supplied by the Christian tradition seen as a normative yardstick for deciding what is or is not truly Christian.

Tradition is not a rigidly fixed _depositum_ constituting the foundations of the edifice of faith; it is not some eternally valid ahistorical set of doctrinal propositions at the base of the structure. Such an architectural model is misleading. Tradition is an ongoing process of doctrinal accumulation, relegation, and removal. But no theoretical hiatus between doctrinal accretions, on the one hand, and the whole burden of tradition seen as the historical accumulation of Christian dogmatic proclamations, on the other, should be tolerated. There is a norm in matters of doctrine; the established legacy of the faith - the apostolic tradition - is the criterion for judging the genuineness of new doctrinal candidates for admission into the corpus of the faith.

While the decision to expose the Church to contemporary intellectual and cultural influences does imply that theologians are at liberty to translate the traditional Christian doctrines into the modern idiom, it does not imply that they may do so in complete isolation from the context of the original birth and formulation of these doctrines. Indeed, the meaning which a restatement is intended to preserve cannot be ascertained unless one can develop an imaginative sympathy with the ideals of those who originally formulated much of Christian doctrine. Secularist interpreters, as we saw earlier, wrongly tear out Christian doctrines from their Christian context and interpret them against the contextual background supplied by an alien anti-ecclesiastical milieu of a fiercely secular culture. It is not surprising that Christianity comes out very badly from the whole affair.

Much more needs to be said about the status of tradition; my remarks here are just a beginning. I do not deny that one would have to show, at greater length, why it is religiously important to remain faithful to the tradition nor that the modernists may, with some tolerable degree of plausibility, argue that one legitimate inference from the traditio of the canonical literature is that faith must, in some way, seek accommodation with non-Christian (including secular) cultures on pain of losing its salvific relevance to peoples fatefully placed in environments indifferent or hostile to the Christian message. Furthermore, one must carefully identify the tradition; under the guise of merely discovering the tradition, one may, perhaps unwittingly, actually impute alien features to it - features that are elements in a writer's own preferred scheme of thought. And there are other difficulties too. One can, for instance, insist neither on requiring complete immutability of doctrine nor on a supra-historical kind of absolute fixity of belief. (Orthodox Islamic theology made both these mistakes in condemning all innovation -bid^{c}a - soon after the end of the creative period of Muslim intellectual culture.) The historicist temper has taken root too deeply for us to require anything of the kind. Even so, however, we cannot ignore the religious importance of achieving theoretical uniformity in doctrine. The problems of continuity and innovation are perennially relevant; a religious institution can resist heresy and preserve the doctrinal unity of the faith only if there is a generally acknowledged or acknowledgeable source of authority. My suggestion is that this source should be the tradition of the faith.

Tillich claims to believe in God - but not in the God of traditional theism. The theist's God is, for Tillich, simply an idol constructed by incompetent metaphysicians. Braithwaite believes in God but gives belief in God a very unorthodox construal. Now, admittedly, we have had different conceptualizations of God through the ages and all have been deeply affected by the dominant culture. (Remember that the problem generated by the collision between tradition and modernity is not an exclusively modern one: it arises afresh in every age as thinkers seek to abandon the myths of tradition while appropriating its insights.) But the departure from the cosmic literalism of the past, inspired by the radical crisis of faith in the modern world, must be constrained by some measured awareness of the limits of such a manoeuvre. We cannot move that far away from the old house: the correct characterization of Christian theism has to be recognisably linked to the older account. The tradition of Christian theism is not authoritative concerning the issue of the truth or even the correct interpretation of traditional doctrines but it is authoritative on the issue concerning what range of beliefs can fairly be labelled as belonging to it.

I shall briefly address the third concern now, namely, the apologetic one. Tradition has rigidly maintained that God is a non-psychological and non-physical reality external to human beings and that "God" is properly to be regarded as a referring expression. "God", on one standard interpretation, is the name of an objectively real being; it refers to that extraordinary being whose creative will is invoked to account for the human condition i.e., to explain and justify various problematic features of the world, such as its existence and the natural evil in it. The concept of God is actually instantiated, we are told by the traditional believer; God is emphatically not just a therapeutic fiction for soothing the tumult of the burdened conscience. The task of proselytization, the traditionalist urges, relies on altering the cognitive content of a man's beliefs, not just the emotive one: religious concerns are acquired primarily through increase in religious knowledge, not change of personal sentiment.

I mentioned in the opening section of Chapter 3 that a significant concern of twentieth century Christian thought has been the attempt to identify the essence of the faith by paring away outmoded pre-scientific cosmologies, culture-bound superfluities, and so on. I suspect that this attempt to separate the central or essential from the peripheral or extraneous has been motivated largely by the apologetic desire to show the philosophical and scientific critics of Christianity that what survives such critiques is actually central to Christian belief while what perishes under critical scrutiny is, in any case, extraneous. Such an attempt is, of course, not inherently dishonest or apologetic. But it is clearly both if one identifies what is essential to Christian theism with precisely what is also acceptable to the philosophical and scientific critics of traditional theism. Such an identification is unacceptable unless it has independent support. There should be grounds rather than motives for establishing a coincidence between the essence of faith and just exactly those scandals to the intellect which today's worldly folk will tolerate.

130

Notes

[1] For an influential statement of logical positivism, see A.J. Ayer's Language, Truth and Logic (London: Gollancz, 1956).

[2] R.B. Braithwaite, "An Empiricist's View of the Nature of Religious Belief", in The Philosophy of Religion, Basil Mitchell (ed.), (Oxford: Oxford University Press, 1971), pp. 72-91.

[3] ibid., p. 73.

[4] ibid., p. 89.

[5] ibid., p. 89.

[6] ibid., p. 86.

[7] ibid., p. 86.

[8] See the following: Kai Nielsen, "Christian Empiricism", in The Journal of Religion, Vol. 61, No. 2, April 1981, pp. 146-167; Antony Flew, God and Philosophy (London: Hutchinson, 1966), p. 23; and C.B. Martin, Religious Belief (Ithaca: Cornell University Press, 1959), Chapter 2.

[9] Friedrich Nietzsche, Twilight of the Idols (Harmondsworth: Penguin Books, 1968), translated by R.J. Hollingdale, p. 69.

[10] Nietzsche, op. cit.

[11] Nietzsche, op. cit., p. 45. Emphasis in original

[12] See John Wisdom's "Gods", in The Logic of God: Theology and Verification, Malcolm Diamond and Thomas Litzenburg (eds.), (Indianapolis: Bobbs-Merrill, 1975), pp. 158-177. My interpretation of Wisdom's position as non-cognitivist is controversial. See also Kenneth Sayre's "A Perceptual Model of Belief in God", in The Autonomy of Religious Belief: A Critical Inquiry, Frederick Crosson (ed.), (Notre Dame: University of Notre Dame Press, 1981), pp. 108-127. Sayre takes his cue from Wisdom.

[13] D.Z. Phillips, Religion Without Explanation (Oxford: Basil Blackwell, 1976), p. 171.

[14] ibid., p. 184.

[15]D.Z. Phillips, "Religious beliefs and Language-Games", in The Philosophy of Religion, Basil Mitchell (ed.), (Oxford: Oxford University Press, 1971), pp. 137-140.

[16]Religion Without Explanation, p. 114.

[17]ibid., p. 150.

[18]ibid., pp. ix-xi, 9-25.

[19]See D.Z. Phillips' Death and Immortality (London: Macmillan, 1970), pp. 71 ff; and Religion and Understanding., D.Z. Phillips (ed.), (Oxford: Basil Blackwell, 1967), p. 66.

[20]See D.Z. Phillips, Faith and Philosophical Enquiry (New York: Schocken Books, 1971), especially Chapters 1, 2, and 13; and see also his The Concept of Prayer (London: Routledge and Kegan Paul, 1965) and his Marett Lecture, "Primitive Reactions and the Reactions of Primitives", delivered in May 1983 at Oxford.

[21]See especially the following: Kai Nielsen, Scepticism (London: Macmillan, 1973), pp. 23-40 and his An Introduction to the Philosophy of Religion (London: Macmillan, 1982), Chapters 3, 4, and 5; J.L. Mackie's posthumous The Miracle of Theism: Arguments For and Against the Existence of God (Oxford: Clarendon Press, 1982), Chapter 12; and Terence Penelhum's "Religious belief and Life after death", in Proceedings of the 8th International Wittgenstein Symposium, August 1983, Part 2, pp. 37-45. For some pungent criticisms of the view that philosophy can neither justify nor refute religious belief, see Michael Durrant's "Is the Justification of Religious Belief a Possible Enterprise?" in Religious Studies, Vol. 9, 1973, pp. 449-455; and see also Kai Nielsen's widely anthologized piece, "Wittgensteinian fideism", as reprinted in Analytical Philosophy of Religion in Canada, Mostafa Faghfoury (ed.), (Ottawa: University of Ottawa Press, 1982), pp. 97-114.

[22]Koran, Surah I, The Opening of the Book, vv. 5-6. A.J. Arberry's translation.

[23]Friedrich Nietzsche, Ecce Homo (Harmondsworth: Penguin Books, 1979), p. 68.

132

24Ludwig Wittgenstein, <u>Philosophical Investigations</u> (Oxford: Basil Blackwell, 1963), para. 66.

25Paul Tillich, <u>Systematic Theology</u> (Chicago: Chicago University Press, 1951), Vol. I, p. 237. Emphasis in original.

26Tillich's characterization of God as "being-itself" or "the ground of being" is obscure beyond any rational excuse. And ironically, in his concern to show that God cannot be identified with any particular finite object in the world or with any dimension of human experience, Tillich advocates a view which, quite apart from the obscurity it has generated when exalted phrases of unclear meaning are thrown about, is also theologically disconcerting: pantheism may well be the last rung on Tillich's ladder.

27Rudolf Bultmann, "New Testament and Theology", in <u>Kerygma and Myth</u>, H.W. Bartsch (ed.), (London: S.P.C.K., 1972), translated by R.H. Fuller, pp. 1 ff.

28Paul van Buren, <u>The Secular Meaning of the Gospel</u> (London: S.C.M. Press, 1963).

29Plato's metaphysic, for example, rests on a division of reality into the sensible world of ordinary realities and the supra-sensible <u>mundus intelligibilis</u> of transcendent realities.

30This is Oliver Buswell's term and is quoted by Francis Lee in the latter's <u>A Christian Introduction to the History of Philosophy</u> (Nutley: The Craig Press, 1975), p. 226.

31Gordon Kaufman, "On the Meaning of 'God': Transcendence without Mythology", in <u>The Harvard Theological Review</u>, Vol. 59, No. 2, April 1966, p. 106.

32Kai Nielsen has argued, at great length, for the view that first-order God-talk is not merely peculiar and problematic but incoherent. See the following works by him: <u>Contemporary Critiques of Religion</u> (London: Macmillan, 1971); <u>Philosophy and Atheism: In Defence of Atheism</u> (Buffalo: Prometheus Books, 1985); and "On Mucking Around about God: Some Methodological Animadversions", in <u>International Journal for the Philosophy of Religion</u>, Vol. 16, 1984, pp. 111-122.

[33] For Wittgenstein's enigmatic views, see a set of notes (which do not constitute a verbatim report of his words) taken by his students, <u>Lectures and Conversations on Aesthetics, Psychology and Religious Belief</u>, Cyril Barrett (ed.), (Berkeley and Los Angeles: University of California Press, 1967), especially pp. 56-57.

[34] John Cook, "Magic, Witchcraft, and Science", in <u>Philosophical Investigations</u>, Vol. 6, No. 1, January 1983, p. 7.

[35] See Patrick Sherry's <u>Religion, Truth and Language-Games</u> (London: Macmillan, 1977), pp. 168-172 for further discussion.

[36] The remark - "l'evangile n'est pas une sagesse, c'est un salut" - is attributed to F. Godet and quoted by Bernard Williams in his "Tertullian's Paradox", in <u>New Essays in Philosophical Theology</u>, Antony Flew and Alasdair MacIntyre (eds.), (London: S.C.M. Press, 1955), p. 210.

[37] David Hume, <u>Dialogues Concerning Natural Religion</u> (New York, London: Hafner, 1969), with an introduction by Henry Aiken, Part XII, p. 94.

[38] Ludwig Feuerbach, <u>The Essence of Christianity</u> (New York: Harper and Row, 1957), translated by George Eliot.

We are accustomed to hearing that reductionist
thinkers tend to lose sight of the true character of
New Testament Christianity. They adapt it to current
secular assumptions even at the cost of mutilation and
distortion; they soften the demands of orthodoxy
incessantly. Instead of defending the exacting traditional versions of the faith, it is alleged, they
espouse accommodating forms of Christianity domesti-
cated within contemporary culture.

Modern European Christianity is, as Kierkegaard
tells us ever and anon, no scandal to the secular
intellect. While we may dispute the scope of Kierkegaard's insight, there is no denying its essential
soundness. It is indeed an indictment of what passes
for Christianity in the modern world that its distinctive (or "offensive") elements are continually pruned
in the attempt to formulate doctrines that are con-
gruent with surrounding secular attitudes. Gone are
the days when it was worthwhile to throw a Christian
to the lions.

Theological reductionists are in good company.
Many secularized believers who reject reductionism are
also subject to Kierkegaard's criticism. Theism, such
secularized believers contend, cannot be reduced to
its attendant moral scheme or to a particular way of
looking at nature (or, more narrowly, human nature).
The propositional character of theology must be
upheld. But theology, as a discipline, must respect
the constraints imposed on it by its contemporaneous
natural and social science. Religious claims must, if
necessary, be attenuated in the face of current scien-

tific and rational philosophical challenge. What
survives secular scrutiny is still, we are told,
genuine theism with sufficient rationally warranted
credal content to sustain a distinctive pattern of
existence and experience. I turn now to an examination of this philosophical position - "theological
revisionism", as I shall, perhaps tendentiously, call
it henceforth - a position characteristic of secularized religious thinkers who reject reductionism.

- I -

Theological revisionism is a half-way house
between a neo-orthodoxy which denies the autonomy of
secular reason by dethroning secular reason in favour
of religious faith, on the one hand, and a reductionism which endorses the supremacy of reason while
failing to preserve the indicative character of
religious belief, on the other. To the revisionists,
the power of reason is all too apparent. Christianity
must, they insist, make its case before the tribunal
of contemporary intellectual culture; otherwise it
stands condemned. But, equally, it must make its case
without relinquishing, under the pressure of critical
scrutiny, its central claim to providing an authoritative and comprehensive truth about God, nature, and
human destiny.

For the revisionist, unlike the reductionist,
theological propositions refer to something over and
above the mundane facts on which they are based. When
the words of a theological remark are used simply as a
pictorial re-description of the mundane phenomena
referred to, they do not, the revisionists urge,
constitute the expression of an orthodox belief in a
purported supra-mundane reality. Thus, according to

the revisionists, theological propositions
 (i) are assertions of fact (or putative fact),
 (ii) have a basis in the world of experience i.e.,
       there is some mundane evidence in their favour,
       and
(iii) encapsulate claims not only about natural
       realities but also about supernatural ones.
In fine, theological propositions are to be expressed
in a transcendentalist idiom with sensible phenomena
as their grounds and the transcendent as their (putative) referent.

    Theological propositions, then, are factual and
reason is sovereign. Now, not every traditional
religious claim is, the revisionists lament, defensible. The sophisticated Judaeo-Christian theist will
endorse only what he regards as defensible - given the
present state of our knowledge. The sophisticated
believer is one who, in Terence Penelhum's words,

        ...accepts the findings of natural science
        and is not prepared to run counter to them
        in his religious beliefs; who is prepared to
        accept the findings of biblical scholarship
        and has, therefore, abandoned the view of
        the infallible divine dictation of the
        Scriptures; and who, finally, is not pre-
        pared to accept beliefs that turn out, upon
        examination, to be self-contradictory or
        confused.[1]

                    - II -
    The historico-critical study of the Old Testament
and the Gospels has revealed the presence, it is
alleged by some Christian and non-Christian scholars,
of numerous contradictions, improbabilities, histo-

138

rical and scientific falsehoods, and morally unworthy
claims even in the definitive canon.[2] Neo-orthodox
thinkers attempt to explode the perceived antagonism
between Judaeo-Christian theism and secular knowledge
by insisting that the presence of apparent discrepancies and alleged errors in the biblical canon is
irrelevant to faith. Revealed knowledge cannot be
brought within the purview of a purely human understanding and logic: a misconstrual of the limits of
natural knowledge accounts for the notorious incompatibility between faith and science in the modern
world.

Both reductionists and revisionists, however,
recognise that some statements of biblical authors
concerning scientific and historical facts are clearly
false if interpreted in the light of recently acquired
knowledge. The crude pre-scientific cosmologies in
Genesis 1 and 2 are, if the contemporary scientific
picture is even remotely true, to put it minimally, a
masterpiece of inaccuracy. Our current biological and
geological knowledge render downright mistaken the
view that the world originated about six thousand
years ago or that its creation took only six days.
Again, the biblical inaccuracies concerning the
evolution of animal life on this planet are truly
gargantuan. But, as Richard Swinburne retorts,

...it seems odd to suppose that the religious message of what is evidently a piece
of poetry was concerned with the exact time
and method of animal arrival on the Earth,
or that that was what those who composed it
were attempting to tell the world. Their
message concerned, not the details of the
time and method of animal arrival, but the
ultimate cause of that arrival.[3]

Swinburne maintains that if a prophet's religious teaching is to be made intelligible, it might need to be embodied in the false historical and scientific presuppositions prevalent in the prophet's culture and era.[4] It is therefore necessary for us to know the context of revelation - that is, a pre-scientific culture, in the case of the creation stories in Genesis, at an early stage of religious evolution - in order to arrive at a valid assessment of its contents. We must distinguish between the religious import of Scripture and the possibly false extra-religious accoutrements needed to convey the message to an ignorant people.

Swinburne's response to the challenge of critical biblical scholarship is characteristic of revisionist believers.[5] A modern sophisticated Christian believer can, the revisionists tell us, read without alarm Paine, Darwin and Marx since their critiques do not damage the true kernel of Christianity. Thus, while the revolutionary ideas of man's ascent from the inorganic or his descent from an animal ancestry are a direct affront to ancient scriptural views about human nature, this does not eviscerate the essential substance of the religious doctrines about man's dependence on God for redemption and salvation. Again, given that the received history in the Bible is only partly accurate, we can cheerfully accept the claim of secular anthropologists of religion that primitive man was a polytheist rather than, as Holy Scripture would lead us to suppose, a monotheist.[6] We must distinguish, then, between the religious message and its culturally specific incarnation. As long as the religious message itself is entirely true, the falsity of any actual embodiment is religiously inconsequential.

A preliminary remark is in order. For Swinburne, Genesis is, as he tells us in the passage quoted earlier, "evidently a piece of poetry". The tradition of Christian apologetics has, however, until comparatively recently, taken Genesis to be literal and infallible truth. I suppose sophisticated modern Christians must think those chaps in the Middle Ages were out of their medieval minds: a stricto sensu interpretation of the Bible lands us in palpable absurdities. And others may think that, given the primitive state of natural science in the Middle Ages, the Medievals could rationally accept literalist accounts of creation but that we, with our recently acquired knowledge of the world, cannot do so. But, be that as it may, the great controversies that raged over the past two centuries between the ancient Church and the nascent scientific establishment were precisely over whether or not Genesis is a piece of poetry. It is surprising that something so evidently poetical should have been mistaken for literal truth for so long and by so many intelligent men. We have paid a high price for distinguishing poetry from prose. In fact, of course, the Church's opposition to science was not misplaced. It mattered very greatly, for example, whether or not men had indeed evolved from a neighbouring (and rather unflattering) lineage in the animal kingdom.

Even a true religious message, Swinburne tells us, may need to be encapsulated in the current false historical and scientific beliefs. Swinburne's suggestion is that we should simply excise the false non-religious trappings and retain the residual religious message. He admits that in practice it may be difficult to distinguish between the true religious

kernel and its concomitant false cultural husk.[7]   I
shall now argue that Swinburne's own way of drawing
this distinction rests on a petitio principii.

Swinburne's criteria for verifying the truth and
profundity of a religious message are predictable:
none of what is taught by the prophet must be evidently false; no factual teaching of the prophet must
be proven false; and such parts of the prophetic
teaching as can be humanly verified must be found to
be actually true, and so on.[8] But the application of
these criteria seems unclear in view of Swinburne's
simultaneous commitment to the view that the true
religious message may need to be encapsulated in false
historico-scientific presuppositions. Why should the
falsity of a particular factual claim made by a
prophet be regarded as detrimental to his religious
credentials if indeed true religious messages can
sometimes have false embodiments?

The reason for Swinburne's confusion on this
point is instructive. The application of Swinburne's
own criteria of truth and profundity to the Christian
message leads one to the obvious conclusion that it
should be rejected: there are factual falsehoods and
palpable inconsistencies galore in the biblical
canon.[9] But this is clearly an unacceptable conclusion. So, Swinburne decides to espouse the view
that these errors are inconsequential for they are
non-religious. And yet he knows that a rational
decision concerning the truth of a religious message
is never effected in vacuo i.e., in utter disregard of
or in irrelation to the truth of the non-religious
claims being proffered.

Suppose a man in a sheet and sandals suddenly
claims to have heard from God. Our judgement about

the validity of his claim to revelation finds a complex basis in, _inter alia_, what we see of his moral deportment prior to any such unusual pretensions, the moral character of his message, the truth of his factual (for example, prognosticatory) claims, and so on. We do not know in advance of such considerations whether or not his claims are genuine. Swinburne's decision to expurgate the religiously irrelevant falsehoods while retaining the religious truths presupposes that the authenticity of the religious substance can be judged independently of any decision about the truth of the surrounding extra-religious paraphernalia. The hope seems to be that the kernel of revealed truth in the Scriptures is separable from the outer layer of falsehood. But, surely, if a putative revelation can contain errors of astronomy and biology, there is no reason _a priori_ why it couldn't contain errors of religious doctrine. If its factual claims are obsolete, why not its religious ones? Swinburne's distinction between a religious message and its contemporaneous presuppositions may be tenable but it can be used to salvage the Christian dispensation only if one assumes the truth of the latter _ab initio_ - which is precisely what Swinburne does.

There is an important distinction Swinburne fails to draw. It is one thing for a prophet to entertain false historico-scientific beliefs; it is another for a (putative) revelation to contain factual errors. Prophets are, like everyone else, the product in part of their age and culture and they may entertain the prevalent false _Weltanschauung_. But this need not prevent a revelation from being wholly true.

A revelation which remained silent on matters of
secular fact and dealt exclusively with religious
doctrine would attain compatibility with secular
history and science. Alternatively, and more plausibly, if it made deliberately vague factual claims to
suit the audience's ignorance, it would not only
achieve compatibility but also impress upon the
audience the relative unimportance of precise factual
details in a religious narrative. Hence, "The world
was created in six periods" (with "period" signifying
an indefinite duration) is true but vague whereas "The
world was created in six days" is precise but outrageously false. Similarly, "Joseph was sold for a
paltry price" is superior to the more precise "Joseph
was sold for twenty shekels of silver".[10] A <u>bona fide</u>
revelation could, then, remain uncommitted on some
factual issues while expressing others in a vague way.
If compatibility with secular knowledge requires that
not too much of the truth be made clear, why not avoid
error by studied ambiguity?

Let us suppose, for the sake of a case, that some
religious truths may need to be enclosed within culturally prevalent falsehoods. Even so, however, only
some kinds of falsehood would be permissible in a
revealed message. There is no harm in having the
occasional "pious fraud" in the interests of some
greater truth. But what momentous truth do the
factual untruths in <u>Genesis</u> serve? The worry is that
the Bible may be only a fraud - and an impious one at
that. Again, while some allowance must be made for
discrepancies which naturally plague any manuscript of
antiquity, there is no rational excuse for accepting
blatant contradictions and incompatibilities[11] and
obviously untrue statements.[12] The fact that God is

not primarily concerned to convey historico-scientific
truths to men does not entail that one should tolerate
every manner of factual untruth in a putative revelation. The liberty to refrain from making preposte-
rous claims also extends to God.

I remarked in the two preceding chapters that a
significant concern of modern Christian thought has
been the attempt to sift out the quintessence of
Christian religious belief by separating what is
central to such belief from what is merely incidental.
Swinburne's attempt is an obvious instance of this
concern. But the worry here is, of course, that as
more and more of the traditional claims are exposed as
false and embarrassingly fantastic, many sophisticated
Christian thinkers disown the suspect parts of Scripture without offering any systematic account - a body
of theory - which would mitigate the arbitrariness of
this procedure.[13] I am not suggesting, of course,
that revelation has to be viewed as a collection of
rigidly unrejectable data. But one should not reject
ad hoc whatever offends modern sensibilities. Thus,
for example, one could reasonably argue that whatever
in Scripture is factually erroneous should be dis-
owned. Arguably, the fog is thicker when it comes to
apparent moral anachronisms - such as biblical verses
about the status of women, the morality of "deviant"
sexual behaviour, and so on.

Now, on a more theoretical level, Swinburne's
distinction between the true religious message and its
false socio-cultural expression trades on a controversial and suspect construal of the nature and scope
of religion. Unlike science and history, religion
claims to be all-inclusive; the former deal respec-
tively with whatever is subject to lawful regularity

and whatever is significant in the human past while
the latter deals, in some important sense, with everything. Swinburne's distinction presupposes for its
tenability that the cultural embodiment of a religion
can be exclusively secular (i.e., extra-religious).
But to presuppose this is to beg the question about
the comprehensiveness of religion. This may appear
like a quibble to readers reared in the West but the
distinction between "the things of God" and "the
things of Caesar" is actually occidocentric: it is
not a feature of every religion.[14] Swinburne's distinction cannot apply to religion in general and is,
even in the case of Christianity, applicable only to a
distinctively modern conception of that faith dating
from the Enlightenment which marks the beginning of
the tradition of modernity.

Whatever may be said concerning the essence of
Christianity, the presence of errors in the Bible
poses a theological problem. It is disturbing that
revelation makes no attempt to correct culturally
prevalent errors and instead accommodates itself to
them. It is surprising, sophisticated Christians to
the contrary notwithstanding, that God's knowledge of
history, science, and logic is inferior to that of a
schoolboy. Surely, God could have managed error-free
revelation. (Is there in this, perhaps, an intellectual trial to test the mettle of the children of
God?[15])

Modern critical biblical scholarship has persuasively argued that the biblical canon cannot be
equated with the divinely dictated Word of God.
Traditionally, many Christians have accepted claims
about the heavenly inspiration and inerrancy of Scripture on the authority of a Church. But it is quite

undeniable that these claims cannot be justified on any grounds of historical probability. The Bible is not a historically totally reliable account of events: the absolute historical authenticity of the Scriptures has to be rejected.

The appeal to the authority of the Christian revelation, however, does not immediately go to the devil. A revisionist could reply that the writings in the Bible are not God's direct formulations of divine beliefs. Revelation, he may urge, is not, for a Christian, primarily informational. The whole model of God revealing himself by dictating his eternally valid beliefs and commands in the unavoidably imperfect and mutable medium of human language is to be rejected as intolerably crude. God reveals _himself_ in gracious relationship with his creatures, his people of Covenant, and so on. Scripture is indeed a record of encounter with God - men's impressions of their commerce with this unique reality. But these records are revelatory only in a secondary sense. What is primarily revelatory is the actual experience of relationship with God i.e., relationship with the personality of Christ. For Jews and Muslims, divine revelation is primarily in the form of a written record in a sacred language; for Christians, revelation finds its primary locus in the experience of relationship with God as Christ. (Remember that the Torah and the Koran correspond not to the New Testament but to Christ.) Thus, one can be in genuinely revelatory relationship with God, the revisionist will urge, even though the content of any written record of this experience be unclear and erroneous. It is not the message but the messenger that really matters.

Now, to be sure, even if God reveals himself in the manner indicated by the revisionists, we still need to theorise about what it is that has thus been revealed to us. And the record of what Christians have interpreted to be their encounter with God simply has to be assessed for authenticity. Moreover, while the distinction between revelation qua divine self-disclosure and revelation qua written record of divine beliefs is not untenable, the Christian believer still has to justify his claim that his religious experience is an experience of relationship with God. My own suspicion is that there is an apologetic motive concealed in this revisionist stratagem: the idea that revelation as acquaintance with the divine personality is more fundamental than revelation as written record of such an alleged acquaintance is itself relatively modern. It is not a coincidence that the idea has gained currency in the wake of unwelcome discoveries in critical biblical scholarship and comparative religion.

There are, in any case, no a priori expectations about what a sophisticated Christian should do in the face of the predicament created by the discovery of what seem at least scientific and historical errors, contradictions, and morally questionable claims in the biblical revelation. He cannot assume a priori (i.e., in the absence of relevant evidence) that the only right course of action is to retain the religious core in the hope that it is true while abandoning the non-religious husk.

Suppose a sophisticated modern Christian decides to consider rival putative revelations. Once he abandons the question-begging assumption that the Christian revelation is true (or uniquely true), he

will need some criteria for choosing between rivals.
If two putative revelations R_1 and R_2 conflict on
matters of religious doctrine, one might reasonably
choose ceteris paribus the one that has fewer factual
errors in it. If, however, we accept, as Swinburne
does, the view that even a truly revealed corpus may
legitimately contain factual errors, then we cannot
use their presence or absence as a criterion for
preferring one (putative) revelation to another.

The fact that there are rival putative revelations in the world poses a serious problem for honest
sophisticated Christians. Unlike their neo-orthodox
co-religionists for whom secular reason is subordinate
to faith, the sophisticated Christians cannot ignore
the fact that the revelatory pretensions of some
related faith - say, Judaism or Islam - may make a
better claim on their reason. (Remember that the
object of our devotion is God - not our beliefs about
God.) Now suppose, for the sake of argument, that the
scripture of some related rival Western religion -
say, Islam's Arabic Koran - is free of the inconsistencies, contradictions, and morally questionable
elements found in the Bible; suppose further that it
contains no discrepancies or errors of its own, and
that its purely religious message is as profound and
appealing as that contained in the Bible. Moreover,
let us suppose that the Muslim scripture has been
carefully preserved (i.e., the purity of its text
guarded[16]), the reputation of God and his prophets
vindicated against biblical accusations,[17] doctrines
such as original sin and vicarious atonement rejected
as false and unjust (thus removing the need to face
morally embarrassing problems about unbaptised infants
burning in hell and children's teeth being set on edge

when the fathers eat the grapes), the religious provin-
cialism of the biblical outlook mitigated by a somewhat more catholic vision, and finally, the presence
of errors and discrepancies in the biblical canon
convincingly explained as being the result of later
human falsification of the Scripture by deletion from
or addition to an originally revealed error-free
corpus. The presence of any such revelation in the
world should be a cause for great concern among sophisticated Christians.[18] A Christian who comes to reject
the authority of the Christian revelation may, of
course, prefer to remain a Christian by embracing a
somewhat jejune deism graced by a Christian morality.[19] But it is far from obvious that his choice is
justified, let alone wise.

- III -

There are several major faiths in the world
today. Unfortunately, the religious beliefs of men in
different religious traditions are incompatible with
one another. Now Christian tradition, unsurprisingly,
has rigidly maintained that the Christian religion has
a de jure claim to unique truth and validity; Christianity provides, it has been thought, a comprehensive
and definitive truth about man, nature, and divinity.

Reductionists, for fairly obvious reasons, handle
the problem generated by the conflicting truth-claims
of the different world religions very differently from
the revisionists. If the cognitive element is
entirely removed, incompatibility between religions
must ultimately be purely verbal rather than substantive. Moreover, if the religious claims of Christianity can indeed be construed as, say, "stories" whose
truth or falsity bears no relation to their religious

function, then the traditional concern with claims to
unique truth is, in any case, bogus. Revisionists,
however, recognise that Christianity is attempting to
deal with matters of truth and reality rather than
subjective import and personal (or cultural) outlook.
But, given the contemporaneous growth of our knowledge
of other rival religious traditions, there is a strong
desire to avoid the insularity implicit in claiming
unique truth for one's own religious belief-system.
And yet one cannot, it seems, talk about Christianity
as a Christian without, in some way, insisting on its
pre-emptive primacy. Certainly, the reasonableness of
the revisionist stance stands out in stark contrast to
the offensive dogmatism of Latin Christianity and to
the complacent and self-indulgent fundamentalism of
neo-orthodoxy in our own day both of which regard
other faiths with unjustified contempt. While sophisticated Christian believers are not all of the same
opinion with respect to other religions, they concur
that the existence of a plethora of faiths in the
world does generate a problem - even a significant
theological puzzle - which needs to be addressed.[20]

Why should anyone deny the orthodox claim that
Christianity alone can provide salvation and fulfil-
ment? Relatedly, why would someone deny the traditional claim that Christianity is a unique repository
of theological truth? John Hick offers a specifically
Christian reason for rejecting the traditional
Christian view: if there is a God who loves all his
creatures, it is incredible that he has decided to
restrict salvation and guidance mainly to a group of
prosperous industrial communities in the Western
world.[21] Extra ecclesiam nulla salus makes a mockery
of God's universal love for mankind. If there is no

salvation outside historical Church Christianity, then God's saving grace is apparently meted out in a remarkably limited if not rather gratuitous fashion. Christianity provides, Hick tells us, the means of salvation for occidental men and women while other religious perspectives have a similar function for the remaining large sections of mankind. Again, Hick avows that he finds it difficult to accept the ancient view that Christianity is uniquely fully true while all other religions are, at best, partially true or, at worst, entirely false.[22] He maintains that the views of different religions are not only not incompatible, they are actually complementary. All the major faiths - i.e., religious traditions with established histories of worship and theological reflection[23] - are expressing genuine albeit partial truths. All the faiths encounter the same immensely fecund divine reality but they do so from differing historico-cultural standpoints. Hick concludes that any person who has coercive or impressive religious experience - be he Jew, Muslim, Buddhist, Christian or whatever - can rationally embrace the appropriate theological outlook.[24]

We can easily understand why Hick opts for the ultimate compatibility - indeed essential unity - of the plurality of faiths. Medieval Christians could conscientiously accept a doctrine such as election with its implied severe restrictions on salvation. Such a doctrine, however, may justifiably be seen as an affront to the Christian ideals of universal human brotherhood and universal divine justice. It is indeed difficult to justify the view - implied in or stated by traditional versions of Christianity, Judaism, and Islam - that most of mankind fall outside

the bounds of the salvific providence of a merciful
God. But one has to put in the balance the fact that
Hick's notion of salvific universalism not only lacks
scriptural support, it is directly contradicted by
prophetic teaching (including Jesus' teaching) about
Hell. Hick's God is some rather sentimental fellow,
so to speak, who saves all and sundry from spiritual
perdition.

Suppose we decide to accept Hick's perspectival
approach to religion; each religious perspective has
validity in its own terms and from its own viewpoint.
The implication of this claim is, of course, that no
given perspective can legitimately lay claim to final
authority or absolute truth. Now, the relativism of
this approach undermines the traditional Christian
claim that God's revelation is uniquely vouchsafed in
the Bible and in the personality of Jesus of Nazareth.
So, Christianity is not valid on its own terms: it is
not valid in its claim to be a uniquely correct perspective uncovering man's true nature and destiny
i.e., a creature destined for redemption and eternal
life. And yet if the traditional understanding of
Christianity as absolute truth is wide of the mark,
then the Christian faith is, to put the point with
moral force, a cheat. Moreover, we have theological
puzzles on our hands: if indeed Christianity is only
relatively true, why does God allow men to think that
it is absolutely true i.e., permit men to remain
misguided on issues of great moment? And, relatedly,
if only one faith is true, why does God tolerate false
ones?

There are other problems with Hick's claim that
all the major religions give access to basically
correct theological insights. This amiable tolerance

overlooks the claim of logic that P and not - P cannot
both be true. If Christianity is true, then some
religions (like Theravada Buddhism and non-theistic
varieties of Hinduism) are well-nigh wholly false
while others (like Judaism and Islam) are only partly
true. The attempt to syncretize the world's religious
traditions would be successful only if the claims of
various faiths were merely different from one another.
But, in fact, of course, they are mutually exclusive
and competitive. Religious conflict is too palpable
to stand in need of careful documentation. Muslims
affirm as passionately the prophethood of Muhammad as
their opponents deny it. Christians uphold the doctrine of the triune Godhead as vigorously as Muslims
deride it. Many Hindus believe in many deities -
which is anathema to Jews, Muslims, and Christians.
Some religious believers conceptualise the ultimate
reality as personal, others as impersonal.

Hick could reply, rather weakly, that all this
perceived incompatibility between the various faiths
is illusory and that there is, appearances to the
contrary notwithstanding, a unique goal for all
genuine religious endeavour. Now, to be sure, the
undeniable fact that some religious doctrines are
thought to be incompatible, no matter how tenaciously
this belief is actually held, does not imply that the
perceived incompatibility is evidence of a deeper
substantive theological conflict. It does not immediately follow that the conflicts are more than
superficial. Nor does it immediately follow that the
conflicts are genuine. But the onus is on the side
whose protagonists claim that the different faiths are
somehow compatible or obscurely united. Perhaps, Hick
is right about the mystical unity of the world reli-

gions; in a future development of our experience,
beyond the grave, evidence may accumulate for the
truth of his conviction. In the meantime, however,
even a cursory glance at the relevant data reveals the
sheer variety of actual religious experience and gives
the lie to any claim about compatibility and unison.
It may fairly be said that, in general, those who
uphold the doctrine of the mystical unity of faiths
either adopt a relaxed attitude towards the constraints of the law of contradiction while studying
the empirically established incompatibilities among
religions or else dispense altogether with the normal
amenities of logic.

The current mood of parity among religions is in
large part due to the felt need for attenuating the
more robust of the traditional doctrines about religious exclusivism. This mood is not universal among
revisionist thinkers; not all sophisticated Christians
have agreed with Hick's claim that Christianity should
abandon its old pretence to proffering religious
truths relevant to all men. Richard Swinburne has
argued that a distinctively Christian theology can and
should maintain that it is more probable that Christianity is true than that any rival is.[25] Swinburne
writes: "We need to show that it is more probable
that God became incarnate in Christ than that Muhammad
was his chief prophet; that the way to worship regularly is by attendance at the Eucharist rather than by
the five daily prayer-times, and so on."[26]

But isn't Swinburne's proposal really just a
counsel of perfection? How precisely does one demonstrate the superiority of one's own faith over that of
others without begging all the crucial questions
against one's opponents? It does seem, at first

sight, to pursue Swinburne's own example, that to show
that Muhammad was the (chief) messenger of God is far
easier than to show that God became incarnate in
Christ. Neither of these unusual claims can be justified wholly on the basis of purely historical evidence
but the claim about incarnation has conceptual difficulties - difficulties I regard as entirely insuperable - which find no parallel in the claim to mere
prophethood.[27]

The conflict between religions, especially between doctrinally related rivals like the sister faiths
of Judaism, Christianity, and Islam, is fierce and
perhaps intractable. To see this clearly, I shall
briefly examine William Paley's attempt, discussed by
Swinburne and partially approved by him, to demonstrate the superiority of Christianity over Islam.
While Islam closely resembles Christianity, Paley
tells us, both in terms of doctrine and in the extent
of its influence, the decisive difference is that
Muhammad, unlike Jesus, "did not found his pretensions... upon proofs of supernatural agency, capable
of being known and attested by others."[28] The argument is not original. St. Thomas produced it in an
earlier age in which Christians, for rather obvious
reasons, very much needed to believe that Islam was an
inferior and false religion and found it rather
difficult to do so.[29] Put in plain language, the
argument is that Muhammad's claim to prophethood has
no divine validation. The only miracles he performed
- the power of his sword and the popular appeal of his
silken Arabian sensuality - are, as many a Christian
commentator gloats, ones not lacking even in tyrants
and robbers.

Putting aside the polemic, let us see if there is any force in the argument. The Muslim apologist will reply that Muhammad did indeed perform miracles. But these are _intellectual_ miracles, if you like, rather than _sensual_ ones.[30] The Arabic Koran, he will say, is a miracle of reason and speech which supersedes the sensual miracles of earlier prophets. Instead of parting the sea or transforming rods into serpents, God has seen fit to close the age of revelation by granting a miracle which fully satisfies the _minds_ of men. Man has come of age: the religious evolution of our species is complete. What distinguishes the age of _realisation_ from the preceding age of _revelation_ is precisely men's ability to discover and to reflect upon the signs of God in nature, history, and the self[31] without any reliance on dramatic contra-natural occurrences designed merely to gratify the senses. Arguably, a reasoned faith based upon calm reflection is likely to be more enduring than one which feeds on dramatic sensual displays or consists merely of "emotion undirected by mind or conscience".[32] And certainly a faith devoid of rational underpinnings is likely to degenerate into a senseless surge of powerful feeling or some thoughtless, even violent, attachment to unworthy ends. In fine, Muhammad can (and indeed did) appeal to the Koran's profundity and supremacy of literary taste as evidence of its supernatural provenance and hence of the authenticity of his mission.

Naturally, the Muslim apologist's reasoning in favour of Islam will seem, particularly to his religious cousins, unconvincing. (In religious dialogue among Jews, Christians, and Muslims, opponents usually see one another as sincere but misguided or, on

occasion, less charitably, as insincere and misguided.) This failure to provide conclusive reasons
indicates the truth of my earlier contention that the
detached standards which could help resolve the
dispute are not available. To be sure, some standards
for assessing the authenticity of religious belief-
systems are indeed available. The internal coherence
of doctrines, antiquity of tradition, and strength of
numbers prima facie count in favour of a particular
candidate just as internal confusion, lack of established tradition (or relative infancy), and paucity of
adherents prima facie count against it. But this set
of criteria cannot be used to settle the issue decisively. Moreover, the criteria themselves may turn
out, upon examination, to be question-begging. Why
should strength of numbers matter? Perhaps, religious
truth is the privilege of the few. And, of course,
the criteria are easy to formulate but far from easy
to apply to actual instances. Ultimately, there may
be no non-questionbegging way of breaking the deadlock
involved in the confrontation between Christianity and
its rivals.

- IV -

The Old Testament, the Gospels, and the Koran
concur that there is ample and entirely convincing
evidence in nature for the existence and activity of a
supreme creative being. The created natural order, it
is thought, clearly reflects the power and wisdom of
God.[33] It is not that there is enough hidden evidence
for God that would convince, say, the scientist who
probes nature's mysteries; rather the existence and
wisdom of the Creator are manifest. No doubt it is an
exaggeration to say that scepticism about the exis-

158

tence of a divine being is entirely absent from the outlook of the authors of the Bible and the Koran or that no arguments at all are proffered in prophetic literature in favour of the view that God exists,[34] but there is enough truth in it for us to regard it as an essentially correct observation.

The traditional religious view, expressed by the apostle Paul,[35] is that God exists and that men know it. When we subsequently refuse to acknowledge and worship God, as we do, the fault is not in any lack of evidence but rather in our irrational and resolute determination not to know him. It is not so much that men overlook the truth about God owing to negligence but rather that they deliberately and wickedly repress whatever, deep down, they know.[36] Indeed, etymologically, the Arabic word for disbelief - "kufr" - means "to conceal what one knows to be true". The knowledge of God, it is thought, makes unwelcome demands on us: to know God and to acknowledge his right to our obedience would imply profound changes in behaviour. And men do not wish to enter into communion with a being who demands worship and righteous conduct. Thus, rejection of belief in God amounts to self-deception and culpable prevarication.

Many religionists insist that all human beings are, by nature, religious. There is ample scriptural warrant for this claim. The Koran, for example, refers to itself as a reminder to the heedless or forgetful (ghafil) souls of men who made a primordial promise of allegiance to the one true God.[37] All men are, according to the author of the Koran, endowed with the knowledge of God in virtue of a divinely implanted semen religionis;[38] this knowledge merely needs to be recollected.[39] Again, in the Christian tradition, the most distinctive feature of human nature - the innate sensus divinitatis - survives the Fall so that men retain a natural awareness of God although they may not fully know him. Thus, all men know God in some weak but nonetheless valid sense. And while only God's eternal power and deity are fully revealed in nature, such limited knowledge is sufficient to remove excuse if any person fails to move on from it to seek God fully.[40]

Men reject God today as they have always done. But the traditional religious explanation for unbelief - that men are purposefully and perversely resistant to the signs of God, that they wilfully reject their Creator suppressing their knowledge of such a reality - seems implausible to many modern religious thinkers. Sinful rebellion, obstinacy and presumption do indeed, it is conceded, account for some men's rejection of God. But it is difficult to believe, as Terence Penelhum points out, that no-one can sincerely reject belief in God for purely intellectual reasons.[41]

Revisionist writers typically go one step further. Theism is not the only reasonable option: the sceptical choice is also viable since, theologically puzzling as it is, it is always possible (except in some unusual circumstances[42]) to reasonably reject faith. The atheist cannot be shown to be mistaken in his refusal to assign any religious significance to the common phenomena of the world and human existence. There is, as it happens, no coercive disproof of theological scepticism. Atheism is, as Penelhum tells us, no less a rational option than religious belief.[43] The experienced world is systematically ambiguous: it sustains both theistic and atheistic interpretations of our experience but lends decisive support to

160

neither.[44] A purely godless <u>Weltanschauung</u> is indeed
an intellectual and moral possibility; and is, moreover, actually prevalent today in the advanced industrial societies.

I believe there are three related yet distinct
worries here:

(1) Is the traditional explanation for rejection
    inadequate?

(2) Are all men naturally religious? If so, what is
    the object of their worship?

(3) What is the religious significance of the
    rational possibility of atheism? And what does
    the fact that such a possibility obtains tell us
    about the character of the world?

I begin by examining (1) against the background
of (2). To the religious mind, rejection of God is
incomprehensible folly.[45] It is thought so incurably
asinine that men are held only partly responsible for
it: surely men cannot be that obtuse, the religionists lament. God, it is said, partially determines
the wills of those who remain estranged from him and,
after repeated rejection, hardens their hearts permanently.[46] Given the assumption about the inherent
religiosity of human nature, which nourishes the
traditional view on rejection, it is easy to see why
disbelief is thought explicable only in terms of
puerile rebellion against the Creator.

Can human beings justly be blamed for rejecting
belief in God? This would be possible only if such
belief is freely espoused or freely rejected. So,
God's existence would have to be manifest without
being coercive or compelling; the proofs must convince
but not overpower by being utterly conclusive. Thus,
it must be possible for a man to witness a rehearsal

of the signs of God, see them as signs of God, and yet
either freely accept them or freely reject them.
Provided that these conditions are met, rejection
could indeed be tantamount to conscious and culpable
evasion since one would be refusing to believe what
one knows very well to be true. And only under these
circumstances (i.e., where unbelief is not sincere)
could God justly punish rejectors for otherwise, in
punishing conscientious rejectors, he would be compromising the moral integrity of his divine nature.

Some form of religious concern is, it has been
urged by religionists, inescapable whether one seeks
to fulfill it through adherence to a recognisably
religious tradition (such as Judaism or Hinduism) or
some current substitute (such as liberal humanism,
Marxism, or Hatha Yoga). Faith and rejection are, it
is said, equally "religious" standpoints since the
"religious" question about the ground and goal of
one's existence is answered albeit differently by
every total metaphysic whether overtly religious or
secular.

Now if we decide to interpret all ultimate human
responses to life as necessarily religious (i.e.,
religious just in virtue of the fact that they are
ultimate), we are employing an essentially question-
begging characterisation of religiosity. And even if
we grant the pervasiveness of such an amorphous human
religiosity, this would not in itself support the
theist's case. That men are religious in some
nebulous manner, that, for example, they give unconditional allegiance to ideals whether ostensibly
secular or religious, does not entail or even indicate
that they are monotheists. And even if it did entail
belief in a unique personal Creator, we would still

need to know whether this being should be identified with the God of austere monotheists like Abraham and Muhammad or with the triune divinity of St. Paul and Pauline Christianity.

The monochromatic view of human nature found in some religious writings is indeed hard to defend. But it is equally difficult to refute. Take, for instance, Kierkegaard's general doctrine about human nature. A certain kind of despair is universal; all men suffer from it even though some artfully conceal it from themselves.[47] Kierkegaard, like Pascal before him,[48] notes the emptiness which lurks behind many of our diversions; the comfortable illusions we create are all part of the larger attempt to avoid the unsettling truth. Kierkegaard argues that men's desire to avoid the emptiness of their lives through idle pursuits is interpretable as evidence of spiritual alienation from their Creator. Now, to be sure, the theological significance that Kierkegaard attaches to human malaise is a contingent, not a necessary, feature of it since an adequate secular explanation also seems to be at hand. But, and this is the important point, the fact that Kierkegaard's account does not exhaust the possibilities of a philosophical interpretation of human nature does not in itself tell against the authenticity of his religious interpretation. It merely shows that alternative explanations are also forthcoming. (Note, incidentally, that Kierkegaard's own tendency to assume at times that only the religious understanding of human nature is truly profound while rival secular analyses are somehow intrinsically superficial is unwarranted.)

Belief in the unity of God (and its corollaries - namely, belief in the unity of nature and of human

destiny) is said to be natural to all human beings.
It is, like moral knowledge, a natural endowment. We
need effort to disfigure or disown this primal monotheistic heritage. Is this indeed true? Do all human
beings today in all cultures believe in an omnipotent
personal Creator? It seems not. Have all human
beings in all bygone ages believed in a supreme transcendent author of nature? Again, it seems not. There
is, after all, a wealth of human types; and there is
an enormous diversity of religious experience. It
does seem, at first sight, as though we are forcing an
artificial unity upon the recalcitrant data in
claiming that one specific form of religiosity is
universal among human beings.

Suppose we ask people about whether or not they
believe in something like what God has usually been
taken to be. It is safe to assume that at least some
tolerably educated and well-informed people in every
culture would reply in the negative. But what does
that show? Why accept their answers at face-value?
After all, even reasonable and sincere human beings
have powerful motives for concealing from themselves
their true condition. And, moreover, research concerning private beliefs and practices (such as those
associated with sexuality and religion) is marred by
the natural human tendency to avow what impresses the
researcher or what obviates embarrassment rather than
what one honestly believes. The worry here is not
just that men will have intractable quarrels over the
significance of the facts which a sociology of religious conviction supplies - although that is also
troubling - but rather that, more fundamentally, it is
difficult to know precisely what the facts are, in
some value-free fashion, so to speak, given that our

personalities at their deepest level are implicated in this area of our lives.

Perhaps, depth-psychology will do the trick. In any case, it is admitted on all accounts that there are concealed and unconscious motives for our actions and that there is a recognisable discrepancy between what we may know and privately avow, on the one hand, and what we allow to influence our behaviour, on the other. What is controversial is whether or not the aim of such self-deception is to conceal (consciously or unwittingly) specifically religious convictions and, more narrowly, Christian ones.

The religionists may be right in claiming that the higher or true nature of man freely confesses, indeed proclaims, the existence and authority of a supreme divine being. It may well be the case that virtually all human beings have a natural inclination to believe in God and that this inclination is systematically frustrated in some societies (such as communist Chinese society) and actively encouraged in others (such as Muslim Iranian society under the Ayatollah Khomeini's leadership). Similarly, the traces of divine activity in the world may be present in every age but harder to find in a secularised era. What makes it difficult to establish these claims is the lack of independent evidence for them. Take, for example, the claim that all men are aware of God or have implicit knowledge of such a reality. Such a claim cannot be treated as a straightforwardly empirical claim or rather, more accurately, if it is so treated, then the view that all men believe in God is a clear instance of an unreasonable inference from the observed evidence. The true character of the claim that all men believe in God may well be empirical and factual. But it is treated by religionists as more of a _religious judgement_ with normative implications about men's culpability in rejecting their Maker. The claim is treated like an _a priori_ truth and has the character of a moral denunciation in the hands of religionists. It is, then, not altogether surprising that the religionists' claim is one for which one can adduce as evidence only comparatively complex data requiring controversial interpretation.

Let me record one more complication before I finally run this to earth. It has been a major _motif_ of apologetics that men can suppress but not destroy their knowledge of God. This, it has been said, is evidenced by their desire to both reject God and yet to invent a substitute deity to take his place. In this way, men come to value lesser realities (such as power, pleasure, and knowledge) and allow these inferior realities to exhaust an allegiance that is properly owed to God alone. This religious defence of the idea that a specific form of religiosity is universal is, for all its popular appeal, quite bank-rupt. For one thing, there is idolatry and there is idolatry. Take, for instance, Faust's pact with the Devil. By selling his soul to the Devil in exchange for knowledge, Faust made a bargain that was expressly condemned by Jesus - "What does it profit a man to gain the whole world and to lose his soul?" Most people, however, who are accused of idolatry by preachers on Sundays (because they prefer the more earthly delights, afforded by the proverbial wine, women, and song, to the Lord's service) are, unlike Faust, not intentional idolaters rejecting God's sovereignty in favour of some inferior reality. To place a lesser reality on the pedestal is not necessarily tantamount to a deliberate decision to replace a higher one.

Where does this leave us? Three brief remarks will have to suffice. Firstly, given that there is no lack of fundamental disagreement concerning various secular issues among what seem, to all appearances, sincere folk, it would be odd (though, to be sure, not impossible) if, of all places, such disagreement were absent from the religious domain. After all, religion has a peculiar power to create controversy. Is it probable that the belief in the existence of God is an utterly uncontroversial one? Is it not more likely that, among sincere human beings, the existence of such a reality would be keenly disputed?

Secondly, one would need to take great liberties with the empirical data to deduce that all human beings who have ever been informed about the God of the prophets of Israel have in fact come to be partially or totally convinced that he exists or is worthy of worship. That no-one can hear of God and yet remain sincerely unconvinced of his existence is, it seems, an unempirical if not false claim. A more reasonable view (i.e., one more responsive to the empirical data) is that, on occasion, the inability to believe in God may well be due to intellectual impediments. Conscientious doubts do occur though they may be unfounded and could perhaps be removed by a successful natural theology. In any case, the religious view that we have only faith and bad faith, never sincere doubt, seems to have been adopted a priori in the service of a particular conception of human nature.

And thirdly, no-one need or should deny that we human beings have a very marked propensity for wish fulfillment, <u>mauvaise foi</u> and hypocrisy whereby we artfully hide from ourselves our true predicament, namely, that of evidently mortal beings destined for some happiness mixed with suffering and followed by inevitable death. We can, do, and perhaps need to suppress such unwelcome truths. Nor, incidentally, is this trait the monopoly of religious believers. As Northrop Frye has clearly seen, both faith and rejection can be insecure and anxious standpoints.[49] Those who already feel committed to a position of acceptance of belief are afraid of being led away from it while those who are antagonistic to such a position are similarly afraid of being led towards it. In practice, then, it is difficult to know whether unbelief is the outcome of sincere reflection or of merely unconscious rationalization.

I turn now to the third problem. What are the implications of the fact, if it be a fact, that atheism may be a rational stance which men can sincerely adopt? Terence Penelhum and other revisionist writers have noted that the events occurring in the natural world (shared by believers and sceptics alike) are inherently ambiguous: they are open to different and incompatible interpretations.[50] Now both theism and atheism as total systems of thought contain certain intellectual mechanisms for explaining the existence of the rival; thus, believers can accuse disbelievers of perversity while disbelievers can accuse believers of wishful thinking. Each interpretive scheme can subsume its rival by absorbing all apparent counterevidence, deflecting the opponent's criticisms, and so on. While each side can explain away the rival position, neither can, Penelhum contends, accuse the other of irrationality without appealing to a controversial standard of rationality. It is impossible to proffer neutral reasons for preferring a secular world-view to a theistic one or for preferring a theistic world-view to a secular one. There is no non-questionbegging way of breaking the deadlock involved in the confrontation between faith and rejection. It is, Penelhum concludes, sheer dogmatism to deny that a man could sincerely align himself on the atheistic side of the impasse.[51]

These are considerable concessions to the modern secular temper. That the experienced world sustains two radically incompatible interpretations equally rationally is contradicted by the scriptural understanding of the natural order. Traditional religious believers have held the view that the world had been endowed with an irreducibly religious character: it bespoke the handicraft of God. The biblical appeal to the wonders of nature, the fate of nations, and the miraculous activity of the prophets by God's leave are all made in an attempt to rupture the otherwise permanent experienced ambiguity of the world.

Now, in a world in which Christian theism were true, "everything becomes", writes Penelhum, "not other than what it familiarly is, but rather what it familiarly is, and more besides."[52] Penelhum's observation is not without a point but it may be lacking in scope. If Christianity were true, the secular explanations for what is the case must also actually be defective independently of whether or not we recognise them to be so. The issue is simultaneously both ontological and epistemological. If there is a God, familiar things remain familiar; but their causal history, the correct explanation for their existence and the right account of their destiny

differ radically from what atheism would lead one to
suppose. Thus, for example, if Christian theism were
true, the concept of sin as a revolt within the universal context of an essentially rational order would be
internally related to the total problem of human
existence so that all secular explanations of the
human condition would necessarily be defective.
Again, the sufferings of God come to Earth would bear
a conceptual relationship to the familiar crises of
warfare and ideological schism that now plague our
luckless world. God's ordinances do not merely serve
to provide one explanation among others for the sorry
scheme of things entire: they render possible the
right explanation by making the world what it truly
is.

This needs explanation. The worry here is that
if the world can be said to be truly ambiguous, then
the supreme being, even if he were to exist, would
presumably be some anaemic deus otiosus whose existence could be added on or subtracted from his
creation without this addition or deletion making any
experienceable difference to our world.[53] The assumption behind such a view is that God should exist while
everything else should be or at least appear to be
exactly what it would be like if God did not exist
and, conversely, that God should not exist and yet
everything else should be or at least appear to be
exactly what it would be like if God did exist. It
was precisely this deistic assumption that was
rejected by the traditional account of God's relation
to the world and to the natural and historical events
occurring in it. The traditional theological appeal
to the providential governance of the world and to
God's direct activity in the world (via miraculous and

significant events) was made in the attempt to establish the <u>religious</u> character of the world.

Now, the world's ambiguity does not seem to be an absolute feature of it but rather relative to our psychology and beliefs. Penelhum avers that a successful natural theology or a "probative revelatory phenomenon" could disambiguate our scandalously ambivalent intellectual situation.[54] Thus, given that a <u>bona fide</u> miracle[55] would be a "probative revelatory phenomenon", the world was not truly ambiguous for those who lived in a religiously charged environment (such as first century Palestine). Several questions arise here, some historical, others conceptual: Did any of the (putative) miracles recorded in the Old Testament and the Gospels actually occur? Do we <u>now</u> have sufficient evidence to believe that any such miraculous events took place several millennia ago? Or should we reject this part of the tradition as false and dispensable? And, moreover, we should ask questions about the need for miracles in this secularised age: Do we need miracles to rupture the otherwise chronic ambiguity of our experience in this secularised epoch? Are any miracles happening in this age? Do we need continuous miraculous activity to render atheism false at every moment in history? What are we to make of the silence of God?

I do not intend to answer these questions. I raise them merely to illustrate the complexity of the issue. The modern secular conception of the natural and historical order (developed under the influence of modern scientific and historical studies) does not leave conceptual room for assigning a role to God. Thus, for example, ever since Darwin's theory of evolution assigned autonomy to the concept of nature, and Hume offered a priori reasons for rejecting as unreliable the historical records of miracles, the purposive religious interpretation of the physical world, so dear to the pre-Darwinian and pre-Humean Christian teleologists, had to be jettisoned. Now, the theist must vindicate the older teleological interpretation of the world; and he must establish the validity of the traditional claim that the natural order is intimately related to the supernatural one by, for example, challenging the a priori Humean judgement that miracles cannot form a reliable part of history. In other words, the religious thinker must develop a philosophy of history that does not despise teleological foundations, and which allows for the possibility of an active transcendent agent working out his sacred purposes in the temporal realm.

The task of resuscitating a religious outlook is an ambitious one. My contribution is in the next chapter. Suffice it to say here that the religious character of the world cannot be sustained if God is some remote spirit in the heavens who disdains to play a role in the world. It is not in vain that Nietzsche - that most far-sighted of philosophers of religion[56] - sought to establish the moral and metaphysical neutrality of the world precisely by killing God. The demand for a determinate world in which God's existence makes a recognisable difference is a religious demand. That is why the radical inaccessibility of God gives rise to a religious problem.

The religious ambiguity of our situation creates, Penelhum notes, a theological problem.[57] The inconclusiveness of the evidence for God's existence is cause for concern among believers. Why doesn't the world unambiguously proclaim the existence of its Maker? If theism is true, why isn't it more obviously true? There are, of course, no traditional answers to these problems. They could not arise at all on the traditional view: the orthodox explanation for men's rejection of God is, significantly, not that the world fails to present an unambiguous aspect to the beholder but rather, as we saw earlier, that men are perverse rejectors. Why does God hide himself equally both from obstinate rejectors and conscientious seekers? The orthodox answer would be, of course, that he doesn't. It is simply that I - the sinful man - am perversely turning away from him whom my heart seeks, not he positively concealing himself from me. "He that seeketh, findeth"[58] - always.

The acknowledgement that men can indeed sincerely experience ambivalence in their commerce with mundane reality is ultimately damaging to the religious outlook. Religious believers are rightly reluctant to concede that atheism can be a genuine rational option for even the conscientious seeker. Atheism, they aver, cannot be an option at all: it is blindness and error. No preacher - unless his orthodoxy were suspect - could admit that the world can retain an optional appearance even to the sincere seeker. In our age, and I don't speak of the age of Pascal or the age of St. Paul, the concession that the world is religiously neutral is asymmetrically damaging to theism i.e., it damages theism more than atheism. Coupled with the demand for ontological economy - a demand which is not prima facie unreasonable or question-begging - such a concession leads one to conclude that, on purely rational considerations, atheism is a more plausible stance than theism.

- V -

If the first step in the modern re-appraisal of atheism has been to give it its due, the second has been to give it no more than its due. Atheism is indeed, it has been said, a rational alternative to faith but faith is not any the less rational for having such a rival. There is indeed, theological revisionists have urged, an epistemic parity between faith and rejection. Both are in the same boat epistemologically: reason cannot demonstrate the truth of religious conviction but equally reason cannot quell sceptical doubts about our (alleged) knowledge of the external world, or about the truth of causal propositions which do not logically follow from the propositions (about conjunctions between events) that are their ultimate grounds, or about the existence of other minds, or about any other funda- mental presuppositions of common life and science. Thus, the argument has run, science rests on an ulti- mately rationally indefensible (and hence arbitrary) faith in the uniformity of nature and much of pure mathematics on unprovable postulates. The justifi- cation that disbelievers demand for belief in God is not available for secular principles such as the consistency of nature or the accuracy of basic arith- metical computations (like, for example, "2+3=5"). Hence, a man whose framework of thought includes (for one reason or another) a belief in a divine reality is entitled to assign the same epistemological status to that belief that he and other men together assign to the secular beliefs of common sense and science. Belief in God is as rationally justified as belief in the existence of other selves[59] or of an independent physical world.[60] In fine, both faith and rejection are epistemically permissible stances but neither can properly be shown to be epistemically obligatory for a rational person.

That we need faith in religious as well as secular life, that faith is a ubiquitous feature of our life and thought, is a view which Penelhum has dubbed "the parity argument".[61] In somewhat different forms, the parity argument has been championed by Pascal and Kierkegaard, among classical writers, and by Terence Penelhum, Alvin Plantinga, Norman Malcolm, and John Hick, in our own day. An argument with so many able defenders should not be despised. Accordingly, I shall now examine it in some detail.

Following Penelhum, we can distinguish two versions of this argument: the classical positive version (found in the writings of Pascal and Kierkegaard) which seeks to convict disbelievers of inconsistency and the modern negative version which seeks to achieve the more modest end of shielding believers against the charge of irrationality.[62] The positive version can be invoked, Penelhum contends, against a writer like Hume who accepts "natural beliefs" (such as the belief in the existence of an external material environment) which, according to Hume, evidence does not justify and yet, inconsistently, rejects religious beliefs on the sole ground that <u>they</u> are not adequately evidenced.[63] Penelhum, however, has his own reasons for rejecting the positive version: even if the commitments of common sense are groundless, restricting oneself to them need not be entirely arbitrary in view of certain recognised considerations of simplicity.[64]

There is, however, a purely defensive version of the parity argument which Penelhum is concerned to

defend.[65] He extracts this version from the works of
Plantinga and Malcolm. Plantinga has argued that
traditional natural theology wrongly made the
concession that belief in God needs to be justified by
or based upon other - basic - beliefs and that , in
fact, it is perfectly rational to class belief in God
as itself already properly basic for some people.
Now, according to the doctrine known as "classical
foundationalism", a belief must, if it is to be rationally entertained, either be basic or be shown to be
justifiable by basic ones. Properly basic beliefs
are, according to this view, restricted to beliefs
which are either self-evident or incorrigible. (Note
that belief in God falls into neither of these categories.) The view that self-evident propositions and
incorrigible propositions are truly basic is,
Plantinga points out, an unjustifiable dogma. Furthermore, continues Plantinga, if one stipulates that no
other sorts of propositions can genuinely be basic for
anyone, one is committed to a self-refuting proposition since this proposition itself is neither self-
evident nor incorrigible and hence cannot be held as
basic. It follows, therefore, Plantinga concludes,
that classical foundationalism is self-referentially
incoherent. And given the collapse of such a foundationalism, belief in God might justifiably be held as
basic i.e., such a belief might be in the foundations
of some rational persons' noetic structure.[66]

Malcolm's version is derived from some perceptive
remarks in Wittgenstein's last work - On Certainty.[67]
Doubt presupposes certainty; doubts can arise only
within a framework of fundamental groundless beliefs
which we all acquire and endorse without proof or
question. A framework-principle, according to

Malcolm, is one which guides all our thinking, provides a matrix for formulating questions and judging
what sorts of questions can legitimately be asked and
what sorts of solutions will be thought acceptable. A
belief such as "The Earth has existed for many years
past", to take one of Wittgenstein's examples, or
"Things do not just vanish without cause", to take one
of Malcolm's examples, cannot be sacrificed without an
ensuing general debacle in our lives; the notions of
proof, justification, and testimony, as we know them
and construe them, would be utterly undermined.
Beliefs of a fundamental ilk neither need nor could
have any demonstration or justification. Justification must come to an end, pontificates Malcolm,
echoing his master, and it ends where life begins.
Wittgenstein and Malcolm are both concerned to give us
some idea of the pervasiveness of groundless conviction - of what the fisherman doesn't see. Malcolm
maintains that a philosophical demand for justification is as out of place with respect to religious
belief as it is with respect to, say, our fundamental
belief in the continuity of nature. In each case, the
demand for justification is the outcome of a misunderstanding of the actual language-games we play.
Religion does not stand in need of justification any
more than science does.[68] Of course, some justification may be in place (as, for example, when appeal
to the Koran becomes relevant in a sectarian dispute
among Muslims) but this is internal to religion.

Before assessing the parity argument, I shall
briefly describe Hick's version of the argument.
(Hick's version is sufficiently similar to Penelhum's
version to warrant an assessment of both in a common
context; the basic aim in both cases is to show that

we can implicate certain fundamental secular convictions as being involved in the same epistemological predicament as their religious counterparts.) There is, Hick tells us, a common epistemological pattern in which religious knowledge, along with other kinds of knowledge, partakes. There is an important similarity in epistemological structure and status between basic secular convictions and basic religious convictions: neither is subject to rational proof and yet each can rationally be defended and reasonably espoused.[69] Hick argues that there is a significant analogy between a religious man's claim to be conscious of God and any man's claim to be conscious of an independent physical world.[70] In each case, a realm of putatively cognitive experience is _assumed_ to be veridical: in both cases, logical demonstrations are unavailable. Descartes failed to provide a proof for our instinctive conviction that our senses relate us to an independent material environment and Hume succeeded in showing that our belief in the existence of an objective world is neither produced by, nor justifiable by means of, purely philosophical reasoning. It is indeed a belief which arises naturally in the normal human mind and, fortunately, most of us have neither reason nor inclination to doubt it.[71] Now, while it is undeniably sane and rational to adopt this normal belief, there is a theoretically possible solipsist alternative. Both in the case of one's alleged experience of the divine and of the physical world, one can affirm _solus ipse_ to the exclusion of the transcendent by denying the existence of a divine personality transcending one's own private consciousness in the former case and by denying the existence of a physical environment transcending one's own private solipsist world in the latter.

We are now in a position to assess the soundness of the parity argument. The central claim underlying _all_ versions of the parity argument is that the _logic_ of the problem of religious faith is, in all epistemologically relevant aspects, _identical_ to the _logic_ of metaphysical puzzles such as the ones concerning the existence of other minds or the regularity of nature or our perception of the external world. The claim is that religious beliefs have the same logical status as certain metaphysical beliefs: both are alike in principle recalcitrant to rational resolution. I shall now argue that this crucially important claim is false.

Someone might, after a cursory glance at the philosophical literature, think that the so-called "problem of other minds" is really just an academic conundrum invented by philosophers to fill their leisure whereas the problem of religious belief is a genuine one - a trustworthy indication of this being the fact that it is _not_ an invention of academic philosophers. It is difficult, after reflection, to remain unsympathetic to this assessment. After all, the ontological basis of our analysis of other minds seems indisputably secure: there are indeed other minds and we know it. The ontological basis of our analysis of religious conviction, on the other hand, does seem insecure: arguably, we do not know that there is a God. With the problem of other minds, the worry simply is to explain _how_ we know that others have minds, not _whether_ or not we know it to be true that others have minds. The outcome of the puzzle is apparently not in dispute. We are not typically plagued with doubts about the truth of the proposition "She has a mind" but rather with doubts about the various epistemological relations that must be examined in the process of answering the doubt. These epistemological relations are thought to obtain among such propositions as "I have a mind", "I have a body", "She has a body", and "She has a mind"; and the problem is to effect an epistemologically acceptable linkage between the first three propositions, on the one hand, and the fourth one, on the other. Since propositions about the minds of others ultimately depend on propositions about the bodily behaviour of others without being logically derivable from them, the kind of support the behavioural evidence gives to the psychological conclusion may be subject to dispute. But what is not subject to dispute is the claim that the behavioural evidence *does* support the psychological conclusion in some way - whether inductively or deductively or otherwise. In fine, then, there are no primary doubts about the existence of other minds, merely secondary worries about how such realities can have the ontological status that they so obviously do.

On occasion, it may be useful, as an exercise in conceptual thought, to prove what one already knows. Thus Bertrand Russell and A.N. Whitehead put their heads together to prove the self-evident mathematical proposition "2+2=4". But, significantly, had they shown during their endeavours that "2+2=5", the success of their project would no longer have been an open question. This very fact would have shown their analysis to be defective; we would not think, for example, that a clever new method of counting had served to refute the time-honoured claim "2+2=4". Similarly, any proof whose last line denies the existence of other selves is reduced to absurdity by its own (apparent) success. In the case of some propositions, what goes to set the standard for judging the adequacy of the analysis of the claim expressed by the proposition is precisely the attainment of a particular independently established outcome.

These are only preliminary remarks. Let us consider now some specific alleged differences between the logic of the problem of other minds (or the external world), on the one hand, and the logic of the problem of religious faith, on the other. (In what follows, what I say about "other minds" applies mutatis mutandis to the other traditional metaphysical puzzles about the external world, the reality of time, the reliability of memory, and so on.) Suppose someone suggests that scepticism about the existence of God is sincere while scepticism about the reality of other selves is merely professional; in the former case, we are concerned, in the latter, merely interested.

This is not an implausible suggestion. Scepticism about other minds appears decidedly forced and unnatural. Belief in such evident realities is so deeply ingrained in human nature, it appears, that the occasional temporary suspension of this belief for purposes of philosophical disputation is recognisably contrived. Is belief in other selves open to serious doubt and, by implication, to possible substantiation? Imagine trying to convince a sceptic of the rationality of belief in other minds. Since it takes great effort to disbelieve or to be agnostic about other minds, it would be hard to find someone who had any natural inclination to doubt the existence of such realities. (Remember that it takes effort only to suspend or dissolve or exceed - not to espouse - the commitments of common sense. It was misleading of

Kierkegaard to insist that even the commitments of ordinary life require an act of will: such commitments are, in a perfectly valid sense, effortless.) But suppose we eventually happen on just such a fellow. We find our man in the relatively sheltered environment provided by a Philosophy Department - a surrounding in which such scepticism may not be entirely unfounded. Now, we need to reason with him. But the process could not even begin let alone convince anyone because, of course, to make a point whose obviousness is embarrassing, our protagonist would refuse to listen to our critique of his scepticism given that such a concession would amount to the somewhat precarious assumption (from his point of view) that we - his confreres - did indeed have minds.

Strictly speaking, of course, the solipsist does not have to concede or assume that what produces that which he interprets to be an argument is necessarily another mind. The solipsist could remain uncommitted on the outcome of the issue concerning the nature of the source which produced what he took to be an argument. And, in any case, we can simply by-pass this problem altogether: someone might retort that each person can experience for himself or herself the doubt about other minds - and that that will do. But, one should reply here, it would be unusual for someone to become any the less convinced about the existence of other minds after a sceptical philosophical challenge. Purely philosophical scepticism has little or no inhibiting effect on the primary practice whose viability is being questioned: it virtually never leads to hesitations in one's ordinary practical commerce with the appropriate reality. Thus, we still claim to know, without undue ambivalence, that our friend Jack has a mind, despite the clever solipsist's contention. It would be odd, though not impossible, for someone (who was mentally stable) to entertain serious doubts about the existence of other selves solely or principally as a result of exposure to sceptical philosophical influences. (Such influences could, of course, contribute to mental disturbance and hence lead to disbelief in other minds.) By contrast, scepticism about religious belief can make serious inroads on first-order religious belief and practical devotion. Priests sometimes leave the household of faith after sceptical encounters. The religious believer facing philosophical critique of his religious convictions (especially for the first time) finds that it takes a very short time - if he is reflective - before his religious beliefs are no longer held instinctively. One becomes conscious that they are held on faith. A reflective believer finds that if he candidly considers the sceptical objections to his faith, he can no longer retain his intuitive religious convictions unimpaired. After such ordeals, the life of faith requires self-conscious effort; the innocence of one's former pre-philosophical days is irretrievably lost.

The distinction between professional scepticism and sincere scepticism may seem question-begging. Certainly, purely philosophical scepticism about other minds and physical objects is reinforced by our occasionally genuine doubts about these realities in certain unusual contexts. Professional scepticism is motivated in part by the recognition of the possibility of genuine scepticism. (Does this explain the perennial charms of this temptress for academic philosophers?) Now, what makes scepticism about religious belief genuine is that typically it has actual logico-metaphysical grounds - How could such a being exist at all? Scepticism about other minds, however, typically has no actual grounds at all; we are just toying with Pickwickian possibilities (- Perhaps, Tom is really just a cleverly constructed robot). The fact that the obtaining of such possibilities is compatible with our experience of the natural and social world does not imply that we should take them seriously.

Perhaps this is too brusque. After all, there is a priori no reason, someone may object, why one cannot be genuinely sceptical of common sense beliefs. Scepticism about common sense can be, it will be said, a thoroughly sincere and practical stance as the ancient sceptics like Sextus Empiricus and the Pyrrhonians have shown us by their example.[72] Not all sceptical doubts are of the methodological variety made famous by Descartes' Meditations. "Sceptical" and "real" cannot be assumed to be antynomous characterizations of doubt.[73] Moreover, it may plausibly be contended, the distinction between professional scepticism and sincere scepticism is a psychological one: the manner in which a doubt is experienced does not entail anything about the logical status of the doubt.

Could one dull the edge of this criticism? Granted that no-one has produced a metaphysically impregnable proof of the reality of other minds, that we do not possess apodictic certainty concerning the truth of the proposition "There exist other minds", it is not at all clear why we need it. One of the lessons we should have learnt from the current debate on the foundations of knowledge is precisely that we don't need absolute Cartesian certainty. The quest

for such certainty was the quixotic ideal of a systematic epistemology concerned to refute the sceptic by
providing indubitable propositions. Ludwig Wittgenstein, G.E. Moore, and Richard Rorty have, in their
different ways, taught us how to silence, even ignore,
the sceptic.[74] We now recognise that proof and
justification are two distinct epistemological
categories such that we can sometimes be fully
justified in believing, even in claiming to know, what
we cannot conclusively demonstrate to be true. Thus,
if we have overwhelming evidence for the truth of a
proposition P and no (or virtually no) evidence
against it, we have rational warrant for affirming
that P.

There is overwhelming evidence for the existence
of some realities. There is, for example, an indisput-
able experiential-phenomenological ground for our
(alleged) knowledge of other selves; and there is a
sensory-perceptual foundation for our (alleged) knowledge of physical objects (such as tables, stones, and
so on). Our experience of the transcendent reality of
other minds is, admittedly, always mediated through
the bodies of "persons" qua their purely physical
character, and through the words they utter and the
gestures they make. But each of us has knowledge of
his own mental life as an experienced reality. This
provides an impressively unproblematic base from which
one can extrapolate to the existence of other minds.

No sceptic can bully us out of some of the
assurances of common sense. Scepticism about other
minds may be logically irrefutable but it is absurd
nonetheless. It may be premature to aver that the
problem of other minds has been "dissolved" by the
later Wittgenstein, that solipsism is demonstrably

incoherent;[75] but it is not at all premature to appropriate for our own purposes the Moorean common sense
insight: there are claims whose truth is so self-
evident that we should reject the sceptical conclusion
which denies their truth rather than the familiar
claim itself. Moore thought that extreme sensory
scepticism was inherently weak; there was more warrant
for accepting our perception of material things as
veridical than there was for endorsing any abstruse
metaphysical sceptical theories which denied this.[76]
I think one can safely appropriate this insight
without committing oneself to any view about the exact
probative force of Moore's notorious "refutation" of
sceptical theories about perception and the external
world.

This is perhaps the place to insert an ad hominem
argument against the defenders of the parity argument.
If the human situation is truly ambivalent in respect
of theistic and naturalistic interpretations, as the
revisionist defenders of the parity argument insist it
is, it seems odd to construct a parallel between our
religious experience and our experience of other
selves. After all, our experience is unambiguously
suggestive of the existence of other minds while our
experience is, being ex hypothesi religiously neutral,
merely compatible with the existence of God. In the
case of other minds, one could say that while it is
logically possible to disbelieve, it is still clearly
irrational to do so. One cannot say so in the religious case for it is, by assumption, as rational to
disbelieve as it is to believe in God.[77] The defender
of parity may reply that while this observation is
correct, it is irrelevant since the parity argument
does not trade on this particular parallel. And this

may be an acceptable response; but one cannot resist
suspicion about the total viability of an analogy
which seems to be failing at so many epistemologically
vital points.

There is another strand of argument I must now
consider. Belief in other minds is, it may plausibly
be claimed, natural to us, almost universal, clearly
rational, and more or less uncontroversial. Moreover,
it is indispensable to successful social intercourse.
Belief in God, on the other hand is, it may reasonably
be said, culture-bound, local, and thoroughly disputed
among men. Moreover, it must be dispensable, it
seems, given that countless human beings claim to
understand the world without believing in God and live
perfectly well without respecting what is thought to
be his moral law. Belief in God may even, arguably,
be irrational. In any case, it is not, any more at
least, a common sense belief grounding ordinary
practice.

Virtually all human beings (with the exception of
very young children, some mentally unstable folk, and
a few overly sceptical thinkers in their professional
moments) have believed in such realities as other
minds, the external world, and the identity of the
self. By contrast, belief in God has never been
universal or even nearly universal in any age.
Sceptics have always existed - a fact which renders
prima facie questionable the claim that disbelief in
God is insane or perverse. But suppose someone says
that some men have been sceptical of the claims of
common sense too. This is, of course, true but the
disturbing fact is that scepticism about the existence
of God has been more widespread than that concerning
the existence of other minds or the external environ-

ment. Nor will it do to retort that, appearances to
the contrary notwithstanding, all men do, deep down,
so to speak, believe in God. The tendency to disbelieve in God cannot be ignored even if there are
religious resources for explaining it. As we saw
earlier, belief in God can be made to seem universally
accepted if one adopts some ad hoc and suspect construal of "belief in God" (such as, say, one according
to which it amounts to adherence to any ultimate
ideals - religious or secular).

It is natural for the secularist to claim that
the ability to cognize the external world or other
minds, or to see the validity of inductive inferences,
is more widely distributed than the ability to cognize
God. But this claim is not, as it stands, supported
by the empirical data. All one can deduce from the
empirical information is that the ability to cognize
God is less widely developed than the ability to
recognise certain secular truths. Perhaps, religious
cognition is the result of an instinct subtler and
scarcer than the instincts necessary for ordinary
physical survival. And this latter concession is
damaging only to those forms of traditional theism
according to which the religious instinct is more or
less fully developed in all (mature) human beings but
consciously suppressed to avoid surrender to the will
of God.

There is something close to a universal consensus
regarding belief in other minds and the external
world. After all, sense-experience reveals a world
that is common to all human beings whereas religious
experience reveals conflicting basic intuitions about
the nature of religious reality - as is evidenced by
the fact that sectarian and interreligious controversy

is commonplace. Someone could quibble that belief in other minds and the external world is actually controversial since the characterization which makes it appear uncontroversial - namely, the one according to which a view is uncontroversial as long as only infants, lunatics, and philosophers take exception to it - is itself controversial. But, conceding this objection for what it is worth, one can still claim that belief in God is controversial both in the sense in which belief in other minds is controversial (i.e., in the sense that lunatics, infants, and some philosophers reject this belief) and also in the stronger sense that people other than lunatics, infants, and some thinkers reject it. Thus, belief in other minds is at least less controversial than the belief in God.

Admittedly, that belief in God is more controversial than belief in other minds may simply be a contingent fact about actual consensus over time. More importantly, however, someone could object that many uncontroversial claims are actually false while some controversial ones may turn out to be true. This is a correct but irrelevant observation: the quarrel is over the pervasiveness of scepticism regarding the existence of some realities, not over the issue of the relationship between the truth of a belief and the extent of its acceptance.

Is belief in God dispensable? Someone could contend that only secular beliefs (like the belief in induction and the external environment) are indispensable to life and that religious ones are superfluous. Take, for example, our normal conviction that there is an external world. We are, if sane, as Hick points out, obliged to interact consciously with the physical environment but not with a spiritual one.[78] Sense-experience does have a coercive quality. It takes effort to suspend belief in the reality of an independently existing world; and even when one succeeds in doing so, one courts disaster. The world is not plastic to our desires; to negotiate successfully with it, to flourish in it, or even to avoid penalty, one needs to believe that the external material environment is roughly as we perceive it to be. Such a belief is pragmatically validated; and this parallel does not seem to hold in the religious case.

Now certainly, secular beliefs are indeed indispensable to secular life-styles. But this is hardly surprising. Some religious beliefs may equally be indispensable to religious life-styles. Every man, whether religious or not, must live in the physical world. But there is no good reason why ordinary physical existence may not be seen as a preparation for a "higher" spiritual end. The indispensability of beliefs cannot be determined in vacuo; rather, it is to be ascertained in relation to some particular metaphysic of man and culture. Thus, as Hick notes, the religious experience of the seminal figures of the monotheistic tradition was of such a compelling and involuntary character that they could ignore their spiritual environment only at great risk.[79] Their experience of the world sustained them in their religious convictions in much the same way that all (sane) men's experience of the physical environment sustains them in their secular common sense convictions. It is also worth noting, though Hick doesn't, that religious men have appealed both to the imminent wrath of God and to the more distant terrors of Hell as being reserved for those who neglect or ignore the spiritual milieu. (God never hesitated in the old

days to deal out immediate calamity to some unrepen-
tant villains[80] - a policy which, if adopted today,
would serve to hasten the conversion of some worldly
folk.)

Is belief in God irrational? It has, significantly, been argued that the existence of evil in the
world renders belief in a Christian deity positively
irrational. Whatever may be said concerning the
merits of this argument, the point to note in this
context is that belief in other minds or the external
world has rarely been accused of positive irrationality.

It is difficult to assess the probative force of
the parity argument. There is an entangled skein of
reasoning here with arguments from both camps inconclusive. The common sense account of our knowledge of
material things, other minds, perception, and even
moral convictions is indeed subject to sceptical
assault. But the kind of scepticism that can properly
arise concerning claims like "This is a chair" or "My
wife has a mind" or even "That was a virtuous action"
is radically dissimilar from the kind of scepticism
directed against claims like "There exists a supreme
transcendent being who accepts our repentance" or
"Christianity is the only true faith".

What is sound about the analogy on which the
parity argument depends is that both secular fundamental beliefs and religious fundamental beliefs are
usually held implicitly. The occasions on which their
grounds are made explicit or the beliefs shown to have
philosophical justification are rare. Moreover, with
some such beliefs, the grounds for holding them are
virtually unknown and yet countless human beings
embrace the beliefs. Certainly, the philosophical

justifications we may offer are not the _cause_ of our holding the beliefs in the first place. And we do feel entitled to rationally accept beliefs for which we have no actual evidence and even, in some cases, no evidence at all.

The recent attacks on classical foundationalism have helped us to realise that it is possible to arrive at a rational stance in several different ways such that the rationality of our believings is not necessarily tied to a foundational construal involving the derivation of inferences from agreed premisses. The parity argument does establish, what is relatively uncontroversial, that the absence (or availability) of a demonstrative proof that _P_ does not entail that a person who believes that _P_ does so unreasonably (or reasonably).

We are not yet at the bottom of the pit. An important part of the insight behind the parity argument in its present form survives the destruction of the argument itself. The parity arguer rightly points out that while religious beliefs are not strictly provable, many fundamental beliefs presupposed by whole significant departments of secular thought are similarly recalcitrant to rational determination. All human knowledge is indeed, to put the point misleadingly, "religious" in character: if human reason is to give us any truths about reality, we must have an initial "faith" that there is an inherent relationship between our bias towards the systematic and meaningful, on the one hand, and reality, on the other. One might say that every cognitive performance with respect to reality is also an act of "faith": the ideas I have of even myself, of other persons, and of external physical objects, may be groundless and fantastic and it is "faith" alone which assures me that they are items of knowledge. The constructions which our reason elaborates upon the material of experience may, as the sceptic has taught us, be utterly illusory. Yet we do feel justified in thinking that we have every right to trust the universe, so to speak; we believe that Nature has not made us such as to be irremediably misled in our thought by the very nature of our minds. Somehow, it seems to us, the acquisition of knowledge is a disciplined affair, not a fortuitous one. And if Descartes' evil demon plays epistemological tricks on us, so much the worse for us. We can only hope that Nature does not epistemologically deceive us. (Wittgenstein remarks: "It is always by favour of Nature that one knows something".[81]) In fine, we have "faith" in the match between intellect and reality.

Now, if we are justified in treating the universe as being made so as to be in good faith with respect to some human intellectual processes, why are we not justified in thinking that the universe is made with a purpose conducive to the fulfillment of our religious and moral aspirations? After all, we live in a kind of world that actually produces beings who discipline themselves by their concern with ideals of value. Many sceptics about religion are not sceptics about science or about sense-experience. And yet any departure from global scepticism involves assumptions concerning the validity of human mental processes with respect to some aspect of reality. Why should one assume that the human mind is capable of attaining any truths about anything whatsoever (including such apparently evident realities as physical objects)? Someone could say that there is pragmatic validation for some of our beliefs and that that is why we know we have got a few things right. But this is an inadequate reply: quite apart from the fact that pragmatically validated beliefs may be false, any such reasoning already involves the mind and hence a belief in its trustworthiness.

In a rather fundamental way, then, "faith" is prior to both rational understanding and knowledge. Some commitments are made by "faith" and only then can reason aid us in advancing towards knowledge of reality. It was this kind of "faith" that F.R. Tennant had in mind when he made the influential but partially misleading suggestion that the practice of science involves faith just as much as the practice of theology, that each rests on presuppositions which are not fundamentally rational yet without which knowledge would be impossible in either. Thus, Tennant reasoned, scientific "faith" (i.e., "faith" in the rationality of the universe) cannot, in any proper sense, be justified, and is thus analogous to religious faith.[82]

Without this kind of faith, reason is indeed impotent. The entire structure of human knowledge, one might say, rests upon certain unproven and unprovable convictions. In a sense, then, one may reasonably claim that all knowledge is inherently "religious" in character: knowledge cannot be fully secularized. But the kind of faith that reason presupposes for its operation is properly characterised as a commitment beyond the limits of rationally established certainty. Faith, in this relatively nebulous sense, is found in many areas of our lives: interpersonal relationships like friendship and marriage, political commitments, the scientific attitude of refusing to prematurely abandon a theory in the face of recalcitrant data, and so on. In this sense of the word, one might say of some Marxist who continued to believe in the political wisdom of the masses even after witnessing the behaviour of a crowd at a football match, that he had "faith" in his vision. But this, of course, is not specifically religious faith. Nor is this a purely terminological point. (It springs too directly from serious concerns to be merely terminological.) Secular faith is faith in its generic sense; it differs from Christian faith in respect of its object, causation, and results. And it is certainly not the kind of faith that used to move mountains.

- VI -

We have a few shards still to gather. I have given a neutral characterization of "revisionism" - a position espoused by many religious thinkers touched by modernity. "Revisionism" is, like "reductionism", a term of opprobrium and is employed in predominantly polemical contexts. My use of this term here is not intended to be question-begging. The secularized believers who espouse the cluster of views I have labelled "revisionism" freely admit, what is impossible to deny, that not all the major traditional elements of Christianity are defensible if secular standards of rationality are employed in assessing the reasonableness of the faith. Revisionists defend what they find defensible - not what there is. If they find some traditional teaching unacceptable or indefensible, they argue that it is either an irrelevant cultural accretion to the faith or else that it is indeed essential to faith and that its presence in the

Christian tradition creates a theological worry for the Christian believer.

Before I offer a final assessment of theological revisionism, I should comment on some of the motivations behind this view. The conviction that a secularized Christianity could successfully absorb the secular scientific culture (just as it had swallowed the Hellenic _Zeitgeist_ in an earlier age) provides part of the impetus behind revisionism. This motivation is, it seems to me, misguided. Christianity is an old faith now; the vigour of its youth has largely been spent. Moreover, it faces opposition in this age not only from rival faiths but also from indifferentism and atheism. If it absorbs modern culture, it can only do so on alien terms i.e., if it effectively abandons its own ideals. One of the aspirations of Christianity, as indeed of all religion, is to offer a critique of existing social reality by identifying the discrepancy between the demands of faith and the actual state of human affairs.[83] But Christianity cannot play a critical role if its doctrines are continually eroded or altered in the larger attempt to accommodate Christian convictions to secular culture.

The tendency to subordinate tradition to harmony with modern thought is one of the defining features of theological revisionism. To be sure, such a tendency is not due to purely defensive motives. Revisionists rightly wish to avoid any compartmentalization of our understanding of religious reality. There is, it is rightly felt, a need for religion to relate itself to the findings of secular science and history and to the implications of those findings. As a result, doctrines such as the Fall and original sin have been freed of all historical reference; the religious heritage of morality has been said to be discredited; and the view that men can sincerely reject God on purely intellectual grounds has been accepted. These concessions seem irresistible in this age but one should harbour no illusions as to their implications.

The concessions made by the revisionists leave Christian theism in a very vulnerable state indeed. It is, as we saw earlier, possible to defend theism against atheistic criticism only to the extent of allowing those within the circle of faith to remain there without fear of being convicted of any distinctive irrationality by the atheist. Thus, Hick thinks that a believer is rationally entitled to interpret his own world theistically and that while he cannot prove that God exists, he can show that it is entirely reasonable for him to believe in God on the basis of his own religious experience.[84] This puts no obligation on anyone else to believe in God but it serves to justify the believer's own adherence to his faith. It is not that a man, on the basis of his religious experience, infers God as the cause of his distinctively religious experience and then recommends to the non-religious man the use of such religious experience as a theoretical foundation for belief in God. On Hick's account, then, the fact that a man's own consciousness of what he takes to be the divine reality is compelling, the fact that he knows where his own shoe pinches, is enough. But Hick's strategy for defending the rationality of faith works by sacrificing an important portion of traditional Christian doctrine about the universality of belief in God.

Hick's position is an instructive instance of the dilemma facing faith in the modern world. The only kind of philosophical justification available for theism is of a relatively weak kind; it shields faith from prejudicially rigorous examination or unfair external assault. The parity argument, espoused in somewhat different forms by both Hick and Penelhum, is essentially an ad hominem one directed against a secular opponent of religious faith eager to convict the latter of some peculiar irrationality. The success of this argument would merely show that religious faith is not distinctively irrational - not that it may not be or is not irrational. It provides a purely negative defence of religious conviction since, of course, the appeal to shared weaknesses or mutual indefensibility cannot provide the basis for any positive defence. Moreover, that homely adage, "Those who live in glass houses shouldn't throw stones at others", may be sound advice but, if one takes it, one forgoes the pleasure of shattering some shared complacencies.

Under these circumstances, there is no convincing reason why any atheist or agnostic should come to religious faith nor indeed, more significantly, why a believer should feel morally or religiously obliged to contend indefinitely with doubts he may experience about the authenticity or truth of his convictions. It is not enough that religious practices or experiences provide sufficient sustenance to reinforce those who are already within the circle of faith: religion must provide something that challenges those who are outside it. To be sure, a man who was independently inclined to believe in God might endorse the view that religious belief is rational but the task of the religionist is to convince the atheist or the agnostic that religious commitment is intellectually respectable.

Where does this leave us? Theological revisionism is a deeply problematic position. As rational and scientific thought expose more and more of the tradition to be superstitious or outrageously false or simply incoherent, Christianity becomes everything by turns and nothing for long. The revisionists disown the suspect parts of the tradition without having any general or principled understanding of the limits of this sacrifice at the altar of secularism. And after all, if one disowns ad hoc whatever offends secular sensibilities, it is not clear what there is left to defend. How much of the tradition do we need?

It is difficult to know precisely what is the theoretical distance between some revisionist accounts and some of the more overt and unpalatable forms of reductionism. Both reductionism and revisionism offer rational reconstructions of traditional Christian doctrine. And, in the process, both destroy certain religiously important facilities - such as the possibility of seeing indifferentism and rejection as morally culpable attitudes from a religious perspective. These facilities are, it seems, only more evidently destroyed by the explicitly reductive accounts; revisionism is also incapable of preserving them. Are revisionists merely reductionists of a more conservative confession?

Notes

[1] Terence Penelhum, *Religion and Rationality* (New York: Random House, 1971), p. 199.

[2] See Thomas Paine's pioneering work, *The Age of Reason* (Secaucus: Citadel Press, 1948, 1974); see the work of the Christian scholar, Cecil Cadoux, *The Life of Jesus* (West Drayton: Pelican Books, 1948) and Maurice Bucaille's epoch-making masterpiece, *The Bible, the Qur'an and Science* (Paris: Seghers, 1983), 10th edn.

[3] Richard Swinburne, *Faith and Reason* (Oxford: Clarendon Press, 1981), p. 182.

[4] *ibid.*, pp. 181-183. This point, Swinburne urges, has been accepted widely only in the past four centuries by Christians but was made by earlier Christian thinkers like St. Hilary of Poitiers and Thomas Aquinas.

[5] See Terence Penelhum's *Religion and Rationality*, Basil Mitchell's *The Justification of Religious Belief* (New York: Seabury Press, 1973), and John Hick's *Faith and Knowledge* (Ithaca: Cornell University Press, 1966), 2nd edn. Penelhum, Hick, and Mitchell are, like Swinburne, "sophisticated" Christians.

[6] David Hume, *The Natural History of Religion* (London: Adam and Charles Black, 1956), edited with an introduction by H.E. Root. First published in 1757.

[7] Swinburne, *op. cit.*, p. 182.

[8] *ibid.*, pp. 183-184.

[9] For example, established archaeological data renders false the claim in *Genesis* that the Flood was a universal cataclysm which destroyed virtually all civilisation flourishing at about the 21 or 22 centuries B.C. Again, one can safely assume that *Genesis* 19:30-36 is making an outrageously false claim if either of *Genesis* 18:23 or *2 Peter* 2:7-8 is true. As for inconsistencies, *Genesis* 6:3 is inconsistent with *Genesis* 11:10-32; and *Matthew* 28:11-15 relates a story that contradicts itself in point of possibility.

[10] Genesis 37:28.

[11] The genealogies of Jesus in Matthew 1:1-16 and Luke 3:23-38 conflict. Moreover, only paternal genealogies are given; and these are, of course, in the case of the Virgin Birth, irrelevant - an exclusively maternal genealogy is needed. Again, John 21:1-14 contradicts Luke 5:1-11; Acts 1:3 contradicts Luke 24:51, and so on.

[12] The claims about the dating of the world's existence (which can be deduced from Genesis) are clearly false.

[13] T.M. Penelhum concedes that such disownment involves a measure of arbitrariness. See Penelhum, op.cit., p. 255.

[14] It is either not drawn at all - for example, in Islam; or it is assigned a different significance - for example, in Hinduism.

[15] See Psalms 7:9 where God is said to try both our hearts and our minds.

[16] The Koran as printed today is identical with the version authorised by Uthman, Muhammad's companion and successor, in the seventh century. The text has universal currency in the Muslim world. The purity of the text is guarded by the use of cryptic code initials at the beginnings of certain chapters (for example, Chapters 2, 3, 7, 10-15, 19, etc.) so that alterations would be detectable. Chapter 74:30 gives the clue to the workings of this extraordinary device.

[17] That God is jealous or suffers because of the iniquities of his creatures or bets with the Devil concerning Job's faith - these seem religiously unacceptable claims. Again, the claim that Lot committed incest with his own daughters in a moment of intemperance (Genesis 19:30-36) strikes most people as being morally outrageous both in itself and doubly so given the fact that Lot is alleged to have been a righteous prophet.

[18] Maurice Bucaille has argued along these lines in his remarkable What is the Origin of Man? (Paris: Seghers, 1984), 3rd edn. Translated from the French by A.D. Pannell and Maurice Bucaille.

[19]This is the alternative which Thomas Paine adopts in his The Age of Reason.

[20]I examine here only the views of Hick and Swinburne on this issue. For Penelhum's views, see his "Irreligion and Religious Variety", in Religion and Irreligion, Hugo Meynell (ed.), (Calgary: The University of Calgary Press, 1985), pp. 7-23.

[21]See John Hick's Arguments for the Existence of God (London: Macmillan, 1971), pp. 117-120.

[22]See Hick's "Theology's Central Problem", pp. 14-15. This was Hick's inaugural lecture delivered at the University of Birmingham on 31st October, 1967, and subsequently published by the University of Birmingham Press.

[23]John Hick, "The New Map of the Universe of Faiths", in Contemporary Philosophy of Religion, Steven Cahn and David Shatz (eds.), (New York: Oxford University Press, 1982), pp. 284-285. This article is reprinted from Hick's God and the Universe of Faiths (London: Macmillan, 1973), Chapter 10.

[24]Note that this view destroys any motivation for proselytizing.

[25]See Swinburne, op. cit., pp. 173-197, for a comparison of creeds.

[26]ibid., p. 176.

[27]I do think, however, that if the doctrine of the Incarnation were free of certain fatal logical infirmities, it could provide useful conceptual resources, lacking in Judaism and Islam, for explaining the nature and origin of evil. And if Christianity could explain the mystery of evil, it would ceteris paribus be explanatorily superior to its related religious rivals.

[28]William Paley, A View of the Evidences of Christianity, Part II, Section 3, first published in 1794, cited by Swinburne, op. cit., p. 193.

[29]St. Thomas Aquinas, Summa Contra Gentiles, Book 1, Chapter 6. See the selections in Classical Statements on Faith and Reason, E.L. Miller (ed.), (New York: Random House, 1970). For another similarly

unjust and savage attack on Islam, see Pascal's
Pensees (Harmondsworth: Penguin Books, 1966),
Remark No. 321.

[30]Muslim tradition relates that the Prophet did indeed
perform some sensual miracles but that what distinguishes him from his prophetic predecessors is the
pre-eminence of the written revelation vouchsafed to
him.

[31]Koran 28:46, 59:21, etc.

[32]John Oman, Concerning the Ministry (New York:
Harper and Brothers, 1937), pp. 44-45.

[33]Psalms 19:1-2; Koran 71:15.

[34]In the case of the Bible, Richard Swinburne urges
that there are indeed passages - such as Romans
1:18-22 and the apocryphal Wisdom 13-15 - which may
be taken as arguing for the existence of God. The
author is here (in each case) ostensibly arguing to
God's nature (i.e., his goodness and power); but to
do so is to argue that there is a god who is God
(i.e., the metaphysically perfect being of ethical
monotheism), and hence that there is a God. See
Swinburne, op.cit., p. 86. As for the Koran, a
simple version of the design argument can be discerned in places - for example, at 71: 14-20 - but,
in general, the existence of Allah is taken as more
or less axiomatic by both Muhammad and his Meccan
detractors, the Koran being mainly concerned to show
that Allah has no partners in his divinity.

[35]Romans 1:18-23

[36]Koran 16:83, 27:14, etc.

[37]Koran 12:3, 38:1, 73:19

[38]Koran 7:172

[39]The similarity between the Koranic doctrine and the
Socratic-Platonic doctrine of anamnesis is obvious.

[40]Christian commentators have generally agreed that
the only exception is invincible ignorance - in
which case a man is exempt though not excused.

[41]Terence Penelhum, God and Scepticism: A Study in Scepticism and Fideism (Boston: Reidel, 1983), p. 156.

[42]Penelhum argues that in a religiously charged environment, rejection may be unreasonable. See God and Scepticism, p. 157.

[43]God and Scepticism, p. 154; Religion and Rationality, p. 86, pp. 203 ff.

[44]God and Scepticism, p. 156.

[45]Koran 2:130, 2:171.

[46]Koran 7:100, 10:74.

[47]Søren Kierkegaard, The Sickness Unto Death (Garden City: Doubleday and Co., 1954), translated with introduction and notes by Walter Lowrie.

[48]See Pensees (Harmondsworth: Penguin Books, 1966), translated by A.J. Krailsheimer, pp. 66ff, especially Remark No. 133.

[49]Northrop Frye, The Great Code: The Bible and Literature (New York: Harcourt Brace Javanovich, 1982), p. xx.

[50]See my discussion of John Hick's philosophy of religion in the next section.

[51]See the following works by Penelhum: Religion and Rationality, pp. 206-207; God and Scepticism, pp. 155-156; and for an overview of his philosophy of religion, see his Problems of Religious Knowledge (New York: Herder and Herder, 1971), and his "Is a religious Epistemology Possible?" in Analytical Philosophy of Religion in Canada, Mostafa Faghfoury (ed.), (Ottawa: University of Ottawa Press, 1982), pp. 17-33.

[52]Terence Penelhum, "Faith, Reason, and Secularity", in Modernity and Responsibility: Essays for George Grant, Eugene Combs (ed.), (Toronto: Toronto University Press, 1983), p. 86.

[53]By "experienceable", incidentally, I do not mean "publicly experienceable at the level of minimally interpreted sense-data" for that would be to endorse a crude version of the verifiability principle. I

do wish to suggest, however, that the propositions
"God exists" and "God does not exist" be somehow at
least weakly testable i.e., some evidence must count
for or against them.

[54] God and Scepticism, p. 157.

[55] I endorse Christine Overall's definition of miracle,
namely, "an event which is a violation of natural
law or which ... is permanently inexplicable". See
p. 348 of her "Miracles as Evidence Against the
Existence of God", in The Southern Journal of Philosophy, Vol. XXIII, No. 3, 1985.

[56] I suspect that one of the reasons for the comparative lack of interest in Nietzsche's philosophy of
religion among contemporary analysts is the conviction that his aphoristic style sets undue limits to
the careful development of his insights. A careful
study would show, however, that there is a full and
coherent intellectual reality behind the pithy
remarks.

[57] ibid., p. 169.

[58] Matthew 7:8.

[59] Alvin Plantinga, God and Other Minds (Ithaca:
Cornell University Press, 1967), p. viii,
pp. 186-271.

[60] John Hick, "Sceptics and Believers", in Faith and
the Philosophers, John Hick (ed.), (New York: St.
Martin's Press, 1964), pp. 242-248.

[61] God and Scepticism, p. 30.

[62] God and Scepticism, pp. 114-116, pp. 147 ff.

[63] See Penelhum's "Scepticism and Fideism", in The
Sceptical Tradition, Myles Burnyeat (ed.), (London:
University of California Press, 1983), pp. 287-318,
and Penelhum's "Natural belief and Religious Belief
in Hume's Philosophy", in The Philosophical
Quarterly, Vol. 33, No. 131, April 1983.

[64] God and Scepticism, pp. 153-154.

[65] God and Scepticism, pp. 147 ff.

[66]Alvin Plantinga, "Rationality and Religious Belief", in Cahn and Shatz, op. cit., pp. 255-277; for a shorter version of this paper, see Plantinga's "Is belief in God rational?", in Rationality and Religious Belief, C.F. Delaney (ed.), (Notre Dame: University of Notre Dame Press, 1979), pp. 7-27.

[67]Norman Malcolm, "The groundlessness of belief", in Reason and Religion, Stuart Brown (ed.), (Ithaca: Cornell University Press, 1977), pp. 143-157; and see Ludwig Wittgenstein's On Certainty, G.E.M. Anscombe and G.H. von Wright (eds.), (Oxford: Basil Blackwell, 1969), translated by D. Paul and G.E.M. Anscombe.

[68]For some criticisms of Malcolm's position, see Kai Nielsen's "On the rationality of groundless believing", in Idealistic Studies, Vol. XI, No. 3, September 1981, pp. 215-229.

[69]John Hick, Faith and Knowledge, pp. 97 ff, pp. 118-119.

[70]John Hick, Arguments for the Existence of God, pp. 109-113.

[71]David Hume, A Treatise of Human Nature, Book 1, Part IV, Section 2, pp. 187-188 of Selby-Bigge edition.

[72]See Myles Burnyeat's introduction to The Sceptical Tradition, Myles Burnyeat (ed.), (London: University of California Press, 1983).

[73]See Penelhum's God and Scepticism.

[74]See G.E. Moore's Philosophical Papers (London: Allen and Unwin, 1959), Chapters II, VII, IX, and X; and see Richard Rorty's Philosophy and the Mirror of Nature (Princeton: Princeton University Press, 1979).

[75]See Ludwig Wittgenstein's Philosophical Investigations (Oxford: Basil Blackwell, 1963).

[76]Moore, op. cit.

[77]Those who regard the existence of evil as an insuperable objection to the existence of a righteous God may think that our experience is not even compatible with God's existence. But that, of course, is a separate objection.

[78]*Arguments for the Existence of God*, pp. 113-116.

[79]*ibid.*, p. 112.

[80]*Genesis* 38:10.

[81]*On Certainty*, Remark Number 505, p. 66e.

[82]F.R. Tennant, *Philosophical Theology* (Cambridge: Cambridge University Press, 1928), Vol. I, pp. 297 ff.

[83]Robert Ackermann, *Religion as Critique* (Amherst: The University of Massachusetts Press, 1985), *passim*.

[84]*Arguments for the Existence of God*, pp. 109 ff.

Chapter VI
The Religious Imagination

In our own despair,
Against our will,
Comes Wisdom,
Through the awful grace of God.
                                    Aeschylus.

So far I have established merely that some influential philosophical defences of the rationality of Christian theism are unsatisfactory. Of these defences, theological revisionism is, it seems to me, the most promising. But, as I hope to have shown in Chapter 5, it is not without its difficulties. I do not know how revisionist thinkers (like Hick and Penelhum) are likely to respond to my criticisms. (I suspect they don't know either.) In any case, my task is almost complete. In bringing this work to a close, I offer some suggestions, in an all too desultory manner, for a defence of Christianity in the modern world and give a brief assessment of its reasonableness as a way of life in twentieth century industrial society. Given the size of this task, some of the argument will be, unfortunately, on occasion, unavoidably inconclusive.

- I -

There was a time when God was thought to be everywhere. Men instinctively believed in him and read his presence in the open book of nature. Intuitions of the divine saturated the ordinary man's experience of the world. Life on earth, it was thought, was simply a temporary probation for testing the mettle of the pious. Human existence was a cosmic drama composed by the dramatist _par excellence_: it had, so to speak, a central theme, a rational plan, and a morally satisfying _denouement_. The task of reason was simply to demonstrate the truth of revealed knowledge by reconciling recalcitrant experience with the rational blueprint of the world vouchsafed by revelation - by forcing the rebellious facts into the pre-ordained categories decreed by the faith.

That age has passed away. Ever since the Enlightenment, it has become a genuine question whether or not belief in the God of the ethical monotheistic tradition is either intellectually defensible or morally necessary. Many people today, and especially the intelligentsia in Western as well as several non-Western societies, conduct their lives in almost entirely secular humanistic terms; religion makes an appearance at tragic or significant events such as birth, marriage, and death. Their total vision of the world differs from that of their predecessors. The natural universe and its denizens are the product of an "accidental collocation of atoms".[1] Man is an undirected being with no omniscient authority to supervise him. There is no superhuman will superimposing an external value and order on the world; there are no ultimate ideals in nature to secrete a normative significance for human conduct. We have here, in effect, shorn of its political inegalitarianism, the Nietzschean programme in action. God is dead. The world is metaphysically and morally neutral. Men must create, not discover ideals. We must eke out an existence in a godless world. The "other world" is simply a fabrication of the alienated man seeking to do something worthwhile with his solitude; the "other world" is merely a figment of the tortured imagination of the homo religiosus.

It is this atheistic world pattern, inspired by belief in a particular cosmic geography, that largely determines the direction and character of modern thought in many societies. Thus, the context in which religion receives a hearing today is vastly different from, say, the context in which the Medievals assessed it. To the Scholastic and the Medieval Jewish and Muslim thinkers, it seemed obvious, for one reason or another, that sensation, reason, revelation, and mystical experience alike were grounds of equally genuine if not equally significant kinds of knowledge. Today, however, given the widespread influence of positivism in one form or another and an increase in the scope and authority of the sciences of nature, there is a marked inclination to regard the scientific method as the only appropriate (or at least the most appropriate) basis for understanding the world and there is a contiguous proclivity to relegate meta-physics, theology, and even some of the human (social) sciences to the status of pseudo-factual disciplines.

The classical frameworks clothed religion in categories derived from speculative metaphysics. After the rise of positivism, however, most proposed frameworks for expressing religious insight have, by contrast, been self-consciously anti-metaphysical; they have sought to interpret religious claims non-cognitively as, among other things, moral poetry or a way of seeing the world. These reductionist frame-works cannot be appropriate for a religious point of view, as I argued in Chapter Four, since, ontologi-cally, they are founded on the assumption that

religious claims can have no basis in reality, i.e.,
that there corresponds to religious beliefs no reality
other than the self-created reality of the religious
life in and of itself.

The positivist conception of rationality is
defined exclusively in terms of considerations drawn
from secular common sense, logic, and (natural)
science. Coupled with an (arguably) essentially
question-begging construal of the nature and scope of
genuine knowledge, this parochial positivist ideal of
rationality provides the larger intellectual context
in which the rationality of religious conviction is
assessed. The contemporary problem of the rationality
of religious faith is set partly by the decline of a
particular classical conception of rationality - which
was defined in terms of considerations deriving from
rationalist philosophy, metaphysical speculation, and
the reality of men's religious experience - and partly
by the rise of a secular and anti-religious conception
of rationality which challenges and seeks to discredit
the older one. If philosophy was the handmaiden of
theology in a bygone age, positivism - understood in a
very wide sense of the term - has become the handmaiden of secularism in this one.

The contemporary climate of opinion, then, is, it
seems, uncongenial to religious conviction; the
secular temper is more pragmatic and empirical than
metaphysical and speculative.[2] Thus, what renders
Scholastic philosophy irrelevant to the man imbued
with the spirit of modern science and secular reason
is not the fact that Scholasticism employed a
different logic (for it didn't) or reached different
conclusions (although it did) but rather the disparity
in total outlook - i.e., the difference between those

instinctively held and culturally acquired precon-
ceptions which constitute any world-view and which
impose upon different communities and thinkers a
characteristic and peculiar use of the intellect.
Hence, while Aquinas' views may be wrong, what really
matters, as far as the modern secularist is concerned,
is that the Saint's views are irrelevant. We have
undergone, if you wish, a Kuhnian "paradigm shift".

- II -

Nowadays virtually every philosophical writer
(whether religious or otherwise) feels obliged to
believe that the existence of God cannot be proved.
Many think that there is no argument, deductively
valid with true premises, for establishing the
existence of God. Others think that no-one has produced even an argument, sound and conforming to the
requirements of strict probability, which would
support the theist's case: no-one has even shown that
the existence of God is more probable than not.

Natural theology, in its most ambitious role, is
the enterprise of providing proofs of the central
tenets of theism; it attempts to show that issues such
as God's existence are decidable by universal rational
criteria and that the proofs offered are comprehen-
sible to and coercive of all rational beings. Traditional natural theology is, in effect, a form of the
positive parity argument: some neutrally describable
facts, presupposed or implied by the ordinary experience of believers and sceptics alike, are seen as
providing incontestable premises for a sound argument
whose success entails the existence of God and hence,
by implication, renders disbelief positively and
demonstrably irrational.

Apart from some professed Thomists, few writers today would argue that theology can give us any kind of knowledge of God let alone that it can be founded on the exercise of speculative reason or that it is demonstrable knowledge. Many thinkers today believe that Kant and Hume effectively destroyed the philosophical credentials of natural theology.[3] There is, it is now widely believed, following Hume and Kant, a conceptual impropriety embedded in the inference from observed features of the natural world or our experience to the existence of a transcendent author of nature. One cannot, that is, proceed from any general analysis of the contingency of finite being or from an analysis of the presuppositions of order and regularity in human experience or from an analysis of our experience of value or indeed, finally, from a consideration of the logical presuppositions of our thought about God, to deduce or make probable the existence of God.

If Hume and Kant offered <u>philosophical</u> grounds for rejecting classical natural theology, it fell to the lot of fideists like Pascal and Kierkegaard to offer <u>theological</u> grounds for undermining the enterprise of establishing God's existence by the unaided human reason. Natural theology, the fideists chanted, was incompatible with the possibility of genuine faith: faith could not co-exist with the possibility of coercive rational argument for God's existence since the availability of such an argument (i.e., the availability of an intellectually compelling case for theism) would make it impossible for men to have <u>faith</u> in God. Moreover, the fideists continued, even if natural theology were possible, it would remain religiously profitless to develop it since it could neither inspire a real faith in God nor help us reach a valid concept of deity. And how, after all, could it do such things when, as the fideists would have us believe, rejection was due not to intellectual doubts but rather to sinful perversity? In fine, natural theology was condemned as irrelevant and pointless at best and impossible at worst.

Let me begin by examining the philosophical critique of natural theology. For Kant, there is, to put it in the form of an influential slogan, "no knowledge outside the realm of sense-experience". "Religious knowledge", if that is the right term, is to be construed, according to Kant, not as a particular theoretical understanding of the world or the transcendent realm but rather as one of the presuppositions of the autonomous moral life. It is simply one of the imperatives of the practical reason that there be a God. Indeed, it is only in and through our apprehension of the moral law that we are assured of the existence of God. As for Hume, all genuine reasoning conforms to a simple pre-conceived blueprint - deduction and induction. Whatever kinds of reasoning do not fit this model are bogus; the product of such bogus reasoning - usually metaphysics - is fit for the furnace. Theistic conclusions, Hume influentially argues, cannot be established by the use of the criteria and presuppositions of secular history. Miracles, Hume tells us, cannot form a reliable part of history; in the famous discussion of miracles in the _Enquiry_, Hume offers _a priori_ reasons for rejecting as unreliable the historical records of miracles.[4] In the _Dialogues_, Hume contends that theistic conclusions cannot be established by an appeal to the criteria employed in natural science:

theology is not an experimental discipline. It follows, for Hume, that theistic conclusions cannot be established at all since, in the words of an influential dictum, "no matter of fact can be a priori"; and there is, of course, no tertium quid which would serve to establish the foundations of religious knowledge.

Now, both Kant and Hume seek to undermine the very possibility of natural theology by the use of reasons deriving from their theories of knowledge. This is an important observation to bear in mind when examining the philosophically motivated rejection of natural theology. Both Kant and Hume, in different ways of course, assess theological and metaphysical theses in accordance with alien criteria derived from, broadly speaking, common sense, natural science and mathematics. In very general terms, the view seems to be that there is a logical contrast between our epistemological situation in science and mathematics, on the one hand, and theology and metaphysics, on the other. Scepticism concerning the pretensions of traditional metaphysics and theology is supported by an appeal to the alleged fact that the possibility of metaphysical and religious knowledge violates certain general epistemological principles about what is or is not knowable. Scepticism about metaphysics and theology is supported by exploiting the possibility of a logical contrast between different epistemological situations, between our alleged epistemological insecurity in theology and metaphysics, on the one hand, and our epistemological security in science and logic, on the other. The Humean-Kantian epistemologies are, then, in effect, a form of mitigated sceptical doctrine since they give substance to some intuitions about the nature of logico-scientific knowledge and then use the resulting criterion to erect a logical contrast between different areas of inquiry i.e., those which satisfy the criterion (and hence qualify as cognitive) and those which do not.

But why should one accept these essentially positivist epistemologies? Humean positivism, for example, seems to provide simply too restrictive and dogmatic a philosophical methodology to do justice to our pre-philosophical intuitions about the range and extent of human knowledge. To make genuine knowledge co-extensive with empirical science and the formal logico-mathematical disciplines is to beg the question concerning its nature and extent. There is a _petitio principii_ at the very root of the Humean doctrine. And, curiously enough, Hume's rigid empiricism is so aprioristic that it does violence to the very intuition of experimental inquiry that it is founded on. It seems unempirical to decide by _a priori_ argument in which areas of human research genuine knowledge is or is not possible.

We see this clearly if we examine the development of Hume's empiricism by the logical positivists. It is a standing reproof to positivist critics of theology and metaphysics that they failed to formulate a criterion of meaning which was a death-warrant solely for these allegedly suspect disciplines and not also, inadvertently, for areas of inquiry the positivists wanted to retain. One must not exaggerate the significance of such a failure but, equally, one must not regard it as entirely insignificant or fortuitous. Unduly restrictive epistemologies are likely to be self-defeating just as excessively liberal ones are apt to be useless.

Now, to get to the central point, there is a self-defeating assumption at the very root of these sceptical epistemological doctrines if they are offered as knowledge-claims. Philosophical "assertions" (including philosophical claims about the status of reason and the extent of our knowledge) and meta-philosophical claims are not part of the subject-matter of any of the special (descriptive) sciences or of mathematics or of common sense. If we strictly adhere to the empiricist positivist conception of knowledge, derived from the writings of Kant and Hume, we destroy not merely the possibility of religious knowledge and metaphysical knowledge but also the possibility of philosophical knowledge. For the strict empiricist (i.e., one who endorses Kant's slogan about the impossibility of knowledge outside the realm of sense-experience), philosophy itself can only be, as one writer so aptly puts it, "either a hermeneutic device for clarifying what other people say or a neutral liaison between branches of inquiry which do have cognitive status".[5] Thus, the Humean and Kantian philosophical schemes cannot coherently be seen as making knowledge-claims unless they permit the possibility of philosophical knowledge - a possibility which is implicitly rejected. If it is conceded that philosophy cannot give us knowledge, then we are under no obligation to accept the epistemological doctrines associated with the Humean and Kantian philosophical systems. If philosophy cannot supply us knowledge, then the assertion of an empiricist criterion of knowledge is merely stipulative and perhaps dogmatic even though it may, of course, enjoy popular support. Relatedly, the adoption of a standard of rationality derivative from science, logic, and the deliverances of ordinary sense would render philosophical beliefs, including the philosophical belief about the legitimacy of such an empiricist criterion of rationality, irrational and unwarranted.

I do not intend to establish the possibility of natural theology. I do hope to have indicated, however, that one of epistemological grounds for denying the possibility of natural theology would also serve to destroy the possibility of philosophical knowledge. If indeed we are to restrict exemplars of genuine knowledge to logic, mathematics, empirical science, and common sense matters of fact, then philosophy itself cannot provide knowledge. And if philosophy is not a cognitive discipline, the assertion of a philosophical criterion of knowledge or of rational belief is itself stipulative. The religious thinker is at liberty to reject it.

The standard objection to verificationism - namely, that no warrant can be given for the status of the epistemological doctrine itself - is also applicable to the Kantian and Humean epistemologies. Both of these epistemologies are, in a broad sense, positivist. My criticisms here are _not_ the outcome of any _confusion_ between the Humean-Kantian critique of the possibility of a rational proof of God's existence, on the one hand, and the positivist dogma that theological claims are factually meaningless, on the other. I am deliberately asserting that there is an underlying affinity between the two positions.

This is an elemental and difficult issue. It is clearly too late in the day for us to join the battle. Two general and highly tendentious comments will have to do for now although I shall return presently to some of the issues raised here. Firstly, to grant the possibility of philosophical knowledge is _ipso facto_ to grant the possibility of some forms of metaphysics. Philosophical knowledge cannot properly be characterised in any non-metaphysical way. Now, if metaphysical reflection is to be seen as intellectually respectable, the older positivist strictures on the nature and extent of knowledge must be relaxed. Perhaps the very prevalence and inescapability of the metaphysical may force upon us the realisation that positivism does not do justice to our intuitions about the true scope of human knowledge. Positivism, after all, in its heyday - and that's the time when a movement shows its true colours - mercilessly outlawed many modes of reasoning (among them, religious and metaphysical) as bogus or else preserved them only in forms utterly distorted and emaciated. Thus, aesthetic, legal, moral, historical, in short, interpretive reasoning, were exiled from the cognitive realm. Critics were not slow to note that such a programme denied the possibility of the human (social) sciences. And, in fact, the possibility of philosophy was also undercut. And, indeed, there is a growing realisation now that a good part of the philosophy of a natural science (like physics) is itself part of the experimental discipline itself, any boundary erected on positivist scruples being merely arbitrary.

Secondly, part of the reason why natural theology is viewed with such scepticism today is that thinkers assess the status of the arguments for God's existence in a predominantly secular cultural environment with its attendant positivist underpinnings. Whether or not such arguments command assent depends, it seems to me, less upon the logic that conveys them than upon the climate of opinion in which they are sustained.

It is important, therefore to bear in mind both the relevance of my remarks (in Section I) about the character of the modern world-view and the fact that philosophical critiques of natural theology are often motivated by assumptions deriving from general epistemological theories whose original context of inspiration is predominantly secular and hence remote from religious concerns. Thus, for example, the criteria of rationality, secreted by broad epistemological theories developed in an attempt to endow substance to intuitions generated by work in secular areas of inquiry, are subsequently applied, somewhat programmatically, to areas like theology and metaphysics.

I turn now to the religious objections to natural theology. A major religious objection is that natural theology is religiously futile. We can reach no valid concept of deity by using the methods of experimental inquiry. Revelation is the only source of true ideas about God. The thinkers may attempt to construct philosophical doctrines about God but, the objection continues, the God of Scripture and tradition, worshipped in church, synagogue, and mosque, and conceived in the minds of believers, is clearly a different reality from any of the anaemic counterparts which the thinkers may invent. (Recall Pascal's passionate protest against confusing the God of Isaac and Abraham with the frail reality concocted by philosophers.)

Moreover, it is said, natural theology cannot inspire a man to have real faith in God: a man's heart must be touched by some experience which is not the result wholly of argument. Relatedly, the argument has run, men's confidence in their own self-sufficiency (as opposed to their confidence in the intellectual self-sufficiency of atheism qua explanatory scheme) must also be shattered. Natural theology cannot do that, the religionists lament. At most it can show us that atheism is false; it cannot make men feel the need for God. In fine, even a successful natural theology need not be capable of producing a specifically religious response to reality. The modern fool hath said in his heart: "God may exist - but his existence is irrelevant to my life." So, the step from presumption to despair is a vital part of the transition to the religious attitudes of faith, worship, and commitment. And natural theology can have no role to play in that part of the process.

The fideists regard the whole enterprise of natural theology as misguided. Rejection is due not to any intellectual doubts which a natural theology would dispel but rather to a sinful perversity which faith alone could remove. Even if natural theology were possible, it would be religiously irrelevant.

Indeed, a successful natural theology would, to turn to another major theological objection, be worse than futile: it would be positively harmful since it would destroy the possibility of genuine faith. The possibility of natural theology is incompatible, it is urged, with the possibility of genuine religious faith. The very nature of faith requires there be available no proof of God's existence. Kierkegaard argues, as we saw in Chapter 2, that the passionate nature of the religious life is guaranteed by the sheer improbability of the beliefs it rests on. The availability of an objective paradox-free knowledge of the divine reality would reduce, Kierkegaard fears, the risk and hence the passion of human faith in God i.e., it would "lower the price of the God-relation-ship" and hence reduce its value.[6] Moreover, as many religious writers have argued, God does not wish to endanger the autonomy of the human personality by any kind of conclusive intellectual proof. In order to extract a voluntary response of faith and loyalty, the Deity must not jeopardise our cognitive freedom; and any fully conclusive demonstration would, it is urged, be coercive and hence compel assent.[7]

Now, certainly, rational argument is, in reli-gious matters, inconclusive. Religious belief is virtually never espoused on purely rational grounds: men rarely come to believe in God solely on the basis of an assessment of the reasonableness of such belief. But it does not follow from the fact that arguments for the existence of God are irrelevant to the life of faith (even supposing this were so, for the sake of argument) that there are no sound arguments capable of establishing the existence of God to those who stand outside the confines of the household of faith. Nor does it follow that rational argument is entirely pointless even in the case of those who are already committed to the faith. While the theistic arguments do not, admittedly, in general, serve to propel men into faith from an initial situation of disbelief or indifference (although a theistic proof like the ontological argument may, if successful, be rationally sufficient to lead some very rational persons to give intellectual assent to God's existence and even perhaps worship him), they do, if successful, offer retrospective justification for an enduring form of life. It is worth noting that, as a matter of histo-rical fact, natural theology was developed long after the faithful had established traditions of worship and devotion. But it was natural theology which served to crystallise their amorphous pre-philosophical intuitions about God into an intellectually powerful and systematic world-picture; the faithful had feeble or confused intuitive convictions of God and felt, naturally enough, justified in thinking that their intuitions were reliable as long as natural theology could deliver the relevant supporting arguments. And, indeed, it was felt, again naturally and reasonably enough, that the absence or unavailability of such arguments would impoverish the convictions of the faithful. Thus, natural theology came to be seen as supporting and confirming the religious beliefs of those already committed to the faith.

Argument, inconclusive or otherwise, does play a role in conversion, lapse, and ordinary religious commitment. Now, to be sure, none of these experiences is describable fully in intellectual terms alone; and the emotions often do play a more dramatic role thus dwarfing the presence of any measured dispassionate judgement. But there is a place both for the emotional and the reflective in religious commitment. The voice of reason may be gentler than that of passion - but it need not be any the less strong for it. It is a cardinal defect of Kierkegaard's thought that he comes close on occasion to exaggerating the importance of religious passion to such an extent that the unwary reader may be forgiven for thinking that, for Kierkegaard, conviction is itself a criterion of truth and passion an adequate substitute for truth. For all its profundity, however, Kierkegaard's talk of emotion and passion in the religious life is incapable of doing the impossible, namely, replacing the logic of faith by the psychology of religious belief.

The search for conclusive reasons in support of religious belief is, Kierkegaard and the fideists tell us, morally reprehensible since it is the outcome of a desire to escape the ineliminable risk of genuine faith. A religious faith which can be proved loses its right to be believed: faith requires that belief be devoid of epistemic certainty. But, as Terence Penelhum has so ably shown, faith can incorporate knowledge just as it can incorporate doubts. Faith and knowledge can co-exist in a religious context just as they can in a secular one. One can believe what one knows, have faith in what one knows. The classical Thomist dichotomy between faith and knowledge is, Penelhum rightly claims, untenable. One can indeed meritoriously believe in, have faith in, P while knowing that P is true. This can happen both in the secular life as well as in the religious one. In a secular context, a child may _know_ that Pythagoras' Theorem is true and yet he may require effort and training to _believe_ that it is true. Similarly, a man may know that there is a God and yet lack faith in him both in the sense that he occasionally experiences doubts about the truth of the proposition "There exists a God" and in the sense that he often fails to live according to the will of God as he understands it. Thus, the availability of a theistic proof would not necessitate faith. The fideists simply misconstrue the implications of the possibility of delivering demonstrative verdicts on religious questions. We can, then, following Penelhum, weaken one of the most powerful religious motives behind the rejection of natural theology.[8]

Penelhum produces an _ad hominem_ argument as well against the fideists. If the fideistic claim (made by

Pascal and Kierkegaard, among others) that rejection is due to sin is actually true, then it is puzzling, Penelhum contends, that intellectual support for belief in God is not overwhelming.[9] Thus, the failure of natural theology is actually a religiously disconcerting fact. Far from dispensing with the problem of faith (as it was intended to do), it actually places it on a new level of seriousness. It generates a theological puzzle: if even the availability of a rational proof of God's existence would not compel faith - sin being the true cause of rejection - why is there no rational proof of God's existence available?

One of the many advantages of Penelhum's model of faith is that we can use it to debunk the powerful anti-intellectualism of popular religious thought. It is often said, by ordinary believers, that men of true faith need no intellectual validation for their religious convictions. (The legendary learned Sheikh at al-Azhar who produced five hundred proofs of Allah's existence must, one simple pious co-religionist remarked with pointed sarcasm at his funeral, have experienced no less than five hundred doubts about the existence of Allah.) But once we realise that the religious opposition to an intellectual defence of faith is in fact the outcome of a misunderstanding about the nature of faith, we can set aside the popular tendency to disparage the intellectual strains in religion. Not only can men of faith legitimately produce proofs to dissipate the doubts of others - for example, those who may not enjoy an intensely religious life - they can also produce them in order to dispel their own misgivings. Faith can co-exist with doubt just as it can with knowledge. Faith requires decision and commitment in the face of inconclusive evidence, says Kierkegaard; faith requires decision and commitment even in the face of <u>conclusive</u> evidence, says Penelhum.

I have examined some of the philosophical and religious objections to natural theology. I conclude that <u>a priori</u> dismissals of natural theology are unacceptable - whether motivated by philosophical concerns, as in the case of Hume and Kant, or by theological ones, as in the case of Pascal and Kierkegaard. It seems to me that a rejection of natural theology should be based on a piecemeal examination of the arguments proffered by writers rather than on <u>a priori</u> claims about the philosophical impossibility of religious knowledge or on theological dogmas about the perversity of the fallen creature. That God's existence cannot be rationally demonstrated is a dogma (unless of course it can be shown that the very concept of God is incoherent). That particular arguments proffered by apologists don't work can indeed be shown: Hume and Kant punctured most of the theistic arguments in their classical forms.

Moreover, the fact that all actual attempts to prove God's existence have been unsuccessful, if indeed that has been the case,[10] does not entail the failure of future attempts. (One would think that Hume's admirers would have noted this point.) To be sure, however, even if it is granted that natural theology is not conceptually flawed, it may still be the case that the likelihood of making a plausible case for natural theology is not very high.[11] More specifically, even if there are no reasons <u>a priori</u> to rule out the possibility of a successful natural theology, there may still be overwhelming empirical difficulties with it. Thus, for example, unless one is prepared to insulate religion from the cruel risks of experience by denying it all standing in experience, one should not under-estimate the weight of contrary empirical evidence. The moral challenge posed by the problem of evil, the problem of religious conflict, the radical inaccessibility of God, and so on, are all likely to provide obstacles to the development of a natural theology.

Before commenting further on the problems just raised, I should say a little about what precisely natural theology is meant to achieve. Classical natural theology was very ambitious in its aspirations. St. Thomas, for example, sought to demonstrate Christian religious truths even to outsiders who rejected the authority of the Christian revelation altogether.[12] In a similar vein, the First Vatican Council pronounced that the existence of God can "certainly [certo] be known by the natural light of human reason from the things which are created."[13] Richard Swinburne has urged, sensibly enough, that this conception of the aims of natural theology may well be untenable. He contends that there are no deductively valid arguments from premises evident to most (or all) rational beings to the existence of God (or to the non-existence of God). Swinburne thinks, however, that there is enough inductive force in those arguments from such premises which can be represented as inductive arguments, taken together, to render the conclusion that there is a God more probable than not. In other words, the theistic arguments, for Swinburne, make their conclusions probable but do not endow certainty.[14]

Modern natural theologians are not likely to accept Aquinas' Five Ways or concur with his claim that the existence of God is _per se notum_ (i.e., self-evident in the sense of being known in and of itself if known at all). But even if natural theology can no longer aim at providing an impregnable rational proof of God's existence, it is still a worthy project. Even if natural theology succeeds merely in making God's existence plausible and probable, it could serve to confirm a faith in which people already participated i.e., it could provide an internal justification for religious practice. And while such a natural theology could not be used to convince staunch atheists and agnostics to come over to faith, it could be used to convince the ordinary reasonable man from becoming an atheist in the first place and to encourage the fellow who sits on the fence to come over to the side of belief. (This is, incidentally, not unlike the role of anti-sceptical philosophy which essentially seeks to prevent ordinary reasonable folk from becoming sceptics in the first place while often acknowledging its incapacity to dissuade the confirmed sceptic.)

And even if all of that fails, we could, while attempting to develop a natural theology, clarify theological concepts, provide a significant way of thinking about God, demonstrate the coherence of the concept of God, help to discredit anthropomorphic tendencies in religious thought, and so on. Thus, even if we cannot show that the concept of God is instantiated or that, less ambitiously, it is plausible or probable that there is a God, it could be the case that in an attempt to develop a natural theology, we could acquire a body of theory which would serve to clarify the basis of the failure of the enterprise.

228

- III -

Theism is not a fashionable cloak to wear in this age. It is often (and rightly) said that the burden of proof rests on men of faith.[15] But one must not forget that the location of such an onus shifts with changes in popular and intellectual culture. (Let us not forget that those who thought atheism rational had to justify their stance in an earlier age.) The problem of justifying religious commitment is, in a crucial way, tied up with the problem of the rightness or wrongness of total world-pictures. Secularism is the dominant outlook today in many advanced industrial societies. Those who defend religious commitment in such societies do so in the larger intellectual matrix supplied by a scientific, anti-metaphysical and, to use a pejorative term, somewhat scientistic culture. Such a scientistic culture with its auxiliary techno- logy and faith in the efficacy of science encroaches daily on the arts and humanities. (Wittgenstein's influential later philosophy is, incidentally, largely a reaction against the excesses of just such a culture.)

I am not suggesting that secularism is just a passing cultural bias or that it is time another prejudice won the day. But, and this is the important point, given the prevalence of the secular atheistic outlook, it is difficult to detect the presence of bad reasons for rejecting the religious Weltanschauung. Of course, there are some good reasons for rejecting the religious outlook - that it is incoherent, false, or fantastic. We can have some imaginative sympathy with the religious vision today and conscientiously reject it as false, perhaps even confused or barely credible. The worry, however, is that some secularists oppose the religious outlook for reasons which are, on careful examination, seen to be bad ones. When this happens, the religionist is entitled to wonder whether the prevalence of secularism is perhaps partly explicable in terms of the fact that we can live with some prejudices but not with others.

The religionist may begin by questioning the characterization of our age as a "secular" one. Is the twentieth century a truly secular age even in the industrialised societies? Private religious experience does occur, he may argue, but, owing to a taboo on religion (as there was on sexuality in Victorian Britain), people conceal it or interpret it atheistically out of fear of ridicule by their secularized compatriots. Similarly, the argument may run, the Middle Ages cannot be taken uncritically to be a truly religious age. It could be that secular proclivities, to walk on the other side of the street, were simply outlawed and hence suppressed for fear of derision. And, perhaps, there is greater genuine religiosity today among individuals than there was in earlier ages when religious observance was legally enforced and hence harder to neglect.[16]

These are all legitimate worries in the empirical sociology of religious belief. I do not know how to resolve them. It seems to me, however, that when all is said and done, twentieth century Western society and many of the industrialised societies in the rest of the world are indeed secularised. Certainly, the intelligentsia in many societies do endorse a secular world-picture. And even religious believers are more secularised than they themselves may imagine: it does not occur even to religious folk today to claim that the intellectual dislocations of the nineteenth century were pre-ordained by God to punish a perverse and stiff-necked generation. Modern audiences - whether composed of believers or atheists - would be very uncomfortable, not to speak of outright embarrassment, at such claims. The scientific world-view has obviously become almost instinctive with all of us.

The religionist will simply have to argue that the rival secular outlook should be rejected. He could argue, among other things, that most contemporary philosophical views opposed to theism do not try to give any rational explanation of the world at all; the world (i.e., the totality of all that there is) is, the secularists claim, just a "brute" inexplicable fact or datum neither susceptible of nor requiring explanation. (How Olympian the serenity with which the modern mind views the mysteries of Nature!) Many varieties of secularism, the religionist may suggest, lack a metaphysic of the ultimate - an eschatology, if you wish. But it is intellectually more satisfying, the defender of religious belief may reasonably argue, to prefer some rational explanation (for the totality of things) to none at all. And we get such a rational explanation if we regard the course of the world as determined by value and purpose than if we do not. Thus, if we adopt the metaphysical principle of seeking to develop a coherent rational system (i.e., of accepting that hypothesis which makes the natural universe more of a rational totality), then theism is a reasonable choice. (Note that this metaphysical principle is characteristically used in natural science). The atheistic alternative according to which there is no rational explanation for the world seems to violate our deepest intuitions - the intuitions of both believers and atheists alike in

some moods. Should we not seek to do justice to the
depth of our intuitions concerning crucial matters?
Does atheism do justice to our desire to seek explanations for what is the case?

These are not meant to be rhetorical questions.
Different people answer them differently. If the
believer wants to win someone over to the side of
faith, he will need to induce a religious vision of
the world. He will have to offer a philosophy of
history which does not despise teleological foundations. It is not unreasonable to suspect that some
atheistic thinkers probably dismiss the very possibility of a teleological interpretation of human
existence for fear that such a possibility may bring
precisely transcendent theism in its train. After
all, why is secularism opposed to the teleological
interpretation of nature if not in deference to the
maxim that my enemy's friend is my enemy? But to
argue, although, of course, no-one has argued so
crudely, that we can't have a teleology of nature
because if we did, we would be committed to some form
of theism, is to assume <u>ab initio</u> the truth of an
essentially atheistic metaphysic.

Resistance to the notion that ultimate meaning or
value somehow reside directly in the nature of things
runs very deep in modern intellectual culture. We
cannot locate any purposes in nature, the secularists
aver. To make sure that no-one tries, they pontificate that questions about ultimate purposes and the
search for supra-naturalistic explanations are, in any
case, incoherent. Questions such as "Why is there
anything at all?" or "What is the ultimate purpose of
man and nature?" are declared incoherent, the outcome
of psychological dislocations attributable to unfortu-

nate early upbringing or unhappy marriage. Believing
writers, predictably enough, respond by asserting that
the question "What is the ultimate purpose of man?"
makes perfectly good sense. It is fairly obvious that
basic intuitions about the nature of the world are
here in uncompromising opposition to each other. That
is the reason, no doubt, for the deadlock involved in
the confrontation between faith and rejection - a
deadlock which has, as I argued in the previous
chapter, disastrous implications for theism in this
secularised era. Believers argue that our experience
of the natural and the social worlds leads reasonable
folk to conclude that the human plight is intelligible, that is, we can conceive an escape from it.
The presence of the religious solution makes our
predicament a meaningful one. It is intellectually
satisfying to know that our lives are grounded in an
ultimate transcendent purpose. (This is not to imply,
by the way, that belief in God is a necessary condition for endowing meaning to our lives.[17]) The
unsympathetic critic will respond by arguing that the
believer is simply muddle-headed, inchoately and
misleadingly expressing certain deep human impulses to
make some sense of this whole nasty affair that life
is[18] - impulses better endowed with expression, more
perspicuously expressed by a more empirically adequate
atheistic humanism which is self-consciously humanistic repudiating as it does the concealed and
pernicious anti-humanism of this monstrous thing
called religion.

There is something deeply unsatisfying about my
discussion of natural theology. It is absolutely
crucial to be clear about the source of this deep-
seated dissatisfaction. In vindicating the possi-

bility of natural theology, one needs to simultaneously vindicate a religious vision of the world.
And the revival of the religious vision of the world
is an all-embracing artistic task involving more than
simply an attack on or a defence of specific controversial claims (although that is, of course, also
necessary).[19]

To vindicate any total vision requires the
support of a total metaphysic. I am suggesting that a
religious metaphysic would need to consist of a teleological interpretation of man and nature. (It may be
a _religious_ task to validate the objectivity of _morals_
and, by implication, to refute ethical subjectivism.)
The theist has to work at _this_ level. The construction of valid arguments for God's existence is a
relatively trivial task. The difficulty is in finding
some uncontentiously true premisses, or even premisses
that it is plausible to believe are true, for a sound
argument. To provide these premisses could itself
hardly be an uncontroversial task.

Would that natural theology were possible! But
perhaps it isn't, the sobering realisation follows.
Now, it is important to see _why_ natural theology is
regarded with scepticism. The scepticism, at its
deepest level, is about the possibility of showing
that the fundamental groundwork of the real - the
essential structure of reality as such - is spiritual
rather than material. And to show that is, of course,
a philosophical task i.e., a task with controversial
metaphysical presuppositions.

The theist's argument is not that since every
metaphysic has some unargued assumptions, therefore
every metaphysic is as good as any other; rather, his
argument is that theism provides the best explanation

for the sorry scheme of things entire. The difficulty, of course, is to locate some Archimedean point
which is neutral between faith and unbelief and hence
capable of supplying detached standards for assessing
the relative merits of radically opposed viewpoints.

Whatever may be said about the possibility,
proper role and content of natural theology, there is
no denying its importance, even indispensability, for
religion.[20] With respect to theism, there are many
sources of universally acknowledged hostile evidence -
the existence, for example, of natural and moral evil,
religious conflict, and so on. A rational defence of
theism would require there to be also, in the balance,
universally acknowledged or acknowledgeable favourable
evidence. To attain this, the theist would need to
search for a metaphysical basis in reality, a basis
which lends objective validity to theological judgements. Only this kind of unequivocal evidence would
suffice since merely permissive evidence (which
allowed the faithful to stick to their religious
convictions without fear of being convicted of irrationality by atheists) would probably cut in the
direction of agnosticism (if not outright atheism)
rather than religious commitment in this secularised
age. A successful natural theology would supply
strong evidence in favour of the religious stance.
And only strong reasons would suffice; impressive
evidence is needed if theism is to be a viable Weltanschauung in competition with a rival as well-
evidenced as atheism.

It is natural to be impressed by the sheer difficulty of the theist's task. And when this happens,
the theist is likely to seek substitutes for natural
theology. The so-called "argument from religious

experience" may, for example, be dragged onto the stage and made to parade as an adequate substitute for more involved theological argument. But this is a poor substitute since the "argument from religious experience" is not really an argument at all. It is a claim to intuitive awareness of what one takes to be a certain kind of reality. The existence of religious emotion or experience does not by itself constitute a valid ground for asserting the existence of God. We need argument to establish that a particular intuitive religious belief is true, that the intuition is genuine. Now, the atheist cannot dismiss the religious claims on the sole ground that they are based on appeals to intuition. One cannot determine by a priori reasoning in which fields genuine intuition is or is not possible. But, equally, the believer must recognise that his private religious experience imposes little obligation on others to accept his truth-claims made on the basis of his religious experience, although the fact that men of unusual integrity and insight have testified to the truth of certain religious claims should give reason for pause to the atheist.

The complexity of the religionist's task is matched only by its importance. The deadlock involved in the confrontation between faith and rejection is a consequence of the failure of natural theology and of, in Plantinga's phrase, a natural atheology i.e., the attempt to show that given what we know, it is impossible or improbable that God exists.[21] A successful natural theology alone could break this deadlock. And it alone could provide intellectual pabulum for the bewildered believer confronted with aggressive atheistic critiques from all sides by

writers like Kai Nielsen, Antony Flew, and A.C. Danto.
Natural theology alone could shoot a fresh woof into
the old warp of faith.

- IV -

An important step in the revival of natural
theology is to establish that faith and reason are
compatible, that there can indeed be such a thing as a
reasonable faith. One often hears people ask "Is
faith compatible with reason?" There is, of course,
no simple affirmative or negative answer to this
question. One needs to subject the terms of the
contrast to a careful analysis.

We heard, in Chapter 2, Søren Kierkegaard's harsh
verdict: there can be no concordat between Christianity and speculative metaphysics, between faith and
reason. Kierkegaard's opposition to combining
Christianity with philosophy is motivated by religious
concerns. His main worry - namely, that any such
combination results in a subordination of Christianity
to secular reason - has already been examined. It is
time now to consider some other reasons Kierkegaard
produces for rejecting a concordat between faith and
reason.

Kierkegaard argues that the academic or rationalist approach to Scripture softens the existential
impact of its truth. The significant changes must,
Kierkegaard counsels us, occur in our motives, intentions, and hopes. The aim of reading Scripture is not
to increase our fund of objective knowledge. A total
change in a man's outlook is needed; and for this
transformation to occur, understanding the truth is
not enough. One does not earn the right to eternal
life merely by understanding what immortality is.

Now, certainly, the emotions and the will must be engaged too if the truth made available by the understanding is to be practically effective in the believer's life. But one has to _know_ the truth (i.e., have an objective theoretical access to it) before one can _appropriate_ it. There is some truth in the claim that rationalist approaches to Scripture dull the keen-bladed impact of biblical imperatives. But it is also true that if one does away with rational assessment altogether or downplays the need for some rationally grounded criterion for judging the authenticity of religious claims, one runs the danger of leaving a believer's will totally defenceless against the onslaught of false but emotionally appealing views. Rationalism in religious thought has borne too many fruits to be lightly dismissed. In very general terms, the emergence of an increasingly purified spirituality in our religious evolution, advances in the rationality and moral quality of religious practice and belief, the greater moral purity of religious doctrine as evidenced by the decline of uncritical dogmatism and exclusivism which plague fundamentalist varieties of any faith - these are all the fruits of a rationalism which we are rightly loathe to abandon.

Kierkegaard is, for rather obscure reasons, fiercely opposed to all metaphysical systems. Reacting against the excesses of an Hegelian rationalism, he argues that all metaphysical systems are anathema to the existentialist thinker. Kierkegaard fears that any systematic metaphysic will have a static character which would preclude the possibility of an individual making free and momentous decisions: there will be no place for the creative variation of

238

the free man whose existential commitments arise unconditioned, as it were, through sheer acts of will. Furthermore, argues Kierkegaard, again rather obscurely, all metaphysical systems have pantheistic implications. And if man is, in any sense, identical with God or with even a moment of God's being, then the passionate God-man encounter is ruined: the stark and pathetic contrast between the "wholly other" God and the despairing subjection of his sinful creatures is lost in a whirl of suspect metaphysics.[22]

No elaborate attempt need be made to counter these objections. Kierkegaard is generalizing illegitimately from the Hegelian rationalist metaphysic to all theoretical systems. While Hegel's metaphysic may well have pantheistic implications, not all metaphysical systems are committed to pantheism. And, with respect to the first objection, the fact that men's actions and acquisition of beliefs can be systematically explained need not entail any lack of freedom in their actions and choices.

But there is, I suspect, a deeper objection to metaphysical systems which underlies these obscure objections, particularly the first one. And it is an objection which is, in a sense, made very frequently by Kierkegaard. Kierkegaard fears that a rational method in theology will result in a finished metaphysical system - a fact which would, Kierkegaard thinks, imply a presumptuous finality in our attempt to understand the world. The fact that the Hegelian metaphysic does seem to presuppose an exact congruity between the natural and the revealed (as if revelation were itself really just a rational occurrence within human history) gives colour to my suspicion. Kierkegaard is, it seems, concerned to attack what he sees

as the intellectual tepidity and complacency of
Hegelian Christianity; he denounces Hegel's overly
rational scheme as a travesty of biblical Christianity
which is replete with emphases on the risks of faith
and the mysteriousness of God.

This is not the place to pursue the question of
whether or not Kierkegaard properly understands Hegel.
All we need to say here is that rational method in
theology presupposes at most a coherent unity of all
experience i.e., that the world is a system rather
than a chaos of unrelated items. It does not presuppose that revelation is unnecessary or that God is
not mysterious or that reason alone can lead us to the
(ultimate) truth. Kierkegaard himself, perhaps
unwittingly, endorses the basic presupposition of
rational method when he says that reality is a system
for God,[23] which implies that no unsystematic view
could be true. (It is worth noting, by the way, that
Kierkegaard's hyperbolic remarks - in which he exalts
the absurd and the unsystematic - obscure the true
import of his fideism. His brand of Christianity is
more rationalistic than either he himself or his
admirers like to think.)

Kierkegaard passionately protests against the
view that scientific knowledge coupled with clarity of
thought will solve the central enigmas of existence.
Reality cannot, he insists, be understood by exclusively intellectual means: reason or intellect alone
cannot lead us to the truth. Theoretical speculation
cannot be a guide for living one's life. But, all of
this notwithstanding, why should we divorce faith from
reason? Surely, the religionist's task is to provide
a synthetic solution to the problem of faith and
reason i.e., to develop a rational metaphysic which

does justice to existential concerns relating to the role of individual decision, God's mysterious nature, the anxiety and risk involved in faith, and so on, without sacrificing the ordinary philosophical concern with objectivity. There is, in principle, no reason why the "objective method" cannot be combined with a due estimate of the place of commitment, passion and risk in the religious life; there is a priori no reason why philosophical objectivity and rational method, on the one hand, should be set in uncompromising opposition to religious "subjectivity" and existential method, on the other.

Both fideism and its rival rationalism are distortions. Each side makes totalitarian claims on behalf of one element - faith or reason - suitably isolated from the other and too exclusively emphasised at the expense of the other. It would be surprising if the whole essence of a phenomenon as complex as religion was to be properly located in one element alone. Clearly, both elements are important. Epistemic concepts (such as those of knowledge, evidence, truth, and justification) cannot be relinquished, the rationalists rightly urge, if theism is to be intellectually respectable. But, equally, of course, the fideists rightly wish to emphasise the limits of our sin-riven reason - the religious analogue to the secular doctrine of the limits of reason - and the role of judgement, decision, and choice in matters of ultimate importance. (It is, however, a little disturbing to note that the fideists place the limits of reason rather suspiciously close to the bounds of their own very Protestant understanding.) The existentialist idiom so favoured by fideists should not, however, be contrasted with the epistemic one so dear to their rationalist opponents; rather, the epistemic or intellectualist element should be supplemented by providing a vocabulary for giving accounts of the relation between religious belief and religious conduct and of how choice, volition and faith somehow interpose between religious belief and religious behaviour.

The total opposition of religious faith and intellectual belief is an exaggeration, and indeed a dangerous one. For Kierkegaard, as for Wittgenstein, the religious use of "believe" is utterly different from the use of the same word in non-religious (for example, scientific or commonsensical) contexts. And this is unsurprising once we divorce faith from reason. That unreason then becomes the hallmark of religious belief is also unsurprising.

The opposition between faith and reason is rooted, it seems to me, in an essential ambiguity in the religious concept of faith derivative from the Bible. On the one hand, there is the conative non-epistemological view of faith (fiducia) which seeks to identify faith exclusively as a personal relationship of trust and devotion. God is seen as the object of such devotion and men are advised to trust in his providential care. It is thought, mistakenly, that there can be acquaintance or encounter with a reality without one's entertaining any implied propositions about the reality in question i.e., that one can know God without necessarily entertaining any true ideas about him. This assumption is rejected by the cognitive view of faith (fides), according to which one should identify faith in terms of its intellectual content, emphasising some distinctive and central truths about God and the created realm. Now, clearly,

both views of faith are, taken singly, false: the
cognitive one because, if faith were indeed a matter
solely of entertaining true propositions about God, if
the intellectualist strain alone were significant,
then only some theologians and philosophers of
religion would be said to have faith - a view patently
contradicted by the history of prophetic religion and,
moreover, inherently incredible; and the conative view
is false because it seems absurd to suppose that the
content of faith should necessarily defy articulation.
(Hebrews 11:6, incidentally, supports a synthetic view
which combines the conative and the cognitive strands
in faith: "For whoever would draw near to God must
believe that he exists and that he rewards those who
seek him."[24])

Let me re-pose the question with which I began
this section: "Is faith compatible with reason?"
Religious thinkers have given very different, sometimes incompatible, answers to this question. Faith
has priority over reason in, for example, the programme associated with Augustine and which dominated
Christian thought, through Anselm, and until the
advent of Aquinas. Understanding is the reward of
faith - not a condition of it. But slogans like
"fides quaerens intellectum" or "Credo ut intelligam"
are not likely to impress those outside the faith or
those who simply happen to regard such views as sympto-
matic of misguided priorities.

A more promising answer to the problem of compatibility is that of St. Thomas Aquinas. The Saint
argues that rational philosophical truths are indeed
different in character and status from revealed ones.
Some religious doctrines are supported by reason but
others are not. These latter are truths guaranteed by

revelation but beyond the power of human reason to discover, <u>fully</u> understand or validate. Such doctrines are not in opposition to reason but rather beyond it; their meaning can coherently be articulated but their truth cannot be established. Thus, one can rationally prove doctrines concerning the existence of God, the unity of God, and the providential ordering of the world. But no rational argument, Aquinas tells us, could prove that there are three Persons of one substance in the Godhead or that the world was created <u>ex nihilo</u> by divine fiat. And yet one needs to entertain both beliefs which reason validates <u>and</u> those beyond its capacity to validate, according to Aquinas, in order to achieve salvation. This ingenious amalgam of faith and reason, of natural and revealed theology, must, I suggest, be the model for Jewish, Christian, and Islamic thought. St. Thomas' monumental <u>Summa Theologiae</u> is an attempt to work out the details of a synthetic solution to the problem of faith and reason; he sets out to establish the foundations of a religious epistemology which can accommodate a non-rational supplementation of reason by assigning a significant place to revelation.

A religion of fanatically intense conviction with little or no resources for self-criticism is not the result of an excess of faith but rather of a theoretical divorce between faith and reason. The fideists mistakenly thought that to remove reason from the religious domain was <u>pro tanto</u> to strengthen faith. In fact, once faith is deprived of its rational foundations, it is enervated. It is more liable to evoke fanaticism and sentimentality thereby falling easy prey to the atheist's charge that religious conviction is ideological. (There is here, incidentally, no

disguised reliance on a persuasive definition of
"faith" or "true faith".) Faith, in the final
analysis, has to be "zeal according to knowledge", in
St. Paul's idiom, not "belief without reason" as one
contemporary essayist has it.[25] And it certainly need
not demand any Kierkegaardian sacrificium intellectus.

- V -

Before giving a final assessment of the rationality of Christian religious commitment in the modern
world, I want to address a number of problems which
may arise during the development of a natural theology
and indeed, more broadly, during the development of a
defence of religious conviction. I restrict my attention to four concerns which bear directly on the task
of justifying religious belief in the modern world.

The first two concerns are best identified by,
for convenience, concentrating on Kai Nielsen's philosophy of religion.[26] The concept of God in non-
anthropomorphic religious discourse is, according to
Nielsen, incoherent - a fact which explains the
perennial failure of natural theology. Application of
a strident verificationism to religious language leads
Nielsen to conclude that it is devoid of factual
significance. Nothing could count for or against the
truth of the non-anthropomorphic religious beliefs of
the mature Judaeo-Christian-Islamic tradition; such
beliefs are, therefore, devoid of factual significance. Nielsen's argument is a linguistic one:
nothing could conceivably correspond in reality to the
concept of God as it occurs in developed monotheistic
thought. No evidence is or could be relevant to the
truth of the claim "God exists" because, as philosophical analysis reveals to us, this claim is,

properly speaking, unintelligible albeit not flatly
so. The search for God is, one might say, like the
search for the married bachelor. One may hear wonderful stories about the blissful abode where men enjoy
the double luxury denied to them in less exotic loca-
tions. But it is all fantasy. So it is with God,
too. Religious discourse is, when properly analysed,
actually incoherent and factually meaningless, though
often endowed with a powerful emotive force.

Part of the reason why both ordinary and sophisticated believers alike fail to see the incoherence of
their religious convictions is that they evade the
issue at some crucial juncture. This brings me onto
our second concern. Believers have generally held
that God is opaque to human reason; a being whose
intentions were penetrable or transparent would, it
has been thought, be the lesser for it. Religious
writers have contended that if there is a God, it is
only to be expected a priori that in regard to a great
deal of what he is alleged to be doing in the world,
we should be puzzled. The subject-matter of religion
is necessarily only partially accessible to human
understanding. Now Nielsen has, in general, very
little sympathy with this kind of reasoning; indeed,
he fulminates against believing writers who argue
thus. "Theologians", he remarks caustically, "speak
of opacity or of mystery when what is actually
involved is incoherence and obfuscation".[27] To be
fair to Nielsen, though, he does not deny that the
concept of a mysterious deity is an ineliminable part
of first-order religious belief.

I begin with the charge of incoherence. Two
preliminary comments are in order. Firstly, Nielsen's
linguistic critique of theism would, if successful,

achieve a colossally important result: it would
decisively undercut the possibility of natural theology and provide a conclusive reason for espousing
atheism. The consequences of its success would be
parallel to those of the success of the _a priori_
ontological argument for God's existence: if
Nielsen's argument is sound, we have an _a priori_
disproof of God's existence, i.e., since the concept
of God is incoherent, God cannot possibly exist. If
the ontological argument turned out to be a sound one,
it would follow that atheism is demonstrably false;
and the need - present in the case of the _a posteriori_
arguments for God's existence - to argue for an identification of this being (whose existence is being
proved) with the perfect God of the Scriptures is also
dissolved. Now, the fact that the success of these _a_
priori arguments (from either camp) would imply an
impressive and decisive refutation or consolidation of
a perenially disputed claim - a controversial claim,
if you will - is itself one of the reasons for remaining sceptical of their alleged success. This is not
cynicism. It is intellectual caution; and we need it
to ensure that in matters of great importance, issues
are not prematurely thought to be resolved for, in
giving the appearance of decisive resolution of keenly
disputed claims, one runs the risk, absent from most
areas of modern philosophy, of misguiding people
concerning matters of moment.

Secondly, the success of Nielsen's case against
theism would _ipso facto_ serve to discredit a number of
fideistic and neo-fideistic strategies for validating
God-talk. Many reductionists and fideists implicitly
accept positivist restraints and, in effect, endorse
the positivist conclusion that theological knowledge-

247

claims are incoherent and then pretend that this is not a disquieting result since one can still believe theological propositions on faith or, in a related strategy, by hoping that they are true. It has been suggested, for example, that religion is to be regarded not as involving beliefs in the supernatural but rather as involving hopes for the realisation of supernatural states of affairs (like immortality or divine judgement).[28] But, for a theological proposition P, if it is incoherent to believe that P or claim to know that P, then it is equally incoherent to have faith that P (or trust that P) or to hope that P. For if P is incoherent or meaningless, then in having faith in its truth or in hoping for it I do not know what I have faith in or hope for anymore than in believing it I know what I believe.[29]

Nielsen argues that for a theological claim to be factually meaningful, there must be some conceivable (empirical) evidence which would serve to confirm or infirm it i.e., it must be at least weakly testable. There is, he argues, no conceivable state of affairs which would or could count as confirming the truth of the proposition "God exists". Nielsen seems to be suggesting that the concept of God is incoherent and that, consequently, no conceivable evidence could be adduced in favour of the proposition "God exists". But it is not clear whether Nielsen regards the concept of God as incoherent because the notion is self-contradictory or whether he thinks that religious claims containing a reference to God are factually meaningless because they are unverifiable. Now, if the worry is that "There exists an infinite, personal individual transcendent to the world" is a meaningless claim, then, of course, the attempt to adduce evidence for it is indeed pointless. But if the sole reason why it is thought meaningless is the absence of evidence for it, it is open to the theist to argue that there is (or at least could be) some evidence in favour of the claim. My own suspicion is that Nielsen is employing a strict version of the verifiability principle so that the incoherence of the concept of God is being deduced from the unverifiability of the claim that it is instantiated. And the unverifiability of the claim that it is instantiated is itself deduced from a prior a _priori_ conviction that the concept is incoherent. Nielsen is playing it both ways.

Now, since we are allowed to construct any logically possible scenarios that would serve to confirm theism, we need not worry about the fact that the kinds of circumstances that would serve to confirm the truth of the theist's contention are themselves so fantastic that the likelihood of their ever actually obtaining is itself something we know, on inductive grounds, to be very remote indeed. Let us suppose, then, that on a bright day during full term, an essay on philosophical theology appeared over the august segment of the sky which clouds Calgary University's Philosophy Department. (I suppose philosophers could argue endlessly over whether or not this would constitute an utterance but I shall simply assume that it does.) It singled out, for special censure, Kai Nielsen and Antony Flew for having published voluminous writings which had become an obstacle to the faith of many an undergraduate. There was no scientific explanation for this event, it seemed; there was, for example, no evidence that the Christians on campus led by Terence Penelhum and Hugo

Meynell had enlisted the services of the Physics
Department to create an illusion. Let us further
suppose that similar essays appeared in other parts of
the world in the windows of disbelieving writers. The
occurrence of this admittedly unlikely set of events
would not only put the truth of theism beyond (reasonable) dispute but also serve to hasten the conversion
of Nielsen, Flew, and their cronies.

I am not saying that it is reasonable to believe
in God only if such miracles really do happen. In
fact, it is religiously inappropriate to make God into
a miracle-worker pandering to the human desire for the
spectacular: an evil and adulterous generation
seeketh after a sign and no sign shall be given unto
them. The point, of course, of constructing such
admittedly bizarre scenarios is to show that there is
a conceivable set of circumstances, empirically identifiable, which would, if it were to obtain, constitute
evidence in favour of the theistic contention.

Nielsen succeeds in making us appreciate the
peculiarity of first-order God-talk. But he fails to
show that theological claims must be without factual
significance. Since Nielsen is committed a priori to
the belief that nothing could even in principle verify
theism, the demand for empirical evidence here is
hypocritical. If one does not allow anything to count
in favour of a religious claim, it cannot be a matter
for any great surprise that nothing is found to do so.
Just as the scientist will not allow anything - any
event or state of affairs - to count as evidence of
disorder in nature, similarly Nielsen will not allow
any conceivable state of affairs to count as evidence
for the claim that God exists or acts. But Nielsen's
imposition of a logical veto on the possibility of

evidence for religious claims renders hypocritical his incessant demand for empirical evidence. The problem of God's existence is not an experimental one, for Nielsen, and hence the demand for evidence is out of place.

Nielsen could, of course, reply that he has discovered the alleged fact that no experience could verify theism. But while it is certainly possible to discover such a thing, the way in which he actually conducts his case seems to suggest that he is not prepared to allow anything to count as evidence for the existence of God. And where such strictures operate, it is hypocritical to demand evidence.

Nielsen claims that where there can be no direct evidence, there can be no indirect evidence either. Direct evidence is, of course, in the theistic case, logically banned since the God of developed monotheism is a non-spatiotemporal entity which cannot be directly observed. Now, it seems to me, what really sustain Nielsen's extravagant view are two controversial epistemological assumptions: firstly, that indirect evidence is impossible to attain unless direct evidence also is or could be available and, secondly, that indirect evidence can never be compelling. As to the first claim, the theist can simply protest that while there is indeed no direct evidence for the existence of God, there can be indirect evidence. As to the second claim, the theist is at liberty to reject it as straightforwardly false: indirect evidence is not always inconclusive.

I cannot pursue this issue any further. But before moving onto the second problem mentioned earlier, I shall make two observations. Firstly, the real problem in this secularised age is not so much the unintelligibility of religious language (or rather, more accurately, the kind of language involved in religious beliefs) but rather the widespread decay of the religious sentiments which such language expresses and masks. "Pious", "sinful" and "righteous" are pejorative words and stand for unfashionable moral postures. There may, in other words, be general cultural reasons for the disrepute into which religious language has fallen. Secondly, and more importantly, the demonstration of the coherence of the concept of God must be a prolegomena to any future natural theology.[30]

I turn now to the second concern. There is one seemingly innocuous demand Nielsen makes on religious thinkers which may actually be an illegitimate one. Nielsen insists on intellectual honesty; he counsels believing writers to shun evasion. Even granted that God is an ultimate mystery, an account of the mysterious need not, Nielsen reminds believers, itself be mysterious.[31]

Now, the concept of an inscrutably mysterious deity is, as Nielsen himself admits and indeed occasionally emphasises, an integral part of primary religious belief. The very first-order religious discourse contains a reliance on the mysteriousness of God and hence on the necessarily partial explication of the central concept. There are special a priori reasons why we cannot understand God in toto. Whatever reality could be fully understood would, for that very reason, fail to be the deus arcanus of religious faith. Thus, while an account of the mysterious need not itself be mysterious, it must be partial since there can be no complete account of the mysterious reality God is taken to be.

The charge of evasion, frequently meted out to believing writers by Nielsen, is, I believe, a deeply problematic one. "Evasion" is a term of philosophical (i.e., artistic) criticism. If "evasion" amounts to a deliberate attempt at remaining ignorant of rational philosophical challenges to one's views or a tendency to be dismissive of the intricacies of philosophical reflection, then it is indeed a deplorable and culpable tendency. Thus, the refusal to become rationally cognisant of contemporary scepticism about the intelligibility and truth of religious claims may justifiably be seen as being evasive. But the theist's refusal to elevate every (apparent) anomaly or paradox into a contradiction on the sole ground that <u>he</u> cannot immediately resolve it is not necessarily tantamount to evasion. Perhaps, on occasion, he may appeal, reasonably, to the fact that someone else can resolve it or that time is needed before a resolution can be achieved. And what appears as evasion to an unsympathetic critic may well in fact be a methodologically defensible reliance on the technique of shelving difficulties in the hope of future resolution. Such a reliance is frequently noted in the case of secular inquirers; we recognise, for example, the right of natural scientists to persist in, say, looking for causal explanations of recalcitrant events and to refuse to abandon their search prematurely. It is easy enough, both in religion and in secular areas of inquiry, to conflate this methodologically justifiable procedure of shelving difficulties which await resolution, on the one hand, with the unjustifiable wish to remain ignorant of or indifferent to sceptical challenges, on the other.

Nielsen endorses the current philosophical assumption that one of the roles of philosophy is the clarification of concepts. There are, however, limits to
conceptual clarification and these are neither identical for all disciplines nor ascertainable a priori.
Now, religious reality is irreducibly mysterious
unlike, say, political reality which is merely indefinitely complex.[32] No methodology of religion could
be adequate unless it recognised the centrality of
mystery in religion. And a recognition of this peculiarity of the religious realm would be empty unless
some provision were made, at a theoretical level, for
taking account of this feature. Hence, it could be,
for example, that some "evasive" moves - and remember
that "evasion" is a term of artistic criticism -
should be allowed as a legitimate part of theological
method. (Is Nielsen smuggling into religion an ideal
of clarity and insight appropriate to politics and
other areas of secular knowledge?[33])

Aristotle is a good guide here. One should
allocate, he advises us, an ideal of rigour appropriate to the nature of the subject-matter.[34]
Perhaps, all we can reasonably expect in religion,
given the essential elusiveness of the subject-matter,
is, as Ian Crombie urged a while ago, a rough sense.[35]

These remarks are liable to be misunderstood.
While believers cannot reasonably be expected to
simply deny the mysteriousness of God (and answer
atheistic critique on that basis), they cannot claim
that the mysteriousness of God's nature is a sufficient explanation for every alleged contradiction or
anomaly the critic produces. The believer should,
for instance, be allowed to claim that a particular
problem (say, the problem of evil) is indeed ulti-

mately resolvable because, say, God has a morally
sufficient reason, unknown to men, for allowing evil.
If, however, the difficulties with theism prove over-
whelmingly intractable - and judgement is needed to
decide when this has indeed happened - then the appeal
to mystery can no longer be a justified one. Such an
appeal is justified only in the context of a generally
viable account of religious conviction. Hence, if
belief in God commits us to a plethora of views independently judged to be implausible - Cartesianism in
the case of God's mental life, the unreality of evil
in attempting to account for the extraordinary amount
of evil on Earth - and if we can believe in God merely
as a bare possibility which is not at all plausible,
then we should abandon the religious stance. Again,
if the enterprise of natural theology turns out to be
a complete failure or issues forth in disappointingly
meagre results or if the concept of divine revelation
runs into intractable difficulties, we should abandon
faith in God. But note that this is not really very
different from the way in which secular Weltanschau-
ungen come to be abandoned.

One final word about evasion. Evasion is not the
monopoly of religious thinkers. Evasion occurs in
many areas of intellectual inquiry although it is
usually more easily detectable when it occurs in an
area whose epistemological pretensions are deemed
unfashionable. When evasion is located, one should
exercise charity. And certainly such charity would
not be out of place with respect to religion: if a
secular understanding of the world is difficult, is a
task, how much more so must the religious understanding be.

The third and fourth concerns arise from the believing side of the street, so to speak. It is too much to expect people to philosophize to the glory of God in an age which regards belief in God as something akin to madness. But there are two temptations the secularist must resist. The first is the temptation to dismiss the problem of God's existence as bogus, to regard it as in some way trivial or unworthy of sustained and serious reflection. The second is the temptation to employ prejudicially rigorous standards for assessing the reasonableness of religious conviction. Unbelieving writers, often men of great intellectual stature, have succumbed to both these temptations.

It is often said that what characterises our age is its rejection of the older supernatural or transcendent order which imposed a normative significance on man in the natural world. But this characterisation, while not wholly false, is not very discerning or truly perceptive. A more accurate characterisation of this era, it seems to me, is the one according to which this age is distinguished by an inherited absence of a concept that conscious atheists like Nietzsche, Schopenhauer, Bakunin, and Marx were vehemently denouncing, in the previous century, as empty. After all, men have rejected God throughout history, albeit in a less extensive and more concealed fashion. To be sure, the biblical fool and his descendants merely denied the relevance of God, not his existential reality.[36] (One supposes that the foolishness involved in denying God's existence, the folly of speculative atheism, if you wish, was reserved for our age.) But whatever may be said on that score, there is no doubt that many modern thinkers regard the problem of God's existence as bogus.

Naturally men have disputes concerning the status of many philosophical problems. For example, as we saw in Chapter 5, there is considerable controversy concerning whether or not certain traditional metaphysical puzzles about the existence of other minds or the external world need be taken seriously. I argued that the outcome of the puzzles was not in serious dispute and that the whole affair was an intellectual pastime for some thinkers. But, surely, one could hardly say the same concerning the problem of the existence of God. This is no mere academic conundrum. It is an important problem if not the most important problem of all. It is not a problem invented by some thinker to fill his leisure.

There is no excuse whatsoever for the shocking degree of frivolity with which the problem of God's existence has sometimes been treated. If men are to reject God, they must earn the right to do so. Otherwise, disbelief may become, as it has for many modern thinkers, merely a cultural prejudice. Unlike a thinker like Nietzsche - who earned the right to reject God if any man ever did[37] - otherwise profound thinkers like Jean-Paul Sartre and Bertrand Russell adopted atheism with remarkably little serious reflection. What characterises our age is not atheism but rather lack of spiritual seriousness.

Take the two modern intellectual giants I have just mentioned. Both Sartre and Russell became atheists in circumstances which are simply laughable. Sartre, for example, boasts that he was liberated from the theistic illusion at the tender age of twelve. While waiting for three Brazilian girls to get dressed

one day, the notion suddenly struck the young Sartre
that God does not exist. Given the incredible obtuse-
ness of these claims, I suspect the reader's credi-
bility will be challenged. Lest parody be suspected,
I quote directly:

> My parents had rented a villa a little way
> out of La Rochelle when I was about twelve,
> and in the morning I used to take the tram
> with the girls next door, three Brazilians
> called Machado who went to the girls' lycée.
> One day I was walking up and down outside
> their house for a few minutes waiting for
> them to get ready. I don't know where the
> thought came from or how it struck me, yet
> all at once I said to myself, "But God
> doesn't exist!" It's quite certain that
> before this I must have had new ideas about
> God and that I had begun solving the problem
> for myself. But still, as I remember very
> well, it was on that day and in the form of
> a momentary intuition, that I said to
> myself, "God doesn't exist." It's striking
> to reflect that I thought this at the age of
> eleven and that I never asked myself the
> question again until today, that is, for
> sixty years.[38]

It is instructive to note that only <u>dogmatic</u>
atheists and <u>dogmatic</u> believers find it unnatural to
see the problem of God's existence as a genuine one.
Religious apologists pontificate that all men know
that God exists and that only self-deception and
perversity can account for atheism. It is obvious, we
are told, that God exists. On the yonder side of the

valley, many atheists assert that, given the modern supremacy of rational scientific techniques for controlling the forces of nature, the continued presence of religion can only be due to early indoctrination and ideological mystification. And once each party settles down for the night, there is little hope of any progress.

Those atheists who do regard the problem of God's existence as worthy of serious attention err, unfortunately, in other ways. One of the most damaging traits of work by sceptical thinkers has been the tendency to engage in prejudicially rigorous examination of theistic claims. Thus, for example, atheists have often tended to demand stricter criteria of rationality and proof in religion than in other areas of inquiry - criteria which are themselves derived from a consideration of various logico-scientific (and hence non-religious) intuitions. Instead of treating religious claims with less rigour (in view of the inherent limitations on our understanding of religious reality), as I suggested earlier, unbelieving writers have often treated religious claims with greater rigour and done so using alien standards developed to give substance to intuitions originally generated in habitats uncongenial to religion.

Take, for example, the principle of verification. This principle was developed by scientists and mathematicians to give substance and formal expression to various intuitions generated, unsurprisingly, by work in natural science and mathematics. Subsequently, it came to be thought that the principle could, with minor qualifications, yield criteria of meaning for more or less all areas of human inquiry. Now, given the history of this principle's development, one would think that writers today would apply it to religious discourse with some misgivings. The opposite is, in fact, generally true. Kai Nielsen, for example, uses a stringent version of the verifiability criterion (which demands conclusive verfication or falsification for purposes of endowing meaning to a claim) at crucial points in his indictment of John Hick's claim that some post-mortem experiences would, if they were to occur, put the truth of Christian theism beyond reasonable dispute; but Nielsen, revealingly, reverts to a liberal version of the same criterion (which demands that some evidence be available in order for a claim to be confirmable and hence meaningful) when discussing our ordinary secular claim to know that there exists an external world. More precisely, in one place Nielsen recognises that a statement about a material object may be confirmed beyond reasonable doubt, although it is not entailed by the sense-datum statements that support it. And yet in his discussion of theism, he insists that the theistic claims can be confirmed beyond reasonable doubt if and only if the experiences jointly entail the truth of the theistic interpretation. As long as the truth of the atheistic interpretation of a particular set of events adduced to confirm theism remains even a logical possibility, Nielsen will opt for the atheistic interpretation.[39]

Isn't this tantamount to using prejudicially rigorous criteria for assessing the validity of theological assertions? Is it surprising that the demands of theological positivism cannot be met by Christian discourse? No doubt, supporting such prejudicial rigour is the belief that somehow the problems encountered in religion are unique and that theology is, in

virtue of its concern with the metaphysical, extraordinarily different from all other branches of human
inquiry. This positivist dogma is surely questionable
quite apart from the fact that the uniqueness of
religious problems - and religious problems are indeed
unique - does not imply that they do not or cannot
share some epistemologically significant aspects with
non-religious problems.

There are, of course, many other problems, both
related and unrelated to these four, which need to be
tackled. I have merely sketched the outlines of a few
which seem to me obviously relevant, important, and
sometimes neglected. It is time now, while bearing
these concerns in mind, to offer an assessment of the
rationality of Christian commitment in the modern
world, and, in doing so, to bring this essay to a
close.

- VI -

There is a motley cluster of issues needing
attention in this final section. I begin with three
unrelated preliminary remarks.

Firstly, if we wish to offer an assessment of the
rationality of religious conviction in the modern
world, we must give separate assessments for different
religious traditions. The cultural situation in which
Christianity, for example, finds itself today is
entirely different from that in which, say, Hinduism
or Buddhism or Islam find themselves. Hence, for
example, while God may be dead culturally and politically in the West, Allah is alive and well in the
East. (It may require a major heretical movement to
create the Muslim response to modernity.)

Religions differ among themselves. They differ in terms of the conceptual and doctrinal claims they make, the moral and political implications of their theologies, and so on. The problems which a philosophy of the Christian religion is concerned to investigate may differ considerably from those which a philosophy of Hinduism, to take just one example, is concerned to investigate. The tendency to generalise to all religions from a consideration of the status of de facto Christianity is one which, given our knowledge of rival religious traditions today, is entirely unjustified. It is unforgivably occidocentric to generalise from the experience of one faith to all others as if the religious experience in Jerusalem or Teheran were the same as in Berlin and Copenhagen.

Someone may think that while my remarks hold for the so-called Eastern religions (which need to be assessed separately from the Western ones), surely one can reasonably lump together the three "heavenly" religions for purposes of philosophical and political analysis. This is an error. The situation of Christianity, Judaism, and Islam is importantly different. Conceptually and doctrinally, problems such as those of original sin or the Incarnation arise primarily in Christian thought; conversely, the moral problem of justifying "holy war" arises predominantly in Islam but not in Christianity. And, similarly, there are aspects of Judaism which differentiate it in a crucial manner from its sister religions. Again, politically, while a religion like Buddhism - if indeed Buddhism is a religion and not just "spiritual hygiene"[40] - tends to neglect its socio-political obligations, Islam, at the other extreme, takes them very seriously. (There are religious religions and political religions, if you like.) That religion is an opiate, that religious belief dulls men's political consciousness, is manifestly false if seen as a general thesis. The political experience of European Christianity, from which social theorists like Marx derived their theories about the political implications of religious doctrines, is not universal. Whatever may be said of the political vigour of the Mosaic dispensation or of the political powers latent in modern Pauline Christianity, Muhammad's political religion, for better or for worse, still topples the dynasties.

Nietzsche alone among nineteenth century thinkers realised that the three heavenly religions are worthy of individual scrutiny. For Nietzsche, only the God of Paul and his followers is a pitiable and ungodlike figure - "Deus, qualem Paulus creavit, dei negatio".[41] The God of the Jews and the Muslims, the being whose power could only be ignored at the risk of terrible consequences, is one that Nietzsche, given his admiration for power, would not have despised to worship if only such a God had existed. Again, in his critique of asceticism, Nietzsche judiciously restricts the scope of his remarks to Christianity, recognising that Islam is not an inherently anti-sensualist faith. (It is noteworthy that the fantastic variety of self-torments invented by Christian ascetics has always been relatively foreign even to the most enthusiastic of Islamic sects.) Finally, it is to Nietzsche's credit that "the two great European narcotics"[42] which ruined Europe, according to Nietzsche, are listed as alcohol and Christianity, not alcohol and religion (or alcohol and the religious instinct), as some less discerning social critic - like Marx, Freud, or Feuerbach - may well have said.

Secondly, in considering the problem of the rationality of religious conviction, we should construe concepts of proof and evidence in a historico-biographical manner so that we can predicate rationality of a man's believings (as opposed to predicating rationality of the propositions believed in). In this way, we can take account of the fact that the socio-psychological bases of different men's belief in God may differ. The rationality of a given believer's commitment is a function of his beliefs and knowledge, not of the actual metaphysical or logical grounds, if such there are, for belief in God. Hence, if I have a proof of God's existence, this fact cannot render someone else's belief in God rational if he or she does not have such a proof even though it may render my belief in God justified and rational. There are two implications of this assumption. One implication is that I can rationally believe a proposition such as "There exists a supreme Creator" while someone else may believe the same proposition and do so irrationally. The rationality of religious conviction is likely to vary somewhat from person to person and indeed from culture to culture even though, no doubt, most people's commitment to their religious beliefs will not be any more or less rational than that of most other members of the community to which they belong. Another implication is that we cannot say sans phrase whether belief in God is rational. And this is indeed a controversial assumption whose truth I shall simply take for granted here.

Thirdly, the sceptic's demand for evidence or proof (in the ordinary sense of these words) is indeed

justified. It is not a question-begging request.
Religion sets out to be rational, the Wittgensteinian
fideists to the contrary notwithstanding; and it is a
critic's right to convict religious belief of irrationality on the ground that it violates some generally
accepted standard of rationality. The defender of
faith must show that, in fact, a thorough examination
of experience reveals evidence to support the claim
that transcendent theism is a more reasonable explanation of the facts than is its rival naturalistic
atheism, that indeed theism is in no sense cognitively
inferior to atheism and is, moreover, morally and
humanly superior to its atheistic rival. Following
Basil Mitchell's lead, he may argue that Christian
theism is the most intellectually appealing alternative among all the coherent options available
although none of these options (including the
Christian theistic one) is demonstrably true. Thus,
the defender of Christian theism may set himself the
task of showing that Christianity, one world-picture
in competition with others, is to be preferred to all
other such systems if it makes the best sense of all
the available evidence or, equivalently, has the most
impressive "cumulative case" in its favour.[43] (This
is, naturally, like all other tasks concerning issues
of moment, a controversial one whose success or
failure will be keenly disputed.) Negatively, the
Christian thinker must argue that those who reject
faith rely on fallacious arguments, ignore relevant
evidence and, more subtly, interpret too narrowly the
meaning or import of "evidence", "rational proof", and
so on.

We are now in a position to offer a brief final
assessment of the rationality of Christian conviction

in the modern world. Now, theology is a systematic attempt to offer reasoned evidence for the truth of controversial religious claims. Interpretation and judgement are needed at crucial points. Theology is, in this respect, no different from most of the human (social) sciences: neither the methods used nor the results obtained escape keen criticism from one quarter or another.

One of the many challenges of modernity is the one posed by the unprecedented amount of secular knowledge, made available by the special sciences, which needs to be integrated into a viable religious _Zeitgeist_. It will be one of the exciting uncertainties of this age whether or not Christianity and the other historical religions can absorb this knowledge without compromising the integrity of their own religious messages. Now, while the methods and conclusions of the sciences cannot be ignored by theologians, they can impose a theological interpretation on the facts discovered by the empirical scientist. Thus, a Christian thinker will seek to assign a Christian significance to claims made by secular historians and psychologists. For example, he may argue that God chose a particular socio-historical mechanism (such as events in the history of ancient Israel) to make himself known to men and to sanctify certain human institutions (such as marriage and legality); he may argue that God finds a basis in the psychological constitution of human nature - our need for security, for example - in order to make himself known to mankind. Again, the findings of archaeology - the ruined habitations, the bygone nations - will be seen, by the religionist, as constituting a vital and relevant lesson about divine judgement. There is no reason in principle why the religious thinker cannot combine some scientific hypotheses (such as the ones proffered by secular science) with some metaphysical religious claims in the manner indicated. Nor is this synthetic technique restricted to the theologian's dealings with secular history and psychology. A Christian thinker may, to give an example from another discipline, appropriate the Marxist claim that the treatment of workers as mere commodities is wrong and do so on the ground that it is contrary to the Christian law of love. That these attempts at synthesis may sometimes appear tortured or artificial or even fail completely cannot be denied. But the alternative - namely, isolation of religion from secular intellectual activity - is not an attractive one.

Faith is a fundamental attitude in the religious life. The religionist's project is to show that it is, for an educated and reasonable man in modern industrial society, a rational attitude, that it has a sound intellectual basis. How do men come to have faith in God? Is it rational to do so today given the prevalence of secular intellectual norms in the advanced industrial societies?

In answering these questions, one needs to bear in mind that religion is not some recently concocted phenomenon. It is, in fact, the basis of an extraordinarily fertile and fundamental aspect of human life and thought throughout history. It has been the dominant factor in the lives of so many who were in other respects obviously among the greatest and best of our species. It is not an unreasoning prejudice to claim that humanism cannot boast of disciples quite so great as St. Francis, Sir Thomas More, Moses, Milton, and Muhammad.

But what does this show? To be sure, simplistic accounts won't do any more. It won't do simply to list the names of famous believers any more than it would to list the names of famous disbelievers. (But doing that is not entirely irrelevant.) Any account of the rationality of religious conviction is bound to be a complex one. I noted in the previous chapter that many religionists regard atheism as obviously irrational - an outcome of obstinacy, ignorance, and self-deception. It is time now to light the candle at the other end. Many atheists think that religion - all religion - is simply an illusion whose true character must constantly be hidden from the believer. Religion is that "heavenly swindle"[44] which obscures our social hopes, causes grief - in fine, costs us half the kingdom. Belief in God, some atheists aver, is always the result of wish fulfillment, self-deception, and the perceived threats implicit in the impermanence of life and the inevitability of death. These causes of religious belief, they argue, could be entirely adequate without in any way involving the truth of religious views.

If one _defines_ religious belief as an essentially pre-rational or anti-rational phenomenon, one begs the question concerning the rationality of religious belief. This is an elementary point. But so much of the scientific study of religion is founded on a neglect of it: writers first assume, for general theoretical reasons, that religion is an inherently irrational and rudimentary attempt to control and placate nature and then offer explanations for the fact that religion persists despite the prevalence of the superior rational techniques of science. Their explanation, unsurprisingly enough, is that religion is a dangerous distortion of reality, an illusion whose true character must be concealed from the believer if the charm is to work.

Now, to be sure, belief in God may well be the outcome of a desire to avoid the harsh realities of life in an indifferent and brutal world. But if there are some factors which would make a man likely to hold a belief in God even if it were false, one should also put in the balance the fact that there are others which would make him likely to reject the belief even if it were true. Psychological explanations provide a double- edged sword. Certainly, the old view that the weak and emotionally crippled folk come to terms with their sordid lives by turning their eyes towards Heaven is a legend which can easily be stripped of its fantasies. It is a colossally simplistic account of the place of religious belief in believers' lives. To be sure, there is such a thing as <u>neurotic</u> religious belief; but there is also such a thing as <u>healthy and emotionally balanced</u> religious belief. And this distinction is available within religion. Religion has some resources for making such distinctions and, more generally, for effecting self-criticism. It has not in general been necessary for believers to convert to Marxism to see their own failings.

Any belief is unjustified if its causal history is suspect: any belief due simply to a desire to hold the belief must be unjustified for the person who thus holds it. Certainly, religious conviction does not always arise out of a desire to believe what is pleasant. In fact, religious beliefs often make unwelcome demands on the believers; and far from removing men's fears, religion contributes greatly to some kinds of fears. The atheist has to show that the history of a particular religious belief is indeed suspect. And even if he succeeds in showing that the causes of a man's beliefs are suspect, it need not enable him to understand the reasons (or the believer's reasons) for holding such beliefs. To understand the socio-psychological needs to which religion is alleged to be a response, for example, may not be sufficient to discredit the beliefs themselves. To explain why men hold religious beliefs is not necessarily tantamount to debunking the beliefs themselves.

The worries still persist: Does God exist? How do we know? Is there an alternative to religion? It is often said nowadays that what we need is an utterly secularised way of life. The nineteenth century materialists thought that once men were better off and understood the true basis of their alienated condition, that is, looked the dragon in the face, religion would wither away; and men would find their new Heaven on Earth. But the promised Shangri-La seems to have eluded us. As religion has decreased in its influence, in the Western world at least, the results have not been encouraging. Sensuality and commercialism have become the chief ends of contemporary godless society. If religion humiliated human nature in the past, humanism plays that role today. It is far from obvious that, even in a godless world, trust is superior to cynicism, love to hate, and reason to prejudice. We have paid a high price for killing God.

Let me put an end to what must seem more of a homily than an observation in the philosophy of religion. There are many questions which still need resolution. No writer who hopes to build the heritage

of faith in the age of reason can avoid asking himself
whether or not men can do without religious convictions. Is religion a fetter on our wills, a monster
of our own creation? (Is man only God's mistake? Or
God only man's mistake?[45]) Or is theism indeed the
noblest humanism in our history? Perhaps, religious
belief is indeed just another of those tragic
illusions of the constructive instinct. But whatever
may be the ultimate truth about the world, there is no
guarantee it will be a familiar one.

Notes

[1] Bertrand Russell, _Mysticism and Logic_ (New York: Longmans Green and Co., 1918), p. 47.

[2] For further discussion of this theme, see Section II.

[3] Bernard Williams is one such thinker. See his review of J.L. Mackie's _The Miracle of Theism_, "Is He or isn't He?", in _Times Literary Supplement_, March 11, 1983, p. 231.

[4] David Hume, "Of Miracles", in _Enquiry Concerning Human Understanding_, Section 10. For some excellent arguments which challenge the _a priori_ Humean judgement that miracles cannot form a reliable part of history, see Gary Colwell's "Miracles and History", in _Sophia_, Vol. 22, No. 2, July 1983, pp. 9-14 and J.C. Thornton's "Miracles and God's existence", in _Philosophy_, Vol. 59, 1984, pp. 219-229.

[5] John Smith, "Faith, Belief, and the Problem of Rationality in Religion", in _Rationality and Religious Belief_, C.F. Delaney (ed.), (Notre Dame Press: University of Notre Dame Press, 1979), p. 58.

[6] Søren Kierkegaard, _Concluding Unscientific Postscript_ (Princeton: Princeton University Press, 1941), p. 207.

[7] John Hick, _Arguments for the Existence of God_ (London: Macmillan, 1971), pp. 104-107 and his _Faith and Knowledge_ (Ithaca: Cornell University Press, 1966), pp. 120-148.

[8] Terence Penelhum, _God and Scepticism_ (Boston: Reidel, 1983), pp. 169-182, especially p. 178. See also his _Problems of Religious Knowledge_ (New York: Herder and Herder, 1971), pp. 112-148. Penelhum's model of faith can easily be developed to capture the Koranic notion of faith (iman), although Penelhum has not noted this application of his analysis. In the story of Joseph, as recited in the Koran (Surah 12, vv. 4ff), Jacob has knowledge (ᶜilm) from God concerning the true circumstances of his son Joseph. Jacob's faith (iman) is on trial despite the assurance given to him that his son Joseph is well and will eventually be caused, by God, to return to his father. The biblical narra-

tive related in Genesis differs from the Koranic one
in that Jacob is apparently convinced that Joseph
has been murdered by his own brothers. His faith
consists in accepting his lot and hoping that God
will show mercy towards him. In the Koranic narrative, he is said to have faith (iman) even though he
is also said to have knowledge (^{c}ilm). It is
interesting that the literal meaning of "iman" is
confirmation (tasdiq) - and this is clearly appropriate if "iman" is an epistemological term.

[9]Terence Penelhum, God and Scepticism, p. 158, 169.

[10]Most believing writers now accept the claim that
classical natural theology was a failure: see John
Hick, Arguments for the Existence of God, p. 101;
Terence Penelhum, Religion and Rationality (New
York: Random House, 1971), Part 1; Basil Mitchell,
The Justification of Religious Belief (New York:
Seabury Press, 1973), Chs. 1 ff. Alvin Plantinga
and Richard Swinburne also regard it as a failure.
And, of course, atheists like J.L. Mackie, Kai
Nielsen, Antony Flew, and A.C. Danto have long
insisted that classical natural theology is an
unsuccessful enterprise.

[11]See for example Clement Dore's recent attempt - in
his Theism (Boston: Reidel, 1984) - to show that
while the a posteriori arguments of classical
natural theology fail, there are defensible versions
of a priori arguments and a sound moral argument
which establish the existence of the maximally great
being of orthodox monotheism. Dore's curious
attempt is, in my view, a complete failure. See my
review of Dore's book in The Journal of Religion,
forthcoming.

[12]See the selections from Aquinas' Summa Contra
Gentiles in Classical Statements on Faith and
Reason, E.L. Miller (ed.), (New York: Random House,
1970).

[13]Vatican I, Constitutio Dogmatica de Fide Catholica,
cap. 2, quoted by Richard Swinburne in his Faith and
Reason (Oxford: Clarendon Press, 1981), p. 179,
n. 2.

[14]Richard Swinburne, The Existence of God (Oxford:
Clarendon Press, 1979).

[15] Antony Flew has argued along these lines in his "The Presumption of Atheism", in Canadian Journal of Philosophy, Vol. II, No. 1, September 1972, pp. 29-46.

[16] This is parallel to the plausible enough view that there may be more instances of genuinely moral behaviour in a permissive society than in a society which legally enforces moral precepts thereby rendering immoral behaviour less likely to occur (or at least less likely to be detected).

[17] To say that the religious explanation for the human condition is intellectually satisfying need not imply that all secular humanistic ones are baseless although, naturally, the religious thinker will wish to argue that the theistic explanation is superior to all atheistic ones. For further discussion, see Kurt Baier's insightful "The Meaning of Life", in The Meaning of Life, E.D. Klemke (ed.), (New York: Oxford University Press, 1981), pp. 81-117.

[18] Professor Jack MacIntosh has objected in conversation that I do not sufficiently appreciate the atheistic mentality and that this comes out clearly in my remark about the nastiness of life. For MacIntosh, only believers view life as nasty. This is, of course, a transparently false claim. Many atheist existentialists were ceaselessly resisting urges to commit suicide; and many believers (especially fundamentalist Christians in prosperous lands) sing joyously about the rather over-rated benefits of the religious lifestyle. In fact, of course, almost all of us have, in one mood or another, thought life a nasty affair. MacIntosh must be a bad student of human nature if he flatters himself with the conceit that his personality is the disbelieving community writ large.

[19] Imaginative literature will play a crucial role in the revival of the religious imagination. Writers like Simone Weil and Fyodor Dostoyevsky are, if you like, religious visionaries.

[20] There is a variety of views on this matter among contemporary philosophers of religion. Hugo Meynell, J.L. Mackie, Richard Swinburne, and Anthony Kenny all agree that religion needs natural theology although there is some disagreement concerning what natural theology can reasonably be expected to achieve. That the availability of a natural theo-

logy is an advantage for religion is endorsed by all the writers mentioned and by most religious thinkers and by atheists. Only Meynell and Swinburne, among those mentioned, think that natural theology, in one form or another, is actually possible; Penelhum and Kenny remain uncommitted on the issue of the possibility of natural theology while Mackie argues that there are strong reasons to regard the enterprise as a failure. For Hugo Meynell's views, see his The Intelligible Universe: A Cosmological Argument (London: Macmillan, 1982), pp. 1-6, and his "On the reasonableness of theism", in Religion and Irreligion, Hugo Meynell (ed.), (Calgary: The University of Calgary Press, 1985), pp. 45-70. For Kenny's views, see his Bampton Lectures, delivered in April 1982 at Columbia University and published as Faith and Reason (New York: Columbia University Press, 1983), Alvin Plantinga thinks, like Penelhum, Hick, and Mitchell, that natural theology is not essential to a defence of the rationality of faith.

[21]Alvin Plantinga, God and Other Minds (Ithaca: Cornell University Press, 1967), p. vii.

[22]Kierkegaard, op.cit., p. 111.

[23]ibid., p. 107.

[24]The quotation is from the Revised Standard Version of the Bible.

[25]Roger Rosenblatt, "Defenders of the Faith", in Time, November 12, 1984, p. 96.

[26]See the following works by Nielsen: Scepticism (London: Macmillan, 1973), Contemporary Critiques of Religion (London: Macmillan, 1971), and his Philosophy and Atheism: In Defence of Atheism (Buffalo: Prometheus Books, 1985). Although Nielsen disowns some of the crudities of his earlier verificationist critique of theism, he still endorses a more sophisticated version of the same critique. See his latest Philosophy and Atheism, p. 8.

[27]Kai Nielsen, "Comments on Empiricism and Theism", in Sophia, Vol. VII, No. 3, October 1968, pp. 12-17. Antony Flew has also levelled the charge of evasion against believing writers. See his "Theology and Falsification", in The Philosophy of Religion, Basil

Mitchell (ed.), (Oxford: Oxford University Press, 1971), pp. 13-22. (Basil Mitchell and R.M. Hare also participated in this famous debate.) In the face of criticism, believers make a "thousand quali-fications": their original claim about, say, God's love for mankind, Flew tells us, is continually modified to evade criticism until all substance has been removed from it. It seems to me, however, that Flew is not counting the qualifications properly. The concession that God is not an empirical reality implies one major qualification - namely, that God differs fundamentally from the world he has created. Believers are entitled, having made this concession, to resist en masse the secular empiricist criteria of judgement. My point about Flew's charge may seem like a quibble. But it is misleading to charac-terise the believer's procedure as a series of endless ad hoc qualifications.

[28]E. Abegg has suggested this in his "Religion as hope for the Supernatural", in Sophia, Vol. IV, No. 1, April 1965, pp. 27-33.

[29]See Kai Nielsen's "Can Faith Validate God-Talk?", in Theology Today, Vol. XX, No. 2, July 1963, pp. 158-173, and his "On the fideist option", in Sophia, forthcoming.

[30]Richard Swinburne has attempted, perhaps success-fully, to demonstrate the coherence of the concept of God in his The Coherence of Theism (Oxford: Clarendon Press, 1977).

[31]Nielsen accuses believing writers of evasion in his "God, Necessity and Falsifiability", in Traces of God in a Secular Culture, George McLean (ed.), (Staten Island: Alba House, 1973), pp. 273-306, and in his "Scepticism and Belief: A Reply to Benoit Garceau", in Dialogue, Vol. XXII, No. 3, September 1983, pp. 398-401. Benoit Garceau, a believing writer, has a reply to Nielsen in Dialogue, pp. 405-413, in the same issue of the journal. Benoit Garceau's initial piece (to which Nielsen responds in Dialogue) is entitled "On Dining with the Meta-Theological Sceptic" and is printed in Analytical Philosophy of Religion in Canada, Mostafa Faghfoury (ed.), (Ottawa: University of Ottawa Press, 1982), pp. 125-137.

[32]Certain ultimate questions - "If theism is true, why isn't it more obviously true?" or "Why doesn't God

forgive the Devil?" or "Why is there evil in the
world" - cannot, in the very nature of the case, be
fully answered. These are questions about the
specific style of the divine art. To be able to
answer them fully would entail the presumptuous
capacity to advise God on how to make an advance in
the practice of an essentially divine art.

[33]Nielsen reprimands two political theorists - Charles
Beitz and Henry Shue - for evading the issue in his
"Global Justice and the Imperatives of Capitalism",
in Journal of Philosophy, Vol. LXXX, No. 10, October
1983, pp. 608-610. (This is an abstract of a longer
paper.)

[34]Aristotle, Nicomachean Ethics, Book 1, Chapter 3,
1094^{b}24.

[35]Ian Crombie, "The Possibility of Theological Statements", in The Philosophy of Religion, Basil
Mitchell (ed.), (Oxford: Oxford University Press,
1971), pp. 23-52.

[36]Psalms 53:1

[37]Perhaps, Nietzsche earned the right to look back
upon his life and remark jocularly that he had never
believed in God, not even as a child because he
"...was never childish enough for it...". See his
Ecce Homo (Harmondsworth: Penguin Books, 1979),
translated by R.J. Hollingdale, p. 51.

[38]Simone de Beauvoir, Adieux: A Farewell to Sartre
(London: Deutsch and Weidenfeld and Nicolson,
1984), p. 434. The translation is by Patrick
O'Brian.

[39]See John Hick's "Theology and Verification", in The
Logic of God: Theology and Verification, Malcolm
Diamond and Thomas Litzenburg (eds.), (Indianapolis:
Bobbs-Merrill, 1975), pp. 188-208. I owe some of
these arguments to Basil Mitchell. See Mitchell's
The Justification of Religious Belief (New York:
Seabury Press, 1973), pp. 11-15.

[40]See Nietzsche's The Anti-Christ (Harmondsworth:
Penguin Books, 1968), translated by R.J. Hollingdale
in one volume along with Twilight of the Idols,
especially Section 20.

[41]The Anti-Christ, p. 163. "God, as Paul created him, is a denial of God." For Nietzsche's views on Islam, see Sections 59 and 60 of The Anti-Christ.

[42]Twilight of the Idols, p. 61.

[43]Basil Mitchell, The Justification of Religious Belief, p. 99.

[44]Kai Nielsen, "Christianity as Ideology", in Sophia Vol. 22, No. 2, July 1983, p. 39.

[45]This is Nietzsche's famous puzzle in Twilight of the Idols, p. 23.

Index

Blasi, Anthony J.

A PHENOMENOLOGICAL TRANSFORMATION OF THE SOCIAL SCIENTIFIC STUDY OF RELIGION

American University Studies: Series 7, Theology and Religion, Vol. 10
ISBN 0-8204-0235-4   205 pp.   hardback US $ 27.85

Recommended prices - alterations reserved

This book develops a theoretical methodology for the scientific study of religion, from the principle of meaning adequacy. Religion is to be understood adequately when the character of its presence in the mind of the religious person is described. This methodology is used to address some major issues in the study of religion in new ways – defining religion, understanding ritual, the connection between religion and morality, religious social morality in the third world, pietism, the value problem in scientific accounts of religion, and types of religious mentalities. These discussions comprise a substantive phenomenology of religion, and a distinctive sociology of religion.

Contents: After developing a phenomenological methodology for the study of religion, the book addresses major issues in the social scientific study of religion. Among these are ritual, morality, and conversion.

PETER LANG PUBLISHING, INC.
62 West 45th Street
USA - New York, NY 10036

Downes, David Anthony

RUSKIN'S LANDSCAPE OF BEATITUDE

American University Studies: Series 4, English Language and Literature, Vol. 4
ISBN 0-8204-0049-1   251 pb.   pp./lam. US $ 24.75

Recommended prices - alterations reserved

This analysis of Ruskin as a critic of art, architecture, economics and literature offers a comprehensive overview for the understanding of a major and prophetic Victorian figure. It augments existing readings of Ruskin's work and contains insights into Victorian culture, art criticism, the theory of criticism, and economic history.
The author places Ruskin's work in the context on his life and relates it to current critical perspective as well. He discusses *Modern Painters, The Seven Lamps of Architecture,* and *The Stones of Venice,* demonstrating how Ruskin established an esthetic standard for religious art to produce the kind of Christian humanistic culture he desired. Examination of *Unto This Last* focuses on Ruskin's view of capitalism while comments on other works provide background on his literary and social criticism. The basic theme of the book underlines Ruskin's understanding of the relationship between esthetic and ethical forces in civilization.

Contents: This book discusses John Ruskin's esthetic ideas of the natural theology of landscape in *Modern Painters* and the liturgy of architecture in *The Stones of Venice* in his attempt to express the ideals of a Christian humanistic culture for modern times.

 PETER LANG PUBLISHING, INC.
62 West 45th Street
USA - New York, NY 10036

Steffen, Lloyd H.

SELF-DECEPTION AND THE COMMON LIFE

American University Studies: Series 7, Theology and Religion, Vol. 11
ISBN 0-8204-0243-5   415 pp.   hardback US $ 45.40 / sFr. 88.55

Recommended prices - alterations reserved

Self-Deception and the Common Life investigates the topic of self-deception from three points of view: philosophical psychology, ethics, and theology. Empirical evidence and an «ordinary language» analysis support the case that the linguistic expression 'self-deception' is literally meaningful and that the language of the common life can be trusted. After critically analyzing the cognition, translation, and action accounts, along with the contributions of Freud and Sartre, Steffen proposes a new synthetic «emotional perception» account, one that avoids paradox. Giving attention to relevant moral issues, he argues that self-deception is not immoral, but represents a peccular form of *akrasia*. Finally, because theologians employ 'self-deception' to describe the cognitive component of sin, Steffen considers the logic of theological self-deception. His study seeks an «intimate acquaintance» with self-deception and exemplifies a method of analysis relevant to constructive theological inquiry.

Contents: «Ordinary language» analysis of self-deception – Accounts: cognition, translation, action, Sartre, Freud, «emotional perception»-self-deception and *akrasia*-theological self-deception: sin, pride, and Kierkegaard's «sin is despair».

PETER LANG PUBLISHING, INC.
62 West 45th Street
USA - New York, NY 10036

DATE DUE

HIGHSMITH   #LO-45220